Janet Malcolm

Marie Winn is the author of thirteen books, among them *Red-Tails in Love: Pale Male's Story* and *The Plug-In Drug: Television, Computers, and Family Life.* Formerly a birdwatching and nature columnist for *The Wall Street Journal* and a contributor to *The New York Times Magazine,* she has also translated plays by Vaclav Havel for performance at the Public Theater in New York. She is married to the documentary filmmaker and palindromist Allan Miller and lives not far from Central Park. Her Web site at www.mariewinn.com has frequent updates on Central Park's flora and fauna.

ALSO BY MARIE WINN

Red-Tails in Love: Pale Male's Story
The Plug-In Drug: Television, Computers, and Family Life
Children Without Childhood

CENTRAL PARK
IN THE DARK

MORE MYSTERIES

OF URBAN WILDLIFE

MARIE WINN

PICADOR

———

FARRAR, STRAUS AND GIROUX

NEW YORK

www.picadorusa.com

Picador® is a U.S. registered trademark and is used by Farrar, Straus and Giroux under license from Pan Books Limited.

For information on Picador Reading Group Guides, please contact Picador.
E-mail: readinggroupguides@picadorusa.com

The illustrations at the chapter openings are the work of Lee Stinchcomb.

Map of Central Park in the dark by Anne Malcolm.

Grateful acknowledgment is made for permission to reprint the following:
"City Greenery," copyright © 1961 by Ogden Nash. Reprinted by permission of Curtis Brown, Ltd.
Ted Kooser, "Screech Owl" from *Delights & Shadows*, copyright © 2004 by Ted Kooser. Reprinted with permission of Copper Canyon Press, www.coppercanyonpress.org.

ISBN-13: 978-0-312-42883-9
ISBN-10: 0-312-42883-9

First published in the United States by Farrar, Straus and Giroux

First Picador Edition: July 2009

10 9 8 7 6 5 4 3 2 1

FOR LEE, NOREEN, JIMMY, NICK,
AND THE GHOST OF CHARLES

CONTENTS

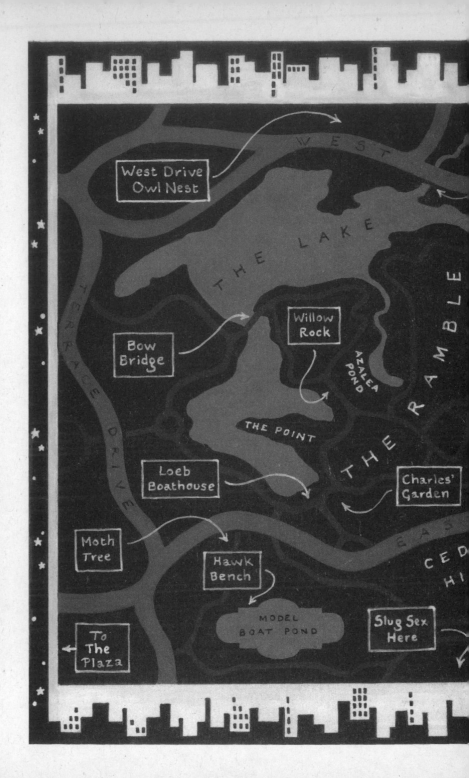

A Word
About
Chronology

This book covers eleven years of night adventures that began with Bug Night in 1995 and ended when I had to stop
following the stories and start writing. Occasionally, new
things would happen, and I'd sneak them in at the last possible
moment, even as the book was going to press.

Everything I've described here is based on notes written in
the dark on small slips of paper that were folded into wads and
dropped into or not quite into a pocket. Any mistakes you find
must be attributed to darkness, bad handwriting, excessive
wadding, and poor aim. But also, I must admit, sometimes events
were so engrossing—slug sex, for example—that I completely
stopped taking notes. Fortunately I also had a small digital camera with a close-focus lens—hundreds of photographs helped
me get the details right. Even more fortunately I've had many
occasions to rehearse the events I describe here with fellow participants, especially the ones to whom this book is dedicated.
Over the years they were helpful in ways I cannot begin to describe, not least of which was retrieving the trail of dropped
notes as well as flashlight, camera, binoculars, backpack, moth
book, daybook, pocketbook, and other paraphernalia I seem to
leave behind wherever I go.

Sometimes I compressed the chronology of those eleven years to suit the purposes of the narrative. You'll find that I rarely mention the year something happened, only the day and month. That's because unlike in human history, exact dates aren't particularly significant in natural history. If a black swallowtail caterpillar turns into a pupa in the Shakespeare Garden on October 2, it really doesn't matter whether it happens in 1908 or 2008. Black swallowtail caterpillars have been pupating in the same way and at about the same time for eons.*

Only one story is told sequentially, year by year, exactly as it happened in Central Park. That's the screech owl saga. Screech owls were introduced into Central Park in 1998 and 1999, and the next two batches in 2001 and 2002. The last madcap scene of the drama covered in this book happened in the spring of 2007. And it still goes on.

*We may be the last generation to enjoy the timelessness of nature. Global warming is beginning to make inroads into the age-old timetables of natural events.

Central Park

in the Dark

Before the Beginning

The night is more quiet than the day and yet we feare in it
what we doe not regard by day. A mouse running, a board
cracking, a dog howling, an owle scratching puts us often in
a cold sweat. —George Herbert, 1657

The first time I walked through the Ramble at night I was
terrified. I had been there in the daytime often enough;
that thirty-seven-acre wilderness in the heart of Central
Park is where I first became a birdwatcher. But the very features
that enchanted me by day—the winding paths, the thicket of
trees blocking out the city in all directions, the rock formations
cropping up out of nowhere, the secret coves, the rustic bridges
and sylvan streams—all looked grotesque and menacing in the
darkness. A shadow looming up ahead brought back a scary illus-
tration from my childhood fairy-tale book, the silhouette of a
horrible, grinning witch about to seize innocent children just
like *me*! And those rustlings to the right of the path and the
small, throaty growls from the bushes near the Lake—was I
imagining them?

No birds to be seen, not even a pigeon or sparrow, no hawks,
no butterflies or dragonflies, no squirrels, no tourists with cam-

eras, no nannies with strollers, no joggers or dog-walkers, no park workers, no cops—nobody. It was too quiet. The Central Park I loved by day made my flesh creep after dark.

That was many years ago. Today the things that once made my heart start pounding are full of possibility. That rustling in the leaf litter could be a white-footed mouse; the odd yips and yowls—squabbling raccoons. Now I recognize the particular rocks and trees that cast ominous shadows on the path. Of course I keep my wits about me walking through the park at night, but not more than I do during the day. You learn to be jungle-smart living in New York.

What made me avoid Central Park at night for so many years? During my childhood and young adulthood the park really *was* a dangerous place, and not only at night. Its decline and neglect began when the economic boom that followed World War II came to an end, and it continued for decades. Eventually the park's bad reputation became a subject of public mockery, as in these lines from a 1961 Ogden Nash poem:

> *If you should happen after dark*
> *To find yourself in Central Park,*
> *Ignore the paths that beckon you*
> *And hurry, hurry to the zoo,*
> *And creep into the tiger's lair.*
> *Frankly you'll be safer there.*

Central Park reached its nadir during the city's fiscal crisis in the 1970s, when the park's budget plummeted and with it police surveillance and patrols. Its reputation as a shabby, neglected, dangerous place was well deserved in those years. The tide turned in 1980 when the Central Park Conservancy began its long program of restoration, which continues to this day.

Still, the park had never been as dangerous as the public perceived it. When, infrequently, a crime is committed within its 843 green acres, whether a robbery or assault or murder, it makes newspaper headlines and the TV news. Meanwhile a far greater number of similar crimes committed in less illustrious neighborhoods go unheralded. Today, though more police cars circle the park's paths and drives than ever before, fear of Central Park in the dark continues to prevail.

"You go into Central Park at night?" people ask, upturn and crescendo on the last word, when I talk about the owls and moths, raccoons and bats, crickets, cicadas, and other wild (non-human) things I've seen in the park after sundown. "But you don't go there *alone*, do you?" they always ask next. When I admit that I've done so on occasion, their eyes widen with horror.

Fear and hatred of darkness: the seed is planted in the first chapter of the Bible, when God says, "Let there be light," and there is light. God does not have to start with "Let there be darkness," for the darkness is already there in that unthinkable, formless void preceding the Creation. "And God saw the light, that it was good," the verse continues. How can one miss the unspoken corollary: that the darkness was not good.

Think how fear of darkness is nurtured in early childhood, the stage of life when patterns of thinking are firmly established. Even in today's psychologically savvy world, toddlers still kneel beside their beds to recite a truly terrifying prayer: "Now I lay me down to sleep, I pray the Lord my soul to keep; if I should die before I wake . . ." Or they learn another prayer that cannot lead to cheerful feelings about the dark: "Lighten our darkness, we beseech thee O Lord, and by thy great mercy deliver us from all perils and dangers of this night."

Surely the years of saying "peril" and "danger" in association with "night" and "darkness" help to create an automatic queasiness about the darkness of night. Since modern neuroscience supports the idea that brain patterns are permanently affected by external stimuli, it stands to reason that frightening words and concepts repeated over a period of time during childhood will have long-lasting neurological and emotional consequences. Nyctophobia, a pathological fear of night and darkness, might be an extreme example of such a consequence.

Yet even the most protected children sometimes believe that there's a monster under the bed at night or a ghost outside the window in the darkness. Nor do adults stop being afraid of venturing into Central Park at night, even when they're presented with rational and incontrovertible facts about its relative safety after dark. Here is such a fact: There's not much crime in Central Park—indeed, the Central Park precinct enjoys the city's lowest crime rate. And more crimes are committed there in the daytime than at night.

Fear of darkness is universal. We are daytime mammals, after all, and evolution has programmed us to respond to failing light by crawling into a safe, snug place and going to sleep. That is what other diurnal mammals do. There are even evolutionary roots for a more specific fear known as nyctohylophobia, fear of dark, wooded areas at night. It makes perfect sense: the predators that threatened humans in their earliest days would have been lurking in those dark woods at night, animals that had evolved with better night vision and keener senses of hearing and smell than *Homo sapiens*.

When daytime animals are forced to leave their protected night quarters and enter the world of darkness, an automatic fear reaction triggers specific hormonal changes that serve as a survival mechanism. Fear triggers adrenaline, for example, which heightens the senses, helping the animal stay awake and alert for signs of danger.

Early in mankind's evolutionary history humans chose to go against the natural order by extending their waking hours long past sunset. Fossil evidence shows that early man used campfires, bonfires, and torches to illuminate the night. Throughout recorded history people have made ever-greater inroads into the darkness—with candles and lanterns, then with the gas mantle, and most dramatically with electricity.

Far greater dangers face us in today's world than our ancestors ever dreamed of, but we are as likely to encounter them in the day as at night. Nevertheless fear of darkness persists as an evolutionary relic, one that may diminish our lives more than it prolongs them. For our instinctive and often irrational fear distances us from the mysteries and wonders of the natural world at night. Central Park offered me my first glimpse into those mysteries and wonders. But not until I'd come to know the place extremely well did my fear of the night recede, though it never disappeared completely. Familiarity breeds content.

Another characteristic is an even more powerful inhibitor of fear: curiosity, the desire to know and to understand. Curiosity, together with our eagerness to learn—a universal human trait— will turn off the automatic fear reaction. Surely this too is part of the mammalian heritage. The impulse to delve into the mysteries of nature must have improved the odds of survival in ancient times, just as it improves the odds of fulfillment in our own day and age.

Night brings out some of nature's most fascinating creatures, and the dramas of their life cycles are enacted in darkness. Curiosity about events that unfold only at night—owls flying off to hunt, bats calling unheard as they circle at the water's edge, spiders spinning elaborate webs, slugs embracing, cicadas unfolding their lacy green wings, hawks falling asleep in concealment, large, colorful moths arriving from the mysterious dark to feed on tree sap—this is what brought a little group of nature lovers I think of as the Night People into Central Park's nocturnal world.

1

PARTY-CRASHERS
AND FLYING MAMMALS

The Loeb Boathouse, located at 74th Street along Central Park's East Drive, is a popular place for parties—you have to book the space months or, for certain holidays, years in advance. Though a shuttle bus is available at the corner of Fifth Avenue and 72nd Street to take infirm or three-inch-high-heeled or merely nervous-Nelly partygoers to the Boathouse at night, some still choose to go by foot. It's a short and romantic stroll along the well-lit drive, with Pilgrim Hill and the model-boat pond visible to the east and glimpses of the rowboat lake to the west.

On most balmy summer evenings these strollers might notice an odd sight—a small band of men, women, and sometimes a few children shining flashlights into a scraggly tree on the drive's east side, just past the point where the 72nd Street transverse goes straight ahead and the drive curves to the north. Indeed, on most summer nights you'll find me there too. Few stop to ask us what we're doing, perhaps because New Yorkers are trained to mind their own business. But the question hangs in the air. The answer: we're watching large, beautiful moths arriving to feed on a special tree.

On a certain summer night a few years ago, just a little after sunset, I happened to be one of those gussied-up partygoers myself. Though it was hard to walk right by the gang at the Moth Tree, I couldn't miss this particular bash. It was being held in honor of a romantic couple close to my heart: Pale Male and Lola, the red-tailed hawks that had been nesting on the twelfth floor of a nearby Fifth Avenue apartment house for more than a decade.

My attachment to Pale Male began in the early 1990s, when red-tailed hawks were rare in big cities. Though hawks passed over Central Park every year during the spring and fall migrations, none had ever nested there. When a light-colored redtail settled in as a year-round resident, hooked up with a mate, and then proceeded to build a nest on an elegant limestone building at Fifth Avenue and 74th Street, it was a newsworthy event. That year I wrote the first of a series of articles about Pale Male in *The Wall Street Journal*, and I continued to cover the redtail beat for years.

Pale Male, the first avian superstar. Pale Male, the red-tailed hawk that tour guides pointed out as he made lazy circles above the model-boat pond. Pale Male—the very name was a crucial ingredient in creating this hawk's celebrity. It fell trippingly from the tongue. Even the echo of Pall Mall—pronounced either as Americans do, to rhyme with *ball*, or as the upper-class British do, *Pell Mell*—gave the name a special zing. People liked to say it—Pale Male. Pale Male and Lola, his third and probably last true love. The names could pull the emotion lever all by themselves.

Over the years twenty-three redtail chicks had hatched and fledged from the Fifth Avenue nest. Later, when this same species of hawk began to proliferate in New York City and other urban centers in the Northeast, Central Park's dedicated hawk-watchers began to half believe that all the other city redtails nesting on buildings and ledges were Pale Male's offspring: the Pale Male dynasty.

Early one rainy morning in December, just as the twice-widowed hawk patriarch and Lola were preparing for a new breeding season, the hawks' huge messy nest was summarily removed from its twelfth-floor ledge by workers ascending on a window-washers' platform. The building's fastidious owners had deemed the accumulation of sticks an unsightly mess and consigned it to the garbage bin.

The ensuing public furor, with crowds parading outside the building chanting, "Bring back the nest!" and car horns honking on Fifth Avenue in support of Hawks' Rights, inspired newspaper headlines and television news stories around the world. Intense public attention was brought to bear on the building's residents, who became public pariahs, while the Fifth Avenue hawks won the city's sympathy and even love. The building's board of directors swiftly relented, and New York City Audubon, the city's leading bird conservation group, helped broker a deal that would allow the hawks to rebuild their nest, or at least to try. In celebration of their success and—why not?—to raise some much-needed funds, the worthy organization was throwing a party at the Boathouse, smack in the heart of Pale Male's territory.

Among the bird-loving guests at the party were three who not only loved birds but loved to eat them. They were raccoons. Thick-tailed members of the Procyonidae family, close relatives of kinkajous, coatis, cacomistles, ringtails, and olingos, raccoons are far from uncommon in Central Park. Some park officials suggest that up to fifty of the black-masked mammals are permanent, year-round residents, and their real population may be twice as high.

Appearing in the bushes behind the Boathouse's outdoor terrace at about 9:45 p.m., the three rather underdressed party-crashers consumed large quantities of chicken and pasta furtively offered them by a few of the invited guests. The raccoons ate noisily, but their benefactors managed to close the terrace doors. Thus they kept the animals' little growls of bestial contentment from disturbing the benefit's co-honorees, Mary Tyler Moore and Parks Commissioner Adrian Benepe. Together with the local Audubon chapter each had helped to resolve the nest-removal crisis. Indeed, Mary Tyler Moore was a resident of the Hawk Building at the time and a vital liaison between the bird lovers and the building's board. Her prepared remarks were being delivered just as the raccoons began feasting.

Five years earlier, more than twenty-five raccoons had been found dead in the northern part of the park. Necropsies revealed multiple lacerations and puncture wounds, probably inflicted by dogs. There were rumors that two large, muscular canines, possibly Rottweilers or Doberman pinschers, had been seen ranging through the northern end of the park. Once, the rumors continued, the dogs had been seen running out of the park and into a waiting car, suggesting that the vicious pair had been loosed in the park to kill for their sadistic owner's amusement. It was a bizarre scenario.

Perhaps the killers were simply feral dogs who belonged to no one. But no stray dog was deemed capable of winning a fight with a strong, aggressive fifteen- or twenty-pound raccoon. Raccoons are known to defend themselves savagely when attacked. They pose no danger to people, however—there has never been a case of a human attacked by a raccoon in Central Park. It's as unlikely an event as a squirrel biting the hand that feeds, and feeds and feeds, it, Fortunately, the dog attacks ceased as mysteriously as they started, and the park's raccoon population seemed to return to its normal number, whatever that might be.

Though they are classified as nocturnal mammals, raccoons are often seen by day in Central Park. Tourists in particular are charmed to come across a wild woodland creature in the park— it's a little nature experience in the heart of the city. Birdwatchers too enjoy raccoon encounters, especially on days when birds are "quiet"—that is, nowhere to be seen. Scanning the trees with binoculars, the park's birders often come upon a raccoon sleeping at the entrance to one of its dens—they have many—or sprawled out on a horizontal branch with its legs and tail dangling. Sightings are less common in winter; though raccoons don't actually hibernate, they go into an energy-conserving winter sleep during the cold-weather months, living off stored fat reserves. Even then they'll emerge on sunny, warmish days for an evening stroll. By ones or twos, and sometimes by nines or tens, they'll venture forth at dusk to harvest the treasure trove of discarded hot dogs, pretzels, half-eaten sandwiches, apple cores, and other goodies available in every garbage can.

The three raccoons who attended the benefit at the Boathouse seemed to like the chocolate petits fours and the miniature cheesecakes from the dessert table above all. They picked up each little pastry with their hands and delicately placed it in their mouths, a behavior that a widely used text describes as characteristic of the species—the manual dexterity, that is, not the consumption of baked goods.

"*Procyon* has a well-developed sense of touch . . . the hands are regularly used almost as skillfully as monkeys use theirs," say the authors of *Walker's Mammals of the World* (none of them, oddly enough, named Walker), adding an observation that seriously undermines the raccoon's scientific name, *Procyon lotor* ("washing bear"): "Although raccoons have sometimes been observed to dip food in water, especially under captive conditions, the legend that they actually wash their food is without foundation."

The raccoon's versatile hands (actually the front feet) are a useful adaptation that allows these highly successful animals to reach into small spaces or turn over stones while looking for prey, as well as to catch and hold on to small animals, fish, and a variety of invertebrates. They enable raccoons to perform the single act for which they are most famous (or infamous) in the human community: opening garbage cans, no matter how securely closed. Raccoons don't have to exert themselves much in Central Park—many of the garbage cans have no lids at all. The nimble animals just climb in and carry off their booty to eat in nearby trees. Sometimes a couple of animals will work in concert to knock over a large garbage can. Then they can dine on the spot. They just crawl in and chow down.

At the Boathouse Pale Male shindig, the three raccoons didn't have to lift a finger. But after the bandit-masked, ring-tailed, pointy-muzzled omnivores had eaten a truly awesome number of rich little confections, some partygoers became concerned for their health. These fears were groundless. Raccoons show up regularly at private Boathouse functions and employees reported that the three were seen again the evening after the Audubon benefit. They were in fine fettle, the men reported, though they seemed a little peckish, if not downright hungry.

☾

There are many more bats than raccoons to be found in Central Park, but the flying mammals' more reclusive hunting habits usually keep them out of human sight. That may be a good thing, since many people are deeply—and needlessly—terrified of bats. Late strollers in the park may glimpse the dark shapes of hunting bats circling over one or another of the park's bodies of water, but unthinkingly they assume the creatures are birds. Being crepuscular—active at dusk and at dawn—as well as nocturnal, bats are rarely seen by Central Park visitors in broad daylight. *Rarely*, however, does not mean *never*.

One of these rare daytime bat encounters was enjoyed by Kellye Rosenheim, a fairly recent addition to Central Park's roster of expert birders. A pretty and stylish young woman, Kellye had been a beginner ten years earlier when she'd gone on one of Wendy Paulson's Nature Conservancy bird walks in Central Park. She just wanted a few hours away from the kids. But those few hours changed her life.

Once bitten by the birding bug, a gifted person can move

ahead quickly. Kellye advanced at breakneck speed. She went on bird walks. She went on birding trips. She studied bird books and field guides and tapes of birdsong. Today she leads the Nature Conservancy* walks in Central Park whenever Wendy is in Washington. This happened frequently after her husband, Henry Paulson, was appointed secretary of the treasury in June 2006.

One late October morning Kellye had a serendipitous encounter with a red bat in the Ramble and sent me a detailed note about it. When I compared some of her observations with scientific accounts of the same species, I appreciated the precision of her description. That ability to observe carefully and remember tiny details, even ones that might seem insignificant, is the sign of unusual talent.

Picture this: 8:30 a.m., Sunday, October 22, a little chilly. A friend and I walked up the hill from the Boathouse and turned toward the Point, where that little path begins. Just where a low railing on the right begins, we stepped out onto the rock cliff there. You know the spot, it's where most birdwatchers begin their watching. Looking down, you see the swampy area below.

As you're standing there, if you look out at eye level, you see the willows on the left. But straight ahead there's a tree—it has oval leaves, pointed at the end, about four inches long, which hang down vertically from the twig branches they grow on. They grow in a line down the branch.

Well, we were watching a cardinal moving around on that tree. All of a sudden something hissed at the bird and I thought it was a snake coming out of the leaves to strike at it. But I put my binoculars on it and saw it was a bat, with its side to me. The "snake's body" that I thought I saw was its wing extended out.

I could see its face. Its little mouth was open with the teeth

---

*A national organization not to be confused with the Central Park Conservancy.

showing. It was hanging upside down, not, I believe, from the branch, but clinging to a big leaf, kind of hiding behind it. The fur was red all over its body (about four inches long) and the skin on its wing was black except where the bones underneath were—there it was reddish, like its fur. That's how I figured it was a Red Bat. It was just awesome. Eventually it retracted its wing and went back into hiding, but not before a hermit thrush dove at it as it would at an owl.

The bat was hanging on to the leaf of that tree near its stem, or so it appeared. I should mention that the leaves on its tree were all still green. The bat itself was at eye level, if you're standing on the cliff there. It looked kind of like a dead leaf behind some green leaves.

The image of a bat looking like a dead leaf in the midst of a cluster of green ones jogged my memory. I looked in a file folder of references to bats in Central Park and there I found what I was looking for: an article in the August 1956 issue of the *Journal of Mammalogy* entitled "Migration Records of the Red Bat," by the late ornithologist John K. Terres. He wrote:

> On September 1, 1955, I caught a live female red bat with my hands that I saw hanging from the branch of a wild black-cherry tree in Central Park, New York City. The bat was only about eight feet above the ground, and bore a striking resemblance to a dead brown leaf. It hung from a twig among a cluster of green leaves, and was asleep when I caught it. I examined it for ectoparasites but found none. I returned it to its perch by putting its feet to the twig, which it clutched, and after a momentary shuffling of its wings, seemed to go back to sleep. When I came back to look for it the next day it was gone.

As I reread the old clipping, an odd question struck me: How had John Terres managed to reach a bat hanging eight feet above the ground? I called an old friend who'd worked with the noted bird expert on his magnum opus, *The Audubon Society's Encyclopedia of North American Birds*, and asked: "Was John Terres an exceptionally tall man?" "No," she answered, "he wasn't particularly tall. Sort of average height." How had he nabbed his bat, then? I wondered. Had he climbed the tree?

A week later I visited the spot Kellye had described, the rocky cliff looking down on a swampy area Central Park's birders call, for unknown reasons, the Oven. It's a favorite birdwatching location, especially during the spring migration, and for a simple reason: you can look down into the treetops and see warblers easily—no neck-craning necessary.

Now, with the willows on the left, I faced directly ahead as Kellye had done. I could see two trees that were taller than the rest: an old black cherry and a hackberry. Based on her description of the leaves and the twig arrangement, Kellye's bat tree had to be the black cherry. And John Terres's tree had been a black cherry too! Eureka. If he'd been standing on that same ledge fifty years earlier he could easily have reached out and removed a sleeping bat, though the creature was actually eight feet above the ground. A coincidence? Or another example of nature's mystery? Just thinking about it gave me a chill.

Discovering a sleeping bat by day requires no unusual equipment—just unusual luck. Finding bats at night is a different matter. Just as binoculars are crucial to a birder's success, so the bat-detector, a device that translates ultrasonic bat songs into frequencies people can hear, is indispensable to Central Park's bat hunters.

Today it's widely known that bats zero in on their insect prey by emitting ultrasonic sounds and then listening to their echoes when they bounce off objects in the air, a process called echolocation. Yet the very existence of ultrasonic sound was not proved until the twentieth century. How bats manage to operate in complete darkness remained a mystery until then.°

More than two hundred years ago Lazzaro Spallanzani, an Italian scientist, came close to solving the mystery. In a series of experiments he compared how bats and owls function at various levels of light. When placed in a partially darkened room, both the bird and the mammal oriented perfectly. In complete darkness, however, only the bat continued to navigate successfully. The owl collided with the wall and with objects in the room. It was evident that when the use of eyesight is no longer possible, bats resort to some other sense to navigate, one that owls do not possess.

In subsequent experiments, Spallanzani demonstrated that while bats he had blinded (alas) continued to hunt as well as those with perfect eyesight, when their ears were plugged they became disoriented and collided with obstacles set in their way. He came to the reasonable conclusion that hearing is the sense crucial to bats' navigation. But the idea was widely ridiculed. "Since bats see with their ears do they hear with their eyes?" a fellow scientist wisecracked.

Spallanzani himself was confounded by his findings. His experiments had shown that bats use their ears to hunt successfully, but how in the world did it work? Without understanding that the seemingly silent flying mammals were actually producing sounds that helped them navigate and hunt, he couldn't make sense of his discovery. His dilemma came to be known as "Spallanzani's bat problem."

Many decades before the discovery of ultrasonic sound, an American poet hinted at its existence. In her poem "The Bat Is Dun," Emily Dickinson wrote, "And not a song pervade his Lips," describing a bat in flight, but she modified the observation by adding, "Or none perceptible." A keen observer of nature,

---

°Echolocation is not unique to bats. The mechanism is used by toothed whales, dolphins, certain cave-dwelling birds such as oilbirds, and possibly by some shrew species.

Dickinson had somehow understood that bats make sounds imperceptible to human ears.

Finally, in 1938, a young man named Donald Griffin solved Spallanzani's bat problem. Griffin, a Harvard graduate student, heard that G. W. Pierce, an eminent Harvard physics professor, had just developed an apparatus able to detect sounds above the human hearing range. It was the first of its kind.

Fascinated by bats from childhood, Griffin was familiar with Spallanzani's enigmatic experiments. Like Emily Dickinson, he had a hunch that bats were not really silent but made sounds that were simply not "perceptible." He applied to Pierce for permission to try the ultrasonic detector on a cageful of bats; until then the apparatus had been used only to detect high-pitched insect sounds. Permission was granted.

In his book *Echoes of Bats and Men*, Griffin describes the moment when his hunch was proved true: "Just as soon as I brought some bats to Pierce's apparatus, it became obvious that they were emitting plenty of sound, but that it was almost entirely above the frequencies that we could hear." For the young bat student it was an auspicious moment and the beginning of the end of Spallanzani's bat mystery. Griffin continues:

> Further experiments showed that covering the mouth of a bat and thus preventing its emission of these high-frequency sounds was just as effective as plugging its ears. Both treatments made bats quite unable to detect large objects or small and they bumped against the walls of the room or anything else in their path. In short, their whole orientation during flight depended on echoes of the high-frequency sounds that they emitted almost continuously while flying about. Because these sounds had shorter wave lengths and consequently higher frequencies than those to which our ears respond, the ability of bats to fly in total darkness had seemed a complete mystery. But once this simple fact became known, all seemed clear.

Poor Spallanzani—close, but no cigar. He blinded the bats, he plugged their ears, but he neglected to cover their mouths. Thus he failed to demonstrate the "simple fact" (as Griffin was unkind enough to remind us in his book) that the bats were not silent after all, that in reality they were making quite a din.

Griffin's fellow graduate student and collaborator Robert Galambos later recalled their historic discovery of echolocation:

> Don divided a sound treated experimental room into equal parts by hanging a row of wires from the ceiling. We aimed the microphone of the Pierce device at this wire array and began to count the number of times a bat flying through the wires will hit them when normal, or deaf, or mute. (The impairments we produced, by plugging the ears or tying the mouth shut, were all reversible.) . . . We also recorded the output of the Pierce device and correlated the bat's vocal output as it approached the barrier with whether it hit or missed the wires. Everything we predicted did happen. Nothing ever went wrong.

Expecting that their claims would be as controversial as Spallanzani's, the two young experimenters made a movie demonstration they hoped would silence the skeptics. And indeed it did. The short movie has been shown and continues to be shown to this day on science and nature television programs around the world. Thanks to Donald Griffin, the once-mysterious world of bats had opened up for nature lovers everywhere, even in Central Park.

☾

I made my official entry into the bat world while taking part in Central Park's first bioblitz. The event is a twenty-four-hour census of all living things to be found in a designated area: insects, reptiles, amphibians, fish, birds, mammals as well as plants and fungi—everything. Volunteers are organized according to the various plant and animal groups, with teams going out at different times throughout the day and night. I picked the last time slot of the day—eight-thirty to midnight— and signed up for the bat team.

On June 27, just before sunset, our team made its way to the Ramble in search of bats. In place of binoculars we used bat-detectors to make our sightings, handheld instruments that can pick up the high-frequency sounds bats emit, between 20 and 200 kilohertz (kHz), and translate them into levels audible to the human ear, frequencies below 20 kHz.

When a bat comes into range, the bat-detector begins to click loudly. And since different bat species emit sounds at different frequencies, the detectors can help identify the bats' species. The little brown bat (*Myotis lucifugus*),* calls at 38 to 62 kHz, the Eastern red bat (*Lasiurus borealis*) at 39 to 50 kHz, and the big brown bat (*Eptesicus fuscus*) at 25 to 51 kHz. You can see there's some overlap. If the bat-detector registers 45 kHz the bat could be any of those three. That's when a quick look at the bat helps. There's usually enough artificial light in Central Park to help distinguish species by size.

The bioblitz team had another trick up their sleeve. Strips of fine nylon netting called mist nets were to be stretched out across some spot, preferably a stream or other body of water, where bats were likely to be hunting. Unable to see the almost invisible nets, or to detect them by means of echolocation, bats in the vicinity tend to fly into them and become tangled in the mesh. One team member would be a mist-net monitor, positioned there to gently untangle the bats and place them into a bat bag for later analysis. The Azalea Pond in the Ramble was the chosen water body. Brad Klein and his wife, Danielle Gustafson,

---

*The little brown bat has been renamed the little brown myotis. Since everybody still calls it the little brown bat, so will I.

both experienced bat-handlers, volunteered to be the mist-net monitors.

I always think of Evelyn Waugh's "bright young things" when I think of Brad and Danielle. Like Waugh's young aristocrats, Brad and Danielle are good-looking, smart, witty, and sharp-tongued. But unlike Waugh's feckless socialites, these two do not find that making a living is "too, too, weary-making." Danielle works for the New York Stock Exchange; Brad is a journalist. He was writing guided tours for museums and galleries at the time of the bioblitz.

Just before real dark descended, Brad's detector went off, clicking away at 40 kHz. Within a few minutes the first bat hit the net—in the lowering light we could actually see it flying overhead—then two more. I was consumed with pity for the poor creatures who had set out to find their evening meal and landed in the mist net instead. This was the moment when our expert Rodrigo Medellin, the "bat guru of Mexico," took over. No harm would come to the animals as a result of their capture, he assured us. Moreover, the momentary interruption in their bat lives was well worth the educational value for humans, who might otherwise fear them and try to eradicate them. Nevertheless I and several others did not breathe easily until the moment came for their release.

It took Brad and Danielle quite a long time to disentangle the bats from the mist nets. Danielle had an anxious look on her face the whole time she worked, and I imagined that, like me, she was afraid of harming the animals. But it wasn't the bats that caused her to furrow her brow. She knew the bats were fine. As she held each hissing and snarling creature in one gloved hand while unraveling the knots with the other, she was worried about damaging the net.

As we watched the mist-net extractions, the tension was broken when first Brad and ten minutes later Danielle managed to fall into the pond. They held the mist net above the water, thus keeping the bats perfectly dry, but they got completely drenched themselves. I'm afraid that I and the other bat-happiness worriers chuckled as the soaked pair pulled themselves out of the pond.

In an e-mail the next day Brad described his experience in detail:

I went to the pair in my net, and the little guy clamped his teeth down on the fingertip of my cotton glove and just started chewing with ardor. I scooted my finger clear of the teeth—but in all the excitement I forgot the first rule of mist netting—determine from which side the bat entered the net before trying to get him out. Plus, he wasn't fully in a pocket of the net so I was afraid of losing him. The idea with these little ones is to grab the body below the head with the gloved hand, then untangle each wing with the bare hand. I learned this on our trip to the Amazon, where some bats have really big teeth and a bite that can take off part of your finger!

The mud in the Azalea Pond was surprisingly glue-like, and I sank in halfway to my knees while working on getting the bat out. It was great fun to mimic the field scientists I've watched in the past, taking care and responsibility not to hurt the animal and taking slight risks (mugging, sprained ankle, rabies) to do the job well.

Our bats here are in many ways less sexy than in the tropics, where they eat fruit, disperse seeds, drink nectar and pollinate plants, build little houses out of leaves, cling to the sides of trees, and drink your blood as you sleep in the hammock on the boat's deck. But to think that a little creature like that could spend 10 to 20 years living in New York City, hibernating in a building during the winter—negotiating traffic and urban lighting during the summer . . . amazing!

Two years later another bioblitz was held in Central Park. This time the bat team's destination was the North Woods.

I was happy that our bat expert that day, a wildlife technician with the New York State Department of Environmental Conservation named Carl Herzog, preferred to gather information by means of acoustical equipment and a computer rather than by mist-net trapping. Also on our team were three local experts familiar with the bat population of Central Park: Chanda Bennett of the American Museum of Natural History, her husband, Tare Gantt, a high school science teacher, and Danielle Gustafson again—Brad was out of town. Then there were four or five amateurs like me, attracted by the romance of bats and the allure of the park in the dark. We were not disappointed.

Thanks to our bat-detectors we were literally detectives. Carl carried a portable computer with a detector attached to it. The apparatus could record and analyze the particular bat emissions being picked up at any given moment, thereby giving a more precise indication of that bat's species.

At 8:30 p.m. the bat team set forth from bioblitz headquarters at the North Meadow Recreation Center, which is just north of the 96th Street transverse. With all detectors turned on, we made our way to the Pool, a little pond between 100th and 103rd streets near Central Park West.

Along the way we inspected every black locust and shagbark hickory we passed. These trees have rough, flaking bark that offers nesting opportunities for local bats. But none had availed themselves, as far as we could see. We noticed several trees with large hollows visible—weren't these promising bat homes as well? No, said Carl, bats avoid large openings. Very small crevices offer better protection from predators. And what predators might bats encounter in Central Park? Raccoons, among others, said Carl. Bad news for Central Park bats given the abundant raccoon population.

At 8:45 we were nearing the Pool when our bat-detectors began clicking wildly. Stopping near a streetlamp, we caught a few fleeting glimpses of dark, erratically flying shapes swooping between trees and water. They looked like birds. But even in the dark something about the creatures' flight pattern revealed that they were bats. They darted and swiveled and wheeled about in the air much more actively than even the most acrobatic avian species, the flycatchers, for instance.

Observers have long distinguished bats from birds simply by the gestalt of their flight, but only recently have scientists succeeded in defining the aerodynamic differences between bat flight and bird flight. In an experiment as inventive as Griffin's landmark study, researchers watched both birds and bats as they navigated in wind tunnels that were filled with manufactured fog. By tracking the displacement of fog particles as the animals flew, the experimenters found that while birds generate thrust using only the downstroke of their wings, bats have developed a twisting wing path that increases the lift during the upstroke as well.

As indicated by our bat-detectors and also by our experts' visual assessment, all our bats at the Pool were little brown bats. Next we headed down a slope and under a handsome bridge called Glen Span Arch. Another water body was at hand—the Loch, a meandering stream that flows through a densely wooded area known as the Ravine. The rivulet passes under the Huddlestone Arch, another of Central Park's thirty historic bridges, and into the Harlem Meer at the park's northeast corner. We were beginning to expect bats in the vicinity of water, and sure enough, as we approached the Meer our detectors began clicking like Geiger counters at a uranium deposit.

When we came to the Meer twenty minutes later, another fusillade of clicks erupted from the detectors. But one bat here was a surprise. Based on a visual impression of the animal illuminated by a streetlamp, as well as by the computer report, Carl believed we had found a northern long-eared bat (*Myotis septentrionalis*). The discovery of a species never before identified in Central Park is what a bioblitz is all about. Our team felt triumphant, as if we had found a new species of bird in the Amazon rainforest or, at least, an ivory-billed woodpecker in some lonesome bayou.

On our way back we ran into the reptile and amphibian team. They did not seem quite as elated. They had only one species on their list: an American bullfrog.

One early October Friday I came home to find a message on my answering machine from Starr Saphir, one of Central Park's most accomplished birders and bird-walk leaders. Even on a recording I could hear her excitement:

> I led a walk for the Linnaean Society this morning in the Ramble. We had stopped at the benches on the east side of the Azalea Pond, and were just heading for the swampy pin oak when we saw a silver-haired bat! This was a life bat for me and for all of us. The bat was in the leaf litter on our left and then flew up to a nearby tree trunk where we all had a chance to observe it.
>
> You know what day today is, don't you? I think having a bat of any species is very nice on Friday the 13th, but I know a silver-haired bat is even better. It's a most unusual species for Central Park. Thought you'd want to know.

A life bird, in birdwatchers' lingo, is a species seen for the first time in one's life. Like many other advanced birders, Starr has a long list of life birds—her grand total is 2,344. "That's on earth," she noted when I asked her for the number, adding in typical Starr fashion, "Of course I've never birded any other planet." In New York alone she has 397 state birds. As she was walking in the park a day earlier, a shorebird called a greater yellowlegs flew overhead on its way from somewhere to somewhere, Central Park definitely not its destination. But a flyover counts, and that brought Starr's Central Park bird list to 244.

But what about life bats? Her Central Park bat list increased by 33 percent with her sighting of the silver-haired bat, the other three being the little brown bat, red bat, and big brown bat. I told her about my only sighting of a silver-haired bat more than ten years earlier. One fall day as I was standing at Belvedere Castle looking down at Turtle Pond below, I saw Starr's future fourth life bat flying low over the water. It was easy to identify because its blackish hair looked as if the tips had just been frosted at the beauty parlor. When I added that the bat actually plunged into the pond and swam for some distance to reach the far shore, Starr didn't bat an eye. (When you talk or even write about Starr Saphir, the urge to pun becomes irresistible.) "He was probably doing the bat-stroke," she quipped instantly.

It's not a coincidence that Starr discovered her silver-haired bat near the Azalea Pond. *Lasionycteris noctivagans* (the scientific name derives from Greek and Latin words meaning "night wandering shaggy bat") prefers to forage near the edges of wooded streams. That's just what the Azalea Pond is—a small enlargement of the Gill, Central Park's quintessential wooded stream. The Gill, to be sure, is not *really* a wooded stream; it turns on and off with a cleverly hidden faucet.

The Ramble retains much of its original Vaux and Olmsted design, but there's an essential difference in the scene today. In place of showy rose and rhododendron displays, you'll find a multitude of carefully chosen trees and shrubs where birds can feed and insects overwinter. At certain times of year you'll find hundreds of songbirds—warblers, vireos, tanagers, cuckoos, kinglets, and grosbeaks—for whom Central Park has become a crucial stopover place during migration. You'll find raccoons wandering and occasional bullfrogs croaking. And if you're lucky, you might come upon a silver-haired bat dozing in the leaf litter.

2

The Ghost
of Charles

Charles Kennedy, one of Central Park's most ardent nature lovers and my accomplice in a variety of wildlife adventures, died in the fall of 2004. A tall, handsome, engaging man, the hero of a book and a film about Pale Male, a gifted photographer and poet, a charmer of all who met him, an admirer of dogs large and small, and most of all a true and loyal friend, Charles was a vibrant presence in Central Park.

When I first met him back in the early 1990s, Charles was trying to become a birdwatcher. His goal was to find every bird mentioned in a book called *Falconer of Central Park*, and I think he was up to 65 out of the book's 150 species on the day I ran into him. When a young red-tailed hawk arrived in the park a few months later, Charles put his list away. He had lost his heart to a single bird. That was when he and I began to follow Pale Male and the wildly successful nest on Fifth Avenue.

From the day Pale Male appeared, Charles egged me on to write the hawk story. If the light-colored redtail brought a rat to his dark inamorata perched in a tree directly above our viewing bench, Charles would nudge me and say, "Take notes."

"Write your own book," I'd grumble. But I'd jot something down anyhow, just to keep Charles happy. Eventually it became a habit.

Meanwhile Charles moved into photography, first taking pictures only of hawks, then of bats and owls, and finally of the mysterious invertebrates we were beginning to follow—cicadas, spiders, slugs, praying mantises, and especially moths.

Charles didn't write his book; he wrote hundreds of striking haiku instead, few of them adhering to the traditional Japanese form but all retaining its intense focus on nature. Here's one about owl-watching:

> *the sun drops*
> *the cold slides in*
> *owl time*

Charles was a cheerful person but he often brought up a subject I found morbid: where he wanted his ashes scattered after his death. He named many specific locations, all in Central Park, of course. Charles loved Central Park with the passion of the Iowa expatriate that he was. The scattering places changed as the years went by; a few lost their magic and were replaced by new ones. Mostly the list just expanded—wherever something happened that delighted or moved him, he'd add that spot to the others. I never took the ashes business seriously—it was just one of my friend's many lovable eccentricities.

During the last months of his life Charles, cheerful even then, continued to refine the scattering list. Death was a natural part of the scheme of things for him, I came to realize, something to be incorporated into daily life. Could he have known all along that scattering his ashes in Central Park would be a gift for his friends?

Charles Kennedy succumbed to lymphoma on the day after his sixty-seventh birthday. Now a year later, five of his friends met at the east side of Balcony Bridge to keep our long-ago promise.

Lee Stinchcomb, Noreen O'Rourke, and Jimmy Lewis, all longtime Central Park regulars, had spent many happy hours with Charles over the years, following the Fifth Avenue hawks by day and owls, moths, and other nocturnal creatures after dark; I was a part of their little night band. The fifth one there was Regina Alvarez. A personable young woman with a deep interest in wildlife, today Regina acts as a liaison between the park's powers-that-be (who might see a dead tree as an eyesore to be removed) and its vigilant community of year-round birdwatchers (who regard the same tree as a potential home for a woodpecker).

Charles pulled Regina into his orbit as soon as they met. She was in her late twenties then and working as a zone gardener at the model-boat pond. It was the year Pale Male first built the nest at 927 Fifth Avenue, and Regina shared many of our hawk adventures during that exciting time. The young woman went on to carve out a shining career, becoming a vice president of the Central Park Conservancy as well as the park's Woodlands Manager. Pale Male made a name for himself: he became the most famous hawk in the world.

On the afternoon of October 19 we gathered at Balcony Bridge to keep our promise. It was almost four o'clock and time to begin, though clearly we wouldn't complete our task in a single day—the list of scattering places was too long. Lee pulled a Zabar's deli container out of her bag. It held the ashes. Then, incongruously, she brought out an ornate silver serving spoon for the task at hand.

Down the steep incline from Balcony Bridge to the Lake's edge we scrambled. Charles had seen his first prothonotary warbler on this very shore. He'd been on a quest for this golden bird for ten years and longed to add it to his life list, but somehow it kept eluding him. Finally the bird and the man intersected on the west side of the Lake near Balcony Bridge. Now, one by one we cast silver spoonfuls of Charles's ashes along the shore there. It's odd—we didn't feel sad at all. We joked around about Charles's devotion to the stunning warbler. Who else would have chosen such a hard-to-spell name for his e-mail address?

Next stop the Moth Tree, our summer mecca. How many hot August and September nights we'd spent there, watching under-wing moths reveal the spectacularly colored hind wings that give them their name. We had a feeling that nobody else but our little band knew they existed in Central Park.

From the Moth Tree we made our way to Cedar Hill, a little slope just south of the Metropolitan Museum of Art. There we scattered a few more ashes, first at the base of the tree where we'd first witnessed the stirring rituals of slug sex, then in the grove where cicadas go through the last stage of their metamorphosis every summer. Our task did not require flashlights this time.

Finally we headed for a small peninsula at the northern end of the rowboat lake—the Upper Lobe. A few years before, a screech owl family had chosen to nest there, the first of that species to breed in Central Park for more than half a century. The four of us and Charles had spent many hours in the messy tangles there, watching the owl parents teach their three fledglings how to succeed in the owl business—how to avoid hitting branches while flying in the woods, for instance, and how to take a proper bath.

Now, a year after Charles's death, the Central Park Conservancy was beginning a grand restoration project that would return the Upper Lobe and the area around it to Vaux and Olmsted's original, pristine conception—the first step of an ambitious restoration of the whole Ramble. Though we were all part of a quasi-official organization called the Woodlands Advisory Board—Regina was its official coordinator—and we'd all participated in the restoration's planning process, still we were uneasy about the project. "In wildness is the preservation of the world," Thoreau had written, and that was exactly what we worried about. Would our favorite birdwatching spots still be wild and messy after the restoration ended? Would they be as wildlife-friendly?

We hadn't been there together for a long time. Somehow, nobody had felt like owling without Charles. That day, a few months before the bulldozers arrived and the major work began, we scattered our spoonfuls at the base of a big willow the owls had often roosted in, and also around the fallen log where we used to sit and watch the owl show. Suddenly we felt sadder than we'd felt before.

Then an eerie thing happened: we heard a couple of blue jays screaming and we raised our binoculars in the direction of the sound. Noreen was the first to spot the little screech owl sitting on a branch almost at the top of the willow. She has an uncanny way of discovering owls—the Finder, Charles had dubbed her. Hardly a minute later Regina exclaimed, "Look! There's another one." The bird was sitting completely still just a few branches away from the first one.

Perhaps owls had been arriving at the Upper Lobe willow every evening for years, and we just hadn't been there to see them. It's possible. But that wasn't what we thought. We *knew* that one of those owls was Charles. We decided to go looking for owls again.

C

The most exciting parts of a night bird's life—hunting, killing, feeding, bathing, fighting, courting, mating, nest-building, child-rearing—take place in the dark of night. If only we had owl eyes!

Owls' eyes are huge and round and richly endowed with the light-sensitive photoreceptor cells called rods that allow nocturnal animals to see in the dark. Owl eyes have almost a million rods per square millimeter; we have only one-fifth as many. The eyes of diurnal mammals—ours, for instance—feature cone-shaped cells. They allow the brain to distinguish colors clearly, an ability advantageous in the daytime but of little use at night when all colors have turned to gray. For most of human history the day began at dawn and ended at twilight, much the way it

still does for most songbirds and diurnal mammals. You don't
need night vision if you keep to the sun's schedule. Only the ad-
vent of artificial light, a relatively recent phenomenon, gave humans the ability to see after dark.

To be sure, owls have a good supply of cones too. Contrary to
popular belief, they can see in the day quite well if they have to.
They just like to stack the deck so they don't have to, preferring
to sleep in the day. They accomplish this by finding day roosts
where they cannot easily be found. With their bark-colored plumage, screech or long-eared or saw-whet owls (the three most common Central Park species) literally blend into the woodwork,
invisible even when you are looking right at them.

Occasionally birdwatchers find a giveaway sign of owl life on
the lower branches of a tree—owl whitewash, or a little pile of
owl pellets at its base. Finding such evidence encourages them
to search more thoroughly, to look and look and look again. It
can't possibly be there. But there it is!

More likely an owl is betrayed by its own classmates (class as
in Aves) through a behavior called mobbing. Many birds are programmed to react aggressively to perched birds of prey; they circle about a perceived intruder, be it a hawk or an owl or indeed
anything with a raptor's outline, even a harmless nighthawk or
whip-poor-will. The avian vigilantes will dart in and out, making
little feints at their target's head or tail, all the while screaming
bloody murder. The message is perfectly clear: *Unwelcome! Get
lost!* The mob's actions may seem foolhardy—many of the at-
tackers are only a fraction of the raptor's size. But small birds
mob with impunity—the mobbee almost never strikes back.

For an owl, mobbing is an annoyance: *Won't those pip-
squeaks stop pecking at me and let me sleep in peace?* For the
birdwatcher, it's a godsend. Hearing the raucous cries of blue jays
(*Thief! Thief!*) or the shrill alarm calls of titmice (*Dee dee dee!*)
and seeing cardinals, robins, or even tiny birds like kinglets, con-

verging on a particular spot, a birder learns to search carefully at the center of the commotion. A raptor in hiding is being outed.

Sometimes you'll find an owl's daytime roost by pure chance. While slowly scanning the greenery for something that caught your eye or ear a moment ago—a small bird that happened to land in a nearby tree, for instance—your brain registers something unexpected: *Wait, what was that?* You move the binoculars back . . . *There, that lump . . . oh my God, look what I found!*

Once an owl is discovered in Central Park, its whereabouts are duly reported. A few birders and quite a few tourists write reports of sightings in the Bird Register, a log that is kept at the Boathouse. But nowadays, most members of the park's birding community send and receive reports via computer, either on *e-birds*, an e-mail newsletter that goes out regularly to a large list of bird enthusiasts in the New York City area, or on the *NYC Bird Report*, a website with up-to-the-minute bird sightings sent in by the park's best birders. The park's serious birders check both daily. The top-notch birders use *Metrobirds*, a Listserv that notes only rare and unusual sightings.

Bird reports usually include detailed directions to help others share the sighting, but in keeping with the strict rules of owl etiquette, the exact location of a roosting owl is never revealed to the general public. It's passed along to other birdwatchers only by word of mouth. If you are a bird-lover and want to locate an owl you've heard about, you must seek out other birders in the vicinity. Your binoculars are the credentials you need. You'll be directed to the owl.

There are good reasons for withholding owl locations from the world at large. While sleeping away their daylight hours in a tree or shrub, owls, especially small ones, are vulnerable. Someone can reach into a low privet bush, for example, and easily remove a sleeping saw-whet owl.

Many years ago someone I know, the former president of a large birding organization, did exactly that. He found a sleeping saw-whet in a shrub one morning, took it to his house on a suburban street several blocks away, and placed it on his Christmas tree in the living room. It slept there all day, to the delight of his children, neighbors, and friends. A little before sunset he let it go again. Actually, owling etiquette wouldn't have saved that bird from becoming a temporary ornament since the owl-borrower was a trusted member of the birding community. But owls need protection, from irresponsible birders as well as from the more usual sources of mischief—for example kids who exclaim, "Oh, how cute!" and take a little owl home as a doomed pet.

☾

Coming upon an owl by day is exciting, but just how long can you watch a sleeping bird and revel in its beauty? You want to see some action! That's why so much attention is paid to the fly-out, that moment toward the end of our human day when owls set forth to begin their owl day.

The fly-out vigil may begin on the very day of an owl's discovery in Central Park. As daylight dwindles, a congregation of human night owls gathers at the owl's tree to watch it wake up and take off. This nightly assembly at a regular owl roost becomes a curious social phenomenon. Though many of the group are birdwatchers, others are simply passersby who have stopped to see what everyone is looking at. Binoculars are offered, they look for themselves, and then they come back the next day and the next and the next. Unlike neighbors or friends thrown together in a common cause, people who gather at owl fly-outs are more like pilgrims moving toward a common destination. Without quite realizing it, they are seeking a transcendent experience, one that will release them, however briefly, from the burdens of humanness.

Back in my earliest years as a Central Park birdwatcher, there were no owl fly-out gatherings. In those days the park was perceived as more dangerous, at night and in the daytime too. When a barn owl stayed for a protracted visit in the early 1990s I dreamed of seeing it spread its wings and fly off into the darkness. But for anyone to linger in the park after sunset was unthinkable in that era.

A few years later, a saw-whet owl roosted for several winter months in the peaceful precincts of the Shakespeare Garden. This little hillside Eden between the Swedish Cottage marionette theater and Belvedere Castle features plantings mentioned in Shakespeare's works. Brass plaques scattered throughout the garden provide appropriate lines: "A rose by any other name" appears beside a rosebush, "Heigh ho heigh ho unto the green holly" by a holly—you get the idea.

The saw-whet owl (*Aegolius acadicus*), the smallest owl in the eastern United States, is only eight inches long. That's two inches smaller than a robin. The adjective usually used to describe it is "adorable," and the group of birdwatchers who began gathering at the garden at day's end to see the owl fly off into the night used it shamelessly. Mary Fiore, a longtime Central Park birder, assigned us a name: The Clandestine and Secret Society of the Saw-whet. Those first Central Park fly-outs were an exhilarating experience: for most of us they marked the transition from being afraid of the park at night to feeling safe there, as safe as we felt anywhere else in the city.

Unlike the cavity-roosting screech owl, Little Adorable sleeps out in the open, in bushes or trees, where it manages to position itself into almost perfect invisibility. Unless you know a saw-whet is there, this tiny creature is extremely difficult to find. Luckily, it often chooses to roost in the same tree day after day, and that knowledge is the key to success for a questing owl-hunter. You can scan a tree with your finest binoculars and swear there's no owl there. Only if you *know* an owl's in a certain tree, because it was there yesterday and the day before, will you continue the excruciatingly careful, inch-by-inch examination necessary to discover that a certain bump on a branch is actually a perfectly camouflaged sleeping saw-whet.

After finding the owl, you'll discover that pointing it out to fellow owlers can be an equally challenging task. "All right, look up the tree trunk until you get to the second fork. Go up the left branch until it intersects a thin, sort of horizontal branch. Go right until you come to a little clump of brownish leaves, just under the spot where the sun is coming through. Go two branches up from there . . ." This can go on for quite a while, until everyone has uttered the gratifying "Ah! There it is. I've got it." Then you wait for the fly-out.

Most owl fly-outs follow the same schedule. As twilight approaches, the owl wakes up from its daylong sleep. It yawns. It stretches its wings. It preens. All at once, as the light continues to fade, the owl comes to attention. It draws itself up and stands erect: the fly-out moment approaches. That's when the worshippers stop their conversations and fall silent. All eyes turn to the owl. Attention—owl on runway!

Sometimes the owl *does* take off at that hushed moment, but sometimes it doesn't. Not infrequently the bird dawdles. *Well, I think I'll preen that left wing one more time.* This is when I, for one, lose my concentration. I take a quick glance at the moon coming out from behind a cloud, or a skein of geese honking overhead. *Who's that whistling on the path? Someone I know?* That's the split second the owl chooses to make its getaway. *Sneaky devil*, as Charles Kennedy used to say.

As the moment of fly-out approaches, someone keeps an eye on the time. Without necessarily understanding why, everyone wants to know to the minute when the owl's takeoff occurs. It *is* important—don't doubt it. Write it down: *Tonight the owl flew out at 6:52 p.m.* When it leaves tomorrow at 6:53 or 6:54, write that down too. Keep track of these changes, compare them as time goes on. Keep track of the sunset. Keep track of the moon's rise and set. All these details make a difference. But why?

Time slows down for fly-out watchers. Though the fly-out occurs just a minute or a fraction of a minute later every day, after two months have elapsed you can't help recognizing that the owl is taking off an hour later than it did when you first started watching.

Yet seeing the clock time of an owl's exit change over the months serves a deeper purpose: it provides a powerful connection with what Thoreau called "the steady progress of the universe." As you stand on terra firma watching the same little drama every day, over time you begin to absorb the realities of life on a planet rotating on its axis. It happens so gradually—the minute-by-minute change, getting earlier and earlier each day from June to December, or later and later from December to June.

Finally you realize that though the owl's fly-out hour changes according to human clocks, by owl time it is always the same. The level of light— almost exactly the moment when we humans can no longer distinguish colors—is the same at fly-out time whether your watch says 4:30 p.m. or 8:52 p.m. I don't know why, but this fact boggles my mind.

Over the years many Central Park nature lovers have enjoyed the quasi-religious exhilaration of an owl fly-out. But few have experienced its arcane reversal, a gathering to observe the early-morning return of an owl to its daytime roost. A fly-in. Charles Kennedy came up with the idea at around the time Palo Male first began building a nest on Fifth Avenue. It was the same year we felt brave enough to watch a saw-whet owl fly out of its tree in the Shakespeare Garden every night for almost two months. After week two of that fly-out stretch, Charles was ready to try something new and more challenging.

On December 15 Charles arrived in the garden at 6:00, an hour before sunrise. It was dark—the nearest working street-light was down the hill. He swept the owl's roost tree thoroughly with a flashlight, branch by branch, diligently searching for the familiar saw-whet shape. Nobody was home.

The challenge of observing a fly-in, he realized then, is greater than that of a fly-out. To witness a bird leaving for the night, you keep your attention on a known spot, the bird at the entrance to its cavity or on its roosting branch. You see it there plainly before it departs. But when waiting for a fly-in, you don't know where to look, since you have no idea what direction the bird is coming from—east, west, north, or south. In the Shakespeare Garden, Charles tried to keep an eye on all directions, slowly swiveling in place, but it was too dark. At 7:10, just as the sky was taking on a pinkish glow, Charles saw the saw-whet sitting peacefully in its usual place in the tree. Sneaky devil.

Later, when Charles began regular fly-in vigils for a pair of long-eared owls we'd found on Cedar Hill, he refined his technique a bit. For one thing, he arrived an hour earlier and positioned himself directly under the roost tree. The task was easier when several owls roosted in one tree—some years as many as seven. You could catch their arrival by hearing their friendly conversation as they landed. Even so, at the end of most of his Cedar Hill morning vigils the words "sneaky devil" could distinctly be heard. The long-eared owls inspired two of my favorite Kennedy haiku:

> *being there*
> *the owl flying in*
> *on the dawn wind*

and

> *5:30 a.m.*
> *owl back on her branch*
> *the dawn the cold*

Lincoln Karim, one of Central Park's most devoted hawk-watchers and nature photographers, carried on the fly-in tradition, but in reverse. His vigils were primarily centered on raptors that fly in at night and fly out in the early morning—the Fifth Avenue red-tailed hawks. During his evening and early-morning visits, he managed to take many photos of the hawks' bedtime and rising rituals. In one remarkable evening shot he caught Pale Male sitting on his nighttime roost tree as the setting sun illuminated the branch; the hawk took on a flaming red color, as bright as a cardinal. After witnessing hawk bedtime, Lincoln often managed to arrive early enough for the next morning's fly-out, capturing the bird waking up, stretching, preening, and flying out for the day in a series of dramatic photos.

What would happen if an owl, heading for its day roost early in the morning, encountered one of those fiery redtails flying out? It would be a disaster for most of the Central Park owls. Long-eared owls, barn owls, screech owls, and saw-whet owls are significantly smaller than redtails; they'd surely lose in a dust-up with a big hawk. But it's not likely to happen. When I compared our available records of owl morning fly-in times with records of the redtails' morning fly-outs, it became clear that the two keep different schedules. The owls return to their day roost in the darkness before daybreak, while the hawks rise and shine quite a bit later, in the twilight before sunrise. Thus does evolution preserve its species.

I was a beginning birdwatcher the year I first fell in love with an owl. I had become aware of Central Park's rich wildlife and its enviable community of nature observers. But I was only an onlooker then; the park had not yet become a place I felt inextricably bound to. That connection required a story, a narrative that kept me coming to the park day after day to see what happened next. Only then would the park become an indelible part of my life.

The first of these stories began at seven in the morning on a long-ago September day as a bird class under the aegis of the American Museum of Natural History made its way through the Ramble. Suddenly a bunch of birds began screaming in the trees somewhere nearby. "Stop, everyone!" said Steve Quinn, a curator in the museum's Exhibitions department and the group's leader. "Those blue jays are mobbing something. It might be a hawk or an owl." He seemed excited. A few moments later Dorothy Poole, a longtime Central Park birdwatcher and one of my future mentors in the park, found what was bothering the jays. Perched on a horizontal branch of a sweetgum tree, exposed and yet invisible, was an owl Quinn immediately identified. It was a barn owl, an extremely rare visitor to Central Park.

While all other North American owls are in the family Strigidae, the barn owl (*Tyto alba*) is in a taxonomic family of its own—the Tytonidae. It is easily distinguished from all other owls by its white or golden heart-shaped facial mask, which gives it a weirdly simian look. That may also explain its "slightly creepy expression," in the words of a popular book about birds. It stands about sixteen inches high, placing it midway down the list of Central Park owls arranged in order of size. Going from smallest to largest, the eight-inch saw-whet owl is first; the screech owl is next, at eight and a half inches; the long-eared owl follows at fifteen inches; and then the barn owl. There are two bigger owls that have visited Central Park: the barred owl, which is twenty-one inches high, and the great horned owl, topping the list at twenty-two inches. The wingspans range from seventeen inches for the saw-whet to forty-four inches for the great horned.

Though not always considered a beautiful bird, the barn owl is an exceptionally useful one: in its life span of about ten years, a single barn owl can consume something like eleven thousand rodents, according to Paul Johnsgard, the author of *North American Owls*. Indeed, the barn owl's entire evolutionary history has designed it for catching rodents—a flying rat-trap, someone once called it. Its eyesight and hearing are perfectly adapted for hunting small prey in the dark. Its wing formation enables it to hover for over a minute without stalling as it homes in on its prey. And thanks to a modification of its first primary feathers, the barn owl's flight is completely silent. It shares these characteristics with most owls.

Accompanying the museum group that morning was a police officer, Daniel Delia of the Central Park precinct. He was there in the line of duty: the Ramble was not deemed a safe place in that era, even during the day, and a police escort was often provided for early-morning walks. But he too was excited about the owl. Indeed, Officer Delia was the first to find an owl pellet at the base of the sweetgum tree.

A few days later the owl moved to a nearby paulownia tree, one of the many exotic species planted in the Ramble by the park's original horticulturists. (Only native trees are planted in the park these days.) The bird sat in the same tree day after day for almost two months, always on the same branch some thirty feet off the ground. "Roost fidelity," the bird books call such behavior. It means that the bird has found a favorable hunting spot.

The barn owl soon became something of a Central Park celebrity. Day after day small crowds could be seen congregating in the clearing where the owl was roosting, and when passersby observed people looking up into a tree, they'd look up in turn and suddenly exclaim, "I see it! My God! It's really an owl!"

Because the owl sat and slept quietly on its preferred roost for most of the day, some people contended that it was a fake, a cardboard decoy. But on one occasion a birdwatcher made mouselike squeaking noises, and suddenly the owl opened its dark eyes. It looked from side to side, swaying weirdly. Then it went back to sleep.

The word *owl*, by the way, is onomatopoeic in origin and descends from the same root as *ululate*, "to howl." Most owls do howl, in some form or other. Some give off the traditional *whoo, whoo* that owls are known for. But the barn owl's howl is closer to a bone-chilling shriek, according to Julio de la Torre, author of *Owls: Their Life and Behavior.*

But during the barn owl's stay in Central Park, no one ever heard it utter a sound, neither a long, drawn-out scream nor a loud raspy *sss-ksch* nor even a snorelike chuckling note, as its various utterances are described in bird books. Nor did anyone ever see it glide silently from its perch after dark to go a-hunting. No one ever saw it raise its long wings and then dive down to grasp an unlucky rat in its talons. No one saw it return to its branch on the paulownia to swallow its prey whole, head first, tail disappearing last. But we were serious victims of owl fever and we found ourselves imagining these events at odd moments of the day, especially at nightfall. That was the best we could do—we were afraid of Central Park after dark in those days.

By the second week of November the paulownia, a deciduous tree, was almost bare. Most of its heart-shaped leaves lay on the ground, and only scattered clusters of its pecan-shaped fruit remained on its branches. I knew the owl couldn't stay there much longer—it had lost its cover. Yet on the day I arrived for my daily visit and found the owl missing, I couldn't accept the idea that it had gone for good. I continued to check the clearing day after day, hoping against hope that the bird would return.

On November 16, a Saturday, I went to look for the owl one last time. As I was leaving, I ran into a man with binoculars.

"You haven't seen the owl?" I asked, without much hope.

"Oh yes, I just found its new tree," he answered. "I asked myself, 'If I were an owl, where would I go?' Then I looked for the most foliated tree I could find in the vicinity of its old roost."

The man turned out to be Curtis Berger, a professor at the Columbia Law School, and a birdwatcher with more than six hundred North American birds on his life list. This, however, was his first barn owl. He led me to a large Norway maple not far from the paulownia. Norway maples are among the last trees in the park to lose their leaves in the fall. And there, sitting on a high branch, was the barn owl! Framed with dark green foliage, it was beautifully visible. The sun glistened on its spotted golden breast, and my heart jumped at the sight.

One winter a spectacular owl showed up in the Big Apple, one that hadn't been seen in Central Park for decades. This owl, however, spent only the briefest part of its New York visit in the park. Instead, it settled into a busy urban neighborhood not far from Vaux and Olmsted's masterpiece: East Harlem, or El Barrio (The District), as its large Hispanic population calls it.

The first to discover the Barrio owl was Brandon Shackelford. Brandon was nine years old and lived with his family in one of East Harlem's largest housing projects, the James Weldon Johnson Houses on 112th Street and Lexington Avenue. The Shackelfords' third-floor apartment, one of 1,307 units in the project, faced a spacious courtyard containing pathways, play equipment, and a few mature trees.

On a Saturday morning in early December Brandon was about to leave for Boy Scouts when he happened to look out the window. Wow! An incredible bird was sitting in the tree just outside his window. It was huge! Every other tree in the plaza was bare, but this one, a red oak, was still full of colorful leaves, which was undoubtedly why the bird had chosen it for its daytime roost.

A little after sunset that evening Brandon, his sister Tawanna, and his mother, Stephanie, saw the bird fly off for its night hunting, languidly flapping its long, long wings. Double wow! The next morning they saw it sitting in the same tree again. It seemed to be asleep.

On Monday, Brandon, a third-grader at a local parochial school, told his teacher about the huge bird outside his window. He must have been persuasive, for the teacher strolled over to the courtyard during his lunch break. He called New York City Audubon the minute he returned. "There's a large bird, I think it's an owl, in a housing project on Lexington Avenue and 112th Street," he told them. That was enough. Word of the Barrio owl spread among birders by means of their efficient and long-established telephone grapevine, the fastest method of communication even in the computer era. The first contingent arrived later that day and had little trouble finding the owl.

And what an owl! Only two eastern owls have dark eyes—the barn owl is the other—and only one has neck feathers resembling a checkered muffler. Brandon's bird was a barred owl, a large nocturnal raptor noted for its spine-tingling vocal repertoire—screams, monkeylike laughter, and a characteristic love song often transliterated as *Whooo cooks for yoooo? Whooo cooks for you all?* The Barrio owl, however, was silent. Most of the time it was asleep.

On Wednesday, December 6, a delegation of Central Park regulars—Tom Fiore, Rebekah Creshkoff, and I—arrived at the owl tree at 7:00 a.m., just before sunrise. We were not the first: John Suggs, a high school math teacher and bigtime birder, gave us a thumbs-up sign, took a last look at the owl, and left for work.

As small crowds of birdwatchers arrived at the owl tree throughout the day, project dwellers took notice. Many looked up and became instant owl-watchers. By 4:00 p.m. quite a crowd—about equal numbers of locals and birders—was gathered around the owl tree.

Part of the pleasure of the sport is letting others in on the show. Though a few birders were uneasy about the safety of their binoculars in this unfamiliar neighborhood, before long the fancy Elites and Trinovids were being passed around the crowd as usual. The project residents uttered exclamations of admiration and wonder at the owl's fine details as revealed by superb optical equipment, while the birders felt sheepish for having worried. In addition to their optical equipment, they shared information about owls with the other spectators—there's nothing birdwatchers like better than passing along their bird knowledge. The locals seemed more interested in learning than most, which led to a heightened feeling of camaraderie among the assorted owl-watchers.

A few of the residents were uneasy about the owl. "Does it bite people?" asked one of a group of overexcited boys, whose names were Robert Crump, Cahiem Harris, Jon Rodriguez, Sadane Parsons, Brian Figueroa, Tyrone Boggs, Brandon Cleckley, Nequan Glover, Anthony Tucker, and José Diaz. I promised to include their names in an article I was writing for *The Wall Street Journal* if they'd stop throwing things at the owl. They did, and I did.

Others were more anxious about the bird's well-being than their own. Victoria Berrios, who was born and raised in the project, looked up and said anxiously, "That bird looks lost and hungry. Maybe we should call the ASPCA." When a birdwatcher explained that the owl was probably feasting on the local rodent population, she was relieved. "I hope he gets plenty of food in his belly so he won't go anywhere else," Berrios declared. "We have plenty of wildlife around here, but only the kind with two feet."

Yet the story of the Barrio owl was not as auspicious as the owl-watchers assumed. A call to Julio de la Torre, president of the New York Linnaean Society at the time, placed the owl's visit to an East Harlem housing project in grave perspective.

"I'm not surprised to hear about a barred owl in the city," he said. "Animals are being discovered in unusual places throughout the Northeast. Bears are walking into supermarkets in major urban centers along the Canadian border. In fact, we are in the midst of the most extraordinary mass movement of birds and other wildlife I have ever encountered." Recent climatological factors, he explained, among them the absence of snowfall and a severe drought the previous year, had led to a near-total failure of virtually every major food item consumed by seed-eating and fruit-eating creatures from Labrador to North Carolina. "There are no seeds, so the seed-eaters at the bottom of the pyramid, mice and voles and shrews, are starving. Consequently the larger creatures that prey on them, the raptors, are fleeing starvation too. Under normal circumstances barred owls do not frequent built-up areas. When you see these birds in an urban environment, you know that the pickings are bad out in the forest." I realized that our saw-whet influx must be part of this weather phenomenon.

"What do you think this owl is catching when it hunts in the Barrio?" I asked. "Would it be eating rats?"

"It might if it's hungry enough," answered de la Torre, "but a barred owl will typically leave a Norway rat alone. City rats are notoriously ferocious, so if that's what the Barrio owl is eating, well, that's an owl *con cojones*. You might want to translate that as an owl with real guts."

I took two owl pellets containing the bones of the Barrio owl's prey to the American Museum of Natural History for analysis. With the help of a mammalogist and an ornithologist, I learned that our owl required fewer cojones than de la Torre imagined: there were no rodent bones in the pellet, only avian remains. The bones belonged to *Columba livia*, a bird that is usually called by its vernacular name—pigeon.

Shale Brownstein, a psychiatrist who had recently come down with a serious case of ornithomania, was one of the last owl-watchers to enjoy a look at the barred owl. At 7:00 a.m. on the bird's fifth day of Barrio residence, Dr. Brownstein saw it sleeping in its usual tree. The next morning it was gone.

Unlike the rare barred owl that shows up in Central Park once in a blue moon, the long-eared owl is a common visitor. In any given year a number of these slender, long-winged owls might arrive in the park in late November or early December and stay till early April. In spring, hormones triggered by the lengthening days impel the birds to head farther north to their breeding grounds.

To be sure, the long, feathery structures that stick up on top of the heads of long-eared owls (and other "horned" owls) are not really ears; they have nothing to do with hearing. The birds' actual ears are situated a bit lower on the bird's face, arranged asymmetrically to help them pinpoint prey accurately. What purpose, then, do the ear tufts serve (apart, of course, from delighting birdwatchers)? Since long-eared owls elongate their ear tufts at times of danger—indeed, they also elongate their bodies—the most likely explanation of the tufts is that they make the owl look bigger and fiercer, thus scaring off would-be predators.

Unfortunately, LEOs, to use local birders' common acronymic shorthand for long-eared owls, are tantalizingly irregular in their visits to Central Park. For three or four years we'll have resident LEOs all winter. And then along comes a LEO-less stretch. Though day after day we search high and low in every possible place an owl might be roosting, though we listen attentively for screaming bird mobs, we fail to come up with a single owl. We're forced to admit that the park has become a LEO desert. Then the next winter, or perhaps the one after that, the long-eared owls will reappear, sometimes in their old haunts and sometimes in new ones. Owl happiness resumes.

Even as I write this, two LEOs are in their fourth week of residency in Central Park after a two-year LEO drought. Without violating owl etiquette—they'll be gone by the time you read this—I can tell you exactly where they were roosting: in

a Korean pine at the northwest corner of the Ross Pinetum—
pronounced *pie-NEE-tum*, by the way. I just hope this marks the
beginning of a long spell of wintering LEOs in Central Park.

Long-eared owls provided my real introduction to owl-watching.
My early years as a Central Park regular coincided with a four-
year LEO winter residency. During year one we grew attached
to a pair that roosted from December to April in a blue spruce at
Cedar Hill. But sometimes there were more owls, many more.
During the third year of LEO winter residence, on a day when
the temperature went down to zero degrees Fahrenheit, we saw
eight long-eared owls clustered on two evergreens just behind
the benches at the base of Cherry Hill.

During those years a small group of us gathered regularly to
see the LEO fly-out. Charles, Lee, Noreen, Jimmy, and I were
there almost every night. Ben Cacace, a birder and amateur
astronomer, often came along, and two or three others. We had
all shared many happy hours at the hawk bench during Pale
Male's most productive years. Now we'd found a way to continue
observing wildlife even after the hawks were asleep for the
night.

After a few weeks of going our separate ways after fly-out, we
became more adventurous. One day, at Noreen's instigation, we
thought we'd see where the LEOs went after leaving their daytime roosts. We followed them to the top of Cedar Hill, Lee and
Noreen in the lead, and found the owls perched in a bare tree
near the drive. They spent a few minutes preening and then took
off again. When we saw them fly westward, across the drive in
the direction of the Ramble, we looked at each other and
thought, Why not? That was our first owl prowl.

We wandered about the Ramble many times thereafter,
sometimes losing owls and then suddenly finding them; Lee and
Noreen seemed to have a seventh sense. But in all those years
only Ben saw an owl hunt successfully. One January evening he

had gone a bit ahead and found himself near Bow Bridge, the graceful span that connects the Ramble with Cherry Hill. As he stopped and waited for the others, he heard a sound and looked around. That was the moment he saw a long-eared owl capture a rat. Just afterward, he said, the owl gave "a demonic call, louder than anything I've ever heard uttered by a bird, and it caused the tiny hairs on the back of my neck to rise."

One year—it was our ninth season at the Hawk Bench and the hawk baby count was up to twenty-one—we began to pursue owls with a new seriousness and sense of purpose. It was the pellet project that helped transform us from hawkwatchers with a casual interest in other birds into dyed-in-the-wool owlers, "ornithological fanatics who have fallen under the owl's spell," in Jonathan Evan Maslow's words. He's a deep-rooted owler himself and the author of a fine book called *The Owl Papers.* Certainly our studies of LEO pellets awakened the dormant dream most birdwatchers share of making a contribution to scientific knowledge.

Owls, you must know, don't go in for fancy food preparation. Down the hatch goes the rat, head first, tail last. The owl's digestive system then spends quite a few hours separating the digestible parts from the indigestible. The process begins in the gizzard, the lower of two enlargements in a bird's stomach. There a little tornado of digestive juices envelops the rat parts and separates the hard, sharp items from the good stuff. The rejects become encased in a rounded mass of feathers or fur—the pellet. The nutritious substances, the blood and meat and some of the internal organs, are transformed into a semiliquid substance called chyme.

The chyme enters the bird's small intestine, where bile and pancreatic enzymes transform it into proteins, fats, and carbohydrates. These nutrients then pass through the intestinal wall into the bird's bloodstream to serve as fuel for all its life processes. We absorb the useful part of what we eat in pretty much the same way.

But the pellet still has a journey to make inside the owl. From the gizzard it moves along into the upper enlargement of the stomach called the proventriculus. The little fuzzy, bony collection—the owl's *salon des refusés*, one might call it—stays there for some hours, up to thirteen in the case of long-eared owls. Finally the owl is ready to get rid of the pellet. It needs to unload it before taking in another meal. When does that happen? Pellets are ejected just before the bird flies off at day's end and in the early-morning hours after returning to its day roost. By boning up (sorry!) on the mechanics of LEO digestion, we came to understand why those are the times for ejection.

Much of the owl's hunting is done at dusk and just before dawn. Say an owl flies out of its daytime roost at 5:00 p.m. and heads for the Ramble. And say it catches a small rat at 6:00 p.m. If the process from consumption to pellet formation takes thirteen hours, then the rat that went down the hatch at 6:00 p.m. will be ejected at about 7:00 the next morning. Similarly, the skull and bones of a victim caught at the predawn hunt will be in the pellet ejected just after fly-out.

Most of the time we found already-ejected pellets under the owl's roost tree. But on rare occasions over the years we actually saw an owl in the act of ejecting a pellet, usually on its first perch just after fly-out. The bird would screw up its head and begin to move it around weirdly in a bump-and-grind kind of motion. The Exorcist meets the Ecdysiast. Then the owl, gagging spasmodically and looking as if it's about to expire, opens its beak wide, and out flies a small cylindrical object. It's slimy when first ejected but quite undisgusting once it dries.

Many people assume that owl pellets are the equivalent of owl shit. In fact, pellets are neat little end products of a remarkable process quite unlike the human body's waste disposal system. But owls do excrete some waste products in the form of a thick whitish goo called whitewash. Now *that's* owl shit. Owls eliminate whitewash through their cloacal vent, located at the end where you'd expect waste products to come from. Pellets, however, are neither excreted nor eliminated; they're thrown up, emerging from the bird's beak. That's why a clever manufacturer of children's science toys is offering a packet of owl pellets for dissection in classrooms or at home under the brand name Owl Vomit. Besides appealing to kids' penchant for the disgusting, school pellet-dissection projects serve the valuable purpose of raising awareness that human digestion is just one of many possible ways food can be converted into energy.

Think about it. Isn't the owl's method much more efficient than ours? Instead of all the chicken-plucking, cow- or pig-skinning, and corn-husking that we do, all the marinating, frying, charbroiling, and finally chewing, chewing, chewing, the owl merely bolts down the food in its original state and lets his insides do the work.

For years we gathered up LEO pellets and tucked them away for eventual study. But somehow we never got around to actually doing it. For one thing we didn't have the right optical equipment. Sometimes we took one or two of the little cylindrical objects to the American Museum of Natural History, where, apologetically, we'd coax a member of the mammalogy department to tell us the specifics of our owl's dinner. But we didn't have the nerve to do it with a hundred pellets.

Then Brad Klein, the bat enthusiast who fell into the Azalea Pond during the first bioblitz, came into the picture. Brad is a scholar and a polymath. Besides bats, he's studying birds, fireflies, dragonflies, and many other aspects of natural history. He also plays the mandolin and the ukulele and knows a lot about art and architecture. When we learned that Brad had acquired a high-quality stereoscopic microscope to further his studies of invertebrates, we knew it was just what we needed to further our studies of owl pellets and their contents.

We spent quite a few evenings with Brad and his wife, Danielle Gustafson. We drank good red wine and nibbled on various artisanal cheeses that Brad and Danielle (who also fell into the pond) just happened to have around, while we studied the tiny bones we'd extracted from our pellets, particularly the intact skulls and mandibles. Skulls have distinctive features that help identify a species. And if the mandibles still contain teeth, that's even better. The patterns on the chewing surfaces of rodent teeth are diagnostic, as they say.

A fascinating finding emerged. An occasional Norway rat turned up in a LEO pellet, but most of the mammal bones came from white-footed mice. On a previous occasion I'd taken a saw-whet owl pellet to be analyzed at the natural history museum, and when they'd found the skull of a white-footed mouse inside, it created a stir. The species had never been found in Central Park before! At least its presence had not been noted on any official Central Park mammal survey. The single mention of a Central Park white-footed mouse appeared in the minutes of a meeting of the Linnaean Society of New York on November 14, 1922. On that day a certain Mr. Woodruff "reported the capture of a White-footed mouse (*Peromyscus leucopus*) in Central Park, New York City." Well, our collection of LEO pellets now revealed that the little rodent is far from uncommon there.

So, ladies and gentlemen, please welcome the white-footed mouse, a handsome little creature with rich, reddish-brown fur above and a snowy white belly below. You already know the color of its feet. It's just a little larger than the common house mouse, the one that inhabits people's homes and elicits *eeks* when unexpectedly encountered. The white-footed mouse, on the other hand, never shares a house with humans, though it may invade your country cottage in winter when you're not in residence. From my own experience with a weekend cabin not far from New York City, I can tell you that this mouse really likes to nest in the fine down comforter you were foolish enough to leave there when you closed for the season. The white-footed mouse likes to eat in bed and doesn't seem to be toilet trained.

Peromyscus leucopus differs from the house mouse and all other local mice in another surprising way: it frequently lives in trees. As good a tree climber as a squirrel, White Foot will often spend the winter in an old woodpecker hole or an abandoned bird nest that it has converted into a perfect, well-protected mouse shelter. Its life span is not long, since just about every owl and carnivorous mammal around depends upon it for sustenance.

White-footed mice are ubiquitous. Indeed, they may be the most widespread and abundant mammal in North America. Why, then, had none of these animals been discovered in Central Park before, when in all likelihood there have always been great numbers of them scampering about? Answer: short of organizing costly scientific studies involving extensive trapping, people have no way of knowing *anything* about the presence or absence of nocturnal creatures in Central Park or indeed in any given area.

To this day rumors abound of another nocturnal mammal's presence in Central Park: the flying squirrel. Nobody can categorically say that flying squirrels *don't* live there. That no one has ever seen one proves nothing. You don't ever *see* flying squirrels, not in the dark of night, not even in a park filled with streetlamps. A few years ago a friend of mine with a weekend house near the city took down a bird box for winter storage. He was amazed to find a little flying squirrel family huddled within, sleeping. He had had no idea this mammal even existed.

Nocturnal implies unseen and therefore unknown. But take apart a large number of owl pellets to find a predominance of *Peromyscus leucopus* skulls, and you've surmounted the shortcomings of human vision. You've penetrated the darkness with the help of an owl's digestive system.

Our little band of owl-watchers had scientific aspirations—most serious birders do. Nevertheless, our fantasies often centered on more romantic matters, as they did the year two long-eared owls roosted all winter in a blue spruce at Cedar Hill. We never doubted that the pair had an amorous relationship and we did our best to celebrate it. On Valentine's Day we read love poems to them as they sat almost touching on the same branch of their roost tree. On New Year's Eve we toasted them with champagne—*To love everlasting!* Charles, Noreen, and I even heard them murmuring sweet nothings to each other very early one morning when we met at their tree an hour before sunrise to watch them arrive from their night's hunt—the fly-in. Well, we didn't really see the moment of arrival—it's dark at five on a winter's morning—but all at once we heard a series of low, beguiling sounds coming from the branches overhead. Charles, a true romantic, called it owl music and attended several more fly-ins on his own just to hear LEO pillow talk.

A little after sunset on a cold Thursday in mid-March, as Lee, Noreen, Charles, and I were waiting for the LEOs to fly out, an apple-cheeked young man with binoculars showed up at the blue spruce. He seemed to know about the owls, about us, and (we somehow got the feeling) about everything else in the world worth knowing. He gave us his card: Mr. Rob Williams, Ecologist, from Norwich, England. He had just arrived in New York to study—what do you imagine?—long-eared owls! In fact he had made his way to Cedar Hill directly from the American Museum of Natural History, he told us, where he'd been looking at the collection of owl skins.

How had he found out about our owls? we asked. The chairman of the museum's ornithology department—a great man, he assured us—had told him of a pair of LEOs in Central Park being monitored by a group of park birders. We exchanged glances. That was us—we were on the map. Before we gave Mr. Rob Williams, Ecologist, a chance to look at the long-eared owls, we peppered him with questions. Could this be the same pair that had roosted in the park last year? (Maybe.) Where did they come from? (Could be anywhere.) And our most burning question: Any chance that they might settle down and raise a family right here in Central Park? (Well, let's have a look at them and we might have an answer.) An enigmatic response. Why should a look at the owls reveal their breeding plans? Did he plan to ask them directly?

At last we pointed out the owl tree, but it took the young man quite a few minutes to find the birds. We were not too helpful—he was the owl expert, after all. But to be fair, the owls were extremely difficult to find in the thick evergreen. The pair had found a perfect hiding place, safe from most inquisitive eyes, though fortunately not our own. To see them you had to stand in one particular spot, directly in front of a trash basket located next to a small rock outcrop halfway up the Cedar Hill east-west path. Once on the spot and not three inches to the right or left of it, you faced east and scanned the tree at midheight, looking for a small window of light in the otherwise densely needled spruce. If you looked at a branch that was visible only through that small opening, you could clearly see the two owls.

Finally we showed mercy and steered him to the right spot. We knew the moment he finally found our owls. "Ah, there you are at last," he said somewhat reproachfully, as if he were chiding a friend who'd kept him waiting on a street corner.

Fastening his binoculars on the owls, he examined them for a long while. "You noticed the coloration of the face, of course," he finally said in a seemingly collegial but unmistakably condescending manner. "Buffy, right? And look at the inside of the ear tufts, they're quite buffy too. That clinches it."

"Clinches what?" we asked.

"They're both females," he stated authoritatively. "The males are much lighter. The male has a white border around the facial disk."

We were speechless.

"The end of romance," Charles muttered, glowering uncharacteristically at the young Brit.

"Are you sure?" Noreen asked, disappointed but not as crest-
fallen as Charles.

"Yes, these are females. They're big, too! Meaty! I'd be interested in what they're eating."

We couldn't resist the temptation to show off—perhaps it's
contagious. Thanks to our pellet project, we knew quite a bit
about what our little carnivores were consuming, and in the
spirit of true forgiveness we shared our knowledge with Rob
Williams. I may have imagined it, but he seemed mildly im-
pressed.

☾

One bitterly cold night in early January I found myself walking home alone from an owl fly-out. A small crowd had
gathered at dusk in the little grove near Willow Rock to see a
great horned owl take off, but that night, for some reason, none
of the owl regulars were there. The other fly-out witnesses had
left along with the owl, the humans walking east toward the
nearest park exit while the owl headed west. Well, west was my
direction too. I hesitated for a moment—widespread disap-
proval of solitary night walks in the park has *some* effect. Besides, I hadn't brought a flashlight. Well, I rationalized, there'll
be plenty of light. It was a crisp, clear evening and directly overhead was a waxing moon, almost full. Besides, why head in the
wrong direction? I crossed the rustic bridge over the Gill, the
meandering little stream that turns on and off, and made my way
through the Ramble toward Central Park West.

But in spite of the visible moon, it was unusually dark as I
walked through the deserted wilderness, or what passes for
wilderness in the center of New York City. I had completely for-
gotten that it's much darker in the park's woodlands on a clear
night than when the sky is overcast. It seems counterintuitive,
but the explanation is simple. Clouds reflect the city's myriad

night lights, making the park and its paths particularly bright on overcast evenings.

I had just come up the little hill from the Azalea Pond and started on the path to the Humming Tombstone when three big, tough-looking guys materialized out of the darkness at the inter-section of a path just ahead. Now they were on my very path, walking very slowly in front of me. I stopped, raised my binoculars, and began to scan the treetops, pretending—to whom? to myself, perhaps—that I was looking for an owl. *Keep going,* I silently urged them. But they stopped too. *Uh-oh.*

This is it, I thought, my heart pounding. I was scared, and I suppose it was obvious, as one of them said: "Don't be afraid. We're undercover cops." They began walking again.

The moment they moved along my fear vanished. Now I was consumed with curiosity. Were they? I walked a bit faster and caught up with them. "Are you really undercover cops?" I asked them.

They laughed. "Well, if we were, we couldn't tell you, could we?" one of them answered. "Then we wouldn't be undercover."

I hardly had time to consider the logic of his answer when an-other one said, "No, we're not really undercover cops. We're like the guys on *21 Jump Street.*"

"What's that?" I asked. The men no longer seemed sinister. Now that I could see them up close, they looked . . . well, okay.

"It's a TV program. Maybe it's not on the air anymore, just re-runs. It's about a bunch of vigilantes, like Curtis Sliwa's group, you know, the Guardian Angels."

"Well, what's your name?" I asked the guy who was doing most of the talking, the one who had looked the scariest at first. I seem to always ask people their names. Maybe I had an idea I'd be writing about this encounter.

"Sahib," he answered. "That's the name I'll be using." He wasn't missing a beat. The other two introduced themselves as "Jerry" and "Bruce."

We chatted for a few more minutes. I told them I thought it might be a great idea to have a bunch of tough-looking volunteers patrolling the park's wooded areas at night. "Actually, why don't you get the Central Park police precinct to help you set up your program?" I asked, trying to be helpful.

The three guys looked at each other. Then Sahib answered, "No, they wouldn't touch us. We've done time."

"You what?" I blurted out.

"Well, I've done five years," he answered. Bruce and Jerry seemed to have done five between them.

"I guess you're right," I finally said. "The cops probably won't help." By now we were on the east-west path to the West Drive, near the Great Lawn. They were going north, while I was heading for the exit straight ahead, at 81st Street and Central Park West. "Well, nice meeting you," I said. "Good luck."

As I waved goodbye, Sahib called after me, "Now you go right home, you hear? Don't go wandering around in the dark."

In all the years I've been walking around the park at night, both alone and with friends, I've had only two scary experiences. This was the first.

3

Much Ado
About Mothing

O ne year a small group of Central Park birdwatchers—I
was one of them—decided to take up the study of night
insects. We were in that tiresome lull between spring
migration and fall migration otherwise known as summer, and
the city was enduring a particularly bad heat wave. With temperatures approaching a hundred degrees, we thought a night expedition might be refreshing. We prevailed upon the American
Museum of Natural History to provide an entomologist and the
necessary equipment for night viewing, while we, in turn, promised to deliver some eager participants. Bug Night was the name
assigned to the event, and it was set for July 14.

At eight-thirty that evening, four minutes after sunset, our
little band assembled in front of the statue of the Prussian naturalist Alexander von Humboldt at the corner of 77th Street and
Central Park West. Charles, Lee, Noreen, Jimmy, and I had
come straight from the Hawk Bench together with Norma
Collin, a longtime park birder. We were all friends thanks to Pale
Male. Though the hawklets had already fledged that year (it was
the first year the Fifth Avenue nest had succeeded), quite a few
hawk fans were still gathering at the model-boat pond every afternoon and evening, hoping for a sighting of one or the other of
the newly famous pair. Five or six other insect enthusiasts were

also there, having heard about Bug Night by word of mouth; one was from the Parks Department and one was a graduate student in biology.

With the museum's expert leading the way, we entered the park through the Naturalist's Gate, appropriately named, from our point of view: it allows easy access to the Ramble. The entomologist was wheeling a portable generator to power a device called a black light. Resembling an ordinary fluorescent tube, this fixture emits light of a far shorter wavelength, the kind of light that insects are particularly drawn to. Its beams would bring in the winged characters of our insect spectacular.

We searched for the darkest possible spot in the Ramble. Without competing light sources the black light would attract more insects. We finally chose a small clearing near the Rustic Summerhouse—three of the four streetlamps that normally light the area happened to be broken, a lucky break for us. As we hung our sheet between two trees, we all fell silent. The city had vanished. The only sounds to be heard were a bullfrog croaking somewhere nearby and the occasional *tseep* of a bush katydid. In the darkness none of us realized that we had set up shop at Warbler Rock, a birdwatching location we knew well. We had spent countless daylight hours looking at migrating songbirds there, but it looked strange and unfamiliar now.

A few fascinating if not entirely conventional people showed up at our light on Bug Night: the man in the Dracula costume, for instance, sporting black pants, black shirt, black cape, and a full set of fake teeth with fangs, who suddenly materialized out of the darkness and caused some consternation. He listened attentively to an explanation about the black light and its attractiveness to insects, and since he didn't seem to know what an insect was—it's odd how many people don't—the museum expert gave us a basic lesson in insect anatomy. The Dracula lookalike stayed the rest of the evening, nodding at each arrival on the sheet in a spaced-out sort of way. He kept muttering something under his breath, a Transylvanian incantation or lycan-thropic spell, I imagined. I sidled closer. Finally I just made out his words: "One, two, three, four, five, six legs . . . insect."

Our first six-legged customer landed on the sheet seconds after the light was turned on: a shiny black click beetle. If you overturn one of these on your hand, it flings itself into the air to right itself. During the process, a hook-and-catch mechanism at the joint between its abdomen and thorax produces a little click, and hence the name. Its order, Coleoptera, is the largest in the insect class. It includes more than 300,000 known species in the world, 28,600 in North America alone. This fact inspired someone to tell an old story about the great British biologist J.B.S. Haldane, one that often comes up when people announce how many beetles there are. When asked by a solemn clergyman, "What can be inferred about the Creator from the wondrous works of nature?" the scientist answered: "An inordinate fondness for beetles."

Our next arrivals were, in order: a caddis fly, a katydid, a leafhopper, a froghopper, an earwig, an ichneumon wasp, and a lovely, pale-green, fragile-looking insect with lustrous eyes and large transparent wings laced with green—a green lacewing, the museum man said. It is also called a stinkfly, he added, though he didn't know why this beautiful creature should have such a lowly name. Later I learned that in 1987 Thomas Eisner, a pioneer in chemical ecology, isolated a compound called skatol that is secreted by members of the Chrysopid family. Skatol shares a linguistic root with the word *scatological* and for good reason. It gives off a distinctly fecal odor. The lovely green lacewing, a member of the Chrysopidae, emits the stinky substance when it's threatened by a potential predator. Mystery solved.

Chrysopids, as it happens, exude another chemical, hexanal, to protect their eggs from ants. Eisner notes that the same substance is found in human ear wax and speculates that it may serve to keep ants out of picnickers' ears. I'd bet my hat on that idea.

The variety of nocturnal insects flying around in Central Park amazed us. But moths were the stars of the show that night. Some of them were astonishingly beautiful—the ailanthus web-worm moth, for instance, a tiny little jewel of bright orange, yellow, and black that curls itself up into a miniature cylinder. "Is that really a moth?" many of us asked in wonder. Others had fernlike antennae or mysterious runic patterns engraved on their wings. One medium-sized moth flashed open its bark-colored outer wings and briefly revealed a bright orange and black pattern beneath. Everything about these wondrous insects intrigued us. Our love affair began on the spot.

Birdwatchers are in the habit of identifying—that's what makes the sport compelling. Consequently everyone at Bug Night wanted to identify the insects that landed on our sheet too. The challenge we faced became clear with our first insect arrival, the click beetle. There happen to be about eight hundred click beetle species in North America (seven thousand worldwide). If there had been a field guide for the click beetle family alone—there is not—we might have had a better chance to nail down the particular insect we were looking at. As it was, we could only be confident that it was a member of the click beetle, or Elateridae, family.

To a birdwatcher this may seem the equivalent of identifying a bird as "a woodpecker" without further determining if it is a downy or hairy or redheaded or red-bellied woodpecker. The difference, of course, lies in the total number of bird species among which we have learned to distinguish the different woodpecker species, as compared to the insect totals. Since in North America there are only 810 bird species altogether, and merely 22 of them in the woodpecker family, it's possible to find them all in a field guide and learn to identify each one. But even a field guide devoted entirely to beetles couldn't include all 28,600 North American beetle species.

Moths presented a similar challenge, but we ended up with some unexpected help.

"Hmmm," the museum man vocalized under his breath, as he examined a medium-sized, narrow brown-and-black moth that had just landed. "It's a Noctuid," he announced, after leafing through a dog-eared volume. "That's the largest family of Lepidoptera—about three thousand of them just in North America. Many noctuids are brownish or grayish like this one." In answer to a question, he added, "Yes, moths are Lepidoptera, just like butterflies. Not much difference between them except that most butterflies are active by day and most moths at night. You might call moths the butterflies' nocturnal cousins, though there are quite a few day-flying moths too."

He peered at the moth again for a few more minutes, then resumed leafing through the book. "Hmm. Looks like it's in the dart subfamily. Let's see . . ." I looked over his shoulder at the page he was studying so intently and saw three columns of illustrations on a light blue background. All the figures on the page looked alike—pale in color, light brown or gray. All appeared in the same pose, spread out with four wings exposed. The one on the sheet didn't look the least like any of those images: for one thing it seemed to have only two wings, not four. It *did* have four, in fact, but like many moths it covered its hind wings with its forewings when at rest. That night the Dracula man was not the only one in the group to learn that almost all insects have two pairs of wings. (The flies are the big exception, having only a single pair of wings. Diptera, the order to which flies belong, means "two-winged" in Greek.)

As the museum expert pored over his book, a youngish man who'd been standing diffidently a few feet behind us ambled up to the sheet. Somewhat stocky in build, he was wearing a light blue T-shirt, khaki shorts, and a Yankees baseball cap. Hadn't I seen him in the park before?

He mumbled something I couldn't make out and shrugged his shoulders in an awkward way, as if apologizing. Then he began to examine the moth on the sheet. Using something like a jeweler's loupe attached to a lanyard, he studied the moth with uncommon intensity. He seemed to be memorizing it, imprinting its pattern on his mind's eye as if it were a poem. Then he extracted a book from his backpack, the same book the museum man had consulted, as it happens, and just as dog-eared. He quickly turned to a page, stared at it, then at the moth again, and then at the page again. Finally he relaxed for the first time. "Yup, that's what I thought. It's a greater black-letter dart." He glanced at an earlier moth arrival, the one that had flashed an orange and black pattern on its hind wings, and said quietly, "I'd say that one is a girlfriend underwing."

The museum man looked in his book at one image and then the other, and finally said with admiration, "You're right. That's what they are."

I turned my eyes to the man in the Yankees cap. Who was he? I wondered. His name, I found out later, was Nick Wagerik. He was to become our moth guru.

Our featured moths of the evening, the ones we assigned names to, were the greater black-letter dart, the ailanthus webworm moth, the lesser maple spanworm, the gypsy moth (a beautiful creature in spite of its devastating habits), the girlfriend underwing, the funerary dagger moth, and the ipsilon dart. We had identified seven moth species! Another entity, a collective one, received a name that night. Inspired by Bug Night, Charles, Lee, Noreen, Jimmy, and I became the core of an informal little band I think of as the Central Park Mothers.

Calling ourselves "the Central Park Mothers" when speaking presents no problem—we pronounce it in a way that makes our meaning clear. But writing the name brings up a verbal oddity called a homograph, defined as one of two or more words that have different meanings and pronunciations but are spelled the same. The word *sewer* is a homograph: when pronounced to rhyme with *bluer*, it's the place where sewage goes; when it rhymes with *rower*, it means one who sews. A more familiar verbal form is the homophone, one of two or more words that have different meanings and spellings but are pronounced the same way. Word pairs like *site* and *sight* and *break* and *brake* are homophones. *Cents*, *scents*, and *sense* are a trio of homophones.

The word *mother* is a homograph. Most of the time it rhymes with *brother* and signifies a female parent. But if it rhymes with *author*, it has an entirely different meaning. The homographic mothers in these pages may be female or male, may be parents or childless. Equipped with flashlights, magnifying glasses, binoculars, cameras, and a maddening field guide, they are engaged in a study of those mysterious, misunderstood, heat- and humidity-loving nocturnal insects known as moths. And since it's almost impossible to read the word *mother* without conjuring up a female parent, I'll try in some way to clarify which one I'm talking about whenever I use one of the homographic pair.

Shortly after Bug Night the Central Park Mothers (rhymes with *authors*) took a step that transformed our nascent love affair with moths from fantasy to reality: we ordered a black light and a battery pack of our own from a California science-equipment company. It was as simple as that. We could stop pestering the museum to lend us expert help. We could go moth-hunting on our own anytime we wanted.

A little garden at the north end of the Loeb Boathouse parking lot became our headquarters. Some volunteers from the Woodlands Advisory Board had planted butterfly- and moth-attracting flowers there—milkweed, joe-pye-weed, purple cone flowers, and the like—vowing to maintain it regularly. But Charles was the only one who continued to put in time weeding and replanting. Eventually everyone simply called it Charles's Garden.

Birdwatchers, insect lovers, and friends, all part of the Central Park nature community, made up the cast of characters at those first Moth Nights, with Charles, Lee, Noreen, and Jimmy the principal organizers. Davie Rolnick, then an exuberant six-year-old, and his engaging young mom, Julia, were charter members—no early bedtime needed for a home-schooled kid. Norma Collin, a hawkwatcher from the early Pale Male days, usually joined us, and so did park regulars Sylvia Cohen, Michael Bonifanti, Charles Matson, and Marianne Girards. A new horizon had opened up for us, and we were eager to learn. But we were starting from scratch. Though we *could* tell a hawk from a handsaw (or even from a heron),* we could hardly tell a moth from a mayfly. I for one didn't yet know that the distinguishing characteristics of moths and butterflies are the scales that cover their body and give them their colors and patterns. Moths have them—mayflies don't. Hence Lepidoptera, meaning "scale-winged" in Greek. We were all rank beginners, and we needed help.

Nick Wagerik was our man—that was clear from the start. On Bug Night he had revealed a special talent for identifying moths. But would he come with us on our first solo voyage? I took it upon myself to phone him and ask—I should say beg. He grumbled and hemmed and hawed on the phone—"I don't know if I can make it. Doubt it. Maybe." For years thereafter he grumbled and hemmed and hawed. That was his way. But he always showed up. Hallelujah, as Charles Kennedy used to say at the slightest provocation.

Once or twice a week we lugged the heavy mothing equip-

---

*When Hamlet says, "I know a hawk from a handsaw" (II.ii.), he offers a comment that has been widely quoted to indicate foolishness. Who but a fool would confuse a large bird of prey with a small wood and metal tool? A more subtle meaning emerges with the understanding that *handsaw* was a common Elizabethan distortion of the word *hernshaw*, or heron. The Prince of Denmark is saying that he is a good enough birder to tell apart a hawk and a heron, two large birds that might be confused with each other, especially in flight.

ment to Charles's Garden. Lee brought an old sheet that had previously served as a drop cloth, and we attached it with clothespins to a chain-link fence at the garden's northern end. We clipped on the black light, plugged it into the battery pack, and instantly the bulb glowed with a weird, pale violet light. Within seconds the insects began to arrive.

On our first night as independent mothers (*authors*), the first visitor was a crane fly. This insect resembles a gigantic mosquito, and many people swat at it when it appears, thinking it will inflict a superbite. In fact, it does not bite people: it bites (and eats) mosquitoes, lots of them. Since crane flies *are* attracted to commercial bug zappers while mosquitoes are not, that particular form of insect control is obviously counterproductive. In spite of the crane fly, quite a few of the insects attracted by our light that evening were mosquitoes. That was the bad news. The good news was that we had moths galore, and Nick was there to help us figure them out. By 11:00 p.m. when we finally called it quits, we had identified nine different species for our brand-new "Moths of Central Park" list.

Nick was always on the lookout for underwing moths, a genus in the Noctuid family he regarded with special passion. The scientific designation, Catocala, derives from the Greek words *kato* (under) and *kala* (beautiful), and if you want to pronounce it the way entomologists do you must put the accent on the second syllable: *kah-*TOCK*-uh-la.* For many years we pronounced it otherwise, with the accent on the third syllable—*kat-oh-*COLL*-uh*—until an expert disdainfully pointed out our gauche mistake. That may be why many of us persist in pronouncing it the wrong way. You should feel free to do the same.

Only one underwing moth appeared at our light that first evening—a species called the ilia (*Catocala ilia*). It didn't stay long, but for a few seconds it opened up its forewings to reveal the radiant orange-and-black ones underneath. Oh! The color came as a surprise, and we wanted more.

Unfortunately for us, most underwings do not gravitate to lights. They're more likely to be attracted by sugary bait. Ever hopeful, Charles began arriving at the garden with a foul-smelling concoction made of rotting fruit, brown sugar, molasses, stale beer, and God knows what else. (Some say that human urine adds a certain *je ne sais quoi* to the stuff.) Using a big paintbrush, Charles glopped it onto a number of tree trunks. The bait did, in fact, draw in a few underwings, whetting our appetite for the en-thralling moths that we were soon to specialize in. But the main beneficiaries of Charles's largesse seemed to be ants.

We knew that identifying moths would be hard. It didn't take us long to understand just how formidable an undertaking it would be. It made the difficulties of birdwatching pale in comparison. Why? To begin with the obvious, you can't tell moths apart by song, as you can with songbirds. You have only their complex markings to go by and, as we were learning, the wing-pattern differences among moth species are frequently inconspicuous. And while all birds of a kind are pretty much the same size (apart from sexual dimorphism) and color (apart from developmental differences), moths of the same species often differ significantly in size and color due to variations in their caterpillars' diet: if there's not enough to eat in the larval stage, a caterpillar will form its pupa early rather than starve; the adult that emerges will be smaller. Color variations within moth species may also re-flect different larval food sources.

To compound the difficulty, a moth you encounter on a tree or a sheet may not be in tip-top condition. It has been spending its precious days (most moths live for a few weeks or less) trying to elude birds, spiders, bats, and other moth-eaters. The ones that manage to escape often do so at a cost. That's why so many moths we see have ragged, incomplete wings. Having managed to wriggle out of a spiderweb by leaving most of its scales be-hind, a moth may appear on a sheet or tree with almost no pattern or color showing—worn, as they say, and thus extremely difficult to identify. Finally, moths can be jumpy and skittish, landing on your sheet for an instant and then disappearing into the darkness, never to return. Scientists solve this problem by "collecting" the moth—that is, killing it. Then they can mount and pin it with outspread wings to study at leisure.

To collect an insect, you need a killing jar, a special glass container with a thick layer of plaster of Paris at its base. Before you go out in the field, you pour in some spoonfuls of cyanide or other lethal substance. Cyanide, the deadly poison used in so many detective stories? Yes, it's easily obtainable from the same entomological equipment shop that sold you the killing jar—no questions asked. The plaster soaks up the cyanide and you're ready to go. Once you've captured your insect, you pop it into the jar and close the cover tightly. The cyanide fumes kill the bug without damaging any part of it that would interfere with identification. Needless to say, every killing jar, as well as the vial of cyanide, has a large skull and crossbones affixed to it.

The *author*-rhyming mothers never acquired a killing jar. Though we were eager to pursue our interest scientifically, this particular way of doing science went deeply against our grain. Instead, we devised strategies to compensate for our tenderhearted avoidance. When a living moth landed on our sheet, we would clap a plastic container over it to allow leisurely examination. We'd release it unharmed when we finished. But lately our task has become easier. We simply take a close-up digital photo of the moth as soon as it lands. If it departs ten seconds later, it doesn't matter—we've got our photo to compare with the pictures in the field guide when we're ready.

The field guide—there's the rub. Birders can find at least ten birding guides—Sibley, Peterson, Kaufman, Stokes, the Golden, Geo, and others. You can buy any number of guides to butterflies, mammals, amphibians, and reptiles, all illustrated with colored drawings or photographs, and all inclusive. That is, they include all the birds or butterflies or frogs or mammals you will find in the geographical area they cover. But for identifying moths in Central Park there is only one field guide, *Eastern Moths*, by Charles V. Covell. It is universally referred to as Covell. It's devilishly hard to use.

A great but understandable shortcoming of Covell may explain why moth-watching has not become a popular hobby like bird- or butterfly-watching. The book shows only a tiny fraction of the moths in the area it covers, the northeastern United States. Imagine searching for a bird in your field guide and not being sure if it's even there. There are about 810 species of birds in North America, according to David Allen Sibley's authoritative guide, while there are more than 10,500 known species of moths in the same area. So how *could* any field guide cover them all? To be sure, Covell *does* include 1,300 of them, and provides pictures of most of the medium and large moths you are likely to find. Mainly the tiny micromoths are omitted. Yet tiny micromoths are what you're likely to see when you're out mothing, since they make up the majority of those 10,500 species. And some of them are breathtakingly beautiful. A few of these *are* in the book, the smallest being only one-fifth of an inch in length. But most of them aren't there. You can search and search and search the pages of Covell, and you won't find the lovely little moth that just landed on your sheet or tree.

One moth that Covell *does* include is the tiny webbing clothes moth (*Tineola bisselliella*). People who detest moths because they think all of them make holes in their cashmeres should know that out of the huge number of moth species known in North America, the major sweater-eater is this very moth and no other. I'm pleased to report that the Central Park Mothers (*authors*) have never once come across the webbing clothes moth in all their years of moth study. (Actually, the creature that eats your sweater is not the moth but its caterpillar. Once the moth emerges from its cocoon, it doesn't seem to eat anything at all.)

Because Covell's moths were all "collected," each and every one is shown in the same position in his illustrations: forewings and hind wings open and spread out. But that's not the way most moths look when you see them in real life. Living moths are likely to do odd things with their wings. They often curl them or hold them up over their abdomens like tents. Sometimes they roll themselves into tight little cylinders. Many moths cover up their hind wings altogether when they rest on a tree or on a sheet. To be sure, a few in the Geometer (or inchworm) family assume a wings-open Covell-like position when at rest. We grew quite fond of those.

We had other quibbles with Covell. Sometimes a living moth has a big furry cowl on its thorax, or thick cottony tufts on its femur or tibia. These features would be useful for identification, but Covell rarely comments on them. For another thing, not all Covell's images of moths are shown in full color. True, the black-and-white pages are often of black-and-white or monochromatic moths. But the noncolor plates are extremely hard to decipher, and . . . I'd better stop here. I can feel my blood pressure going up. I hate Covell.

This is totally unfair. How can I blame Charles V. Covell, Jr., for our difficulties? If there's anyone to blame, it's the moths— they're so numerous! In fairness, Covell *does* provide a great deal of valuable information in his written text. And though living moths look hugely different from the plates of the pinned dead ones, by looking meticulously, you learn to glean information from the little corpses too. Besides, he's the only game in town. So hurrah for Covell after all.

The difficulties of moth identification bring up an inevitable question: Why bother doing it at all if it's so maddeningly hard? Why not just enjoy the creatures for their beauty?

To understand why moth enthusiasts expend so much energy on identifying species that differ from one another so slightly, it helps to know something about taxonomic classification. In a common misconception, people tend to think that the category "moth" must be the equivalent of a category such as "dog." This would mean that the various moths we identify—the clouded underwing or the greater black-letter dart—are actually sub-species of a single species of insect called a moth, as Chihuahuas or Saint Bernards are variations of the mammal species known as *Canis familiaris*, the dog. In fact, each moth found in the field guide is a species of its very own. The proof: a Saint Bernard can (theoretically) breed with a Chihuahua, but a clouded underwing moth can breed only with another clouded underwing and not with any of the thousands of other moths known or unknown to science. This may explain why we take such pains to distinguish the bent-line gray from another moth that looks almost identical, the double-lined gray. At the heart of it lies biophilia, an appreciation for nature's diversity, though a soupçon of lunacy may lie there too.

The Catocalas—our chosen favorites among the moths—provide a perfect example of what moth identifiers are up against. Though differences in their black-and-white or brightly colored hind wings can reveal their identity at a glance, the ornery critters rarely choose to provide such a glance: there they are with their wings tightly closed and only their somber, cryptic forewings visible. Consequently, a would-be moth identifier who does not want to collect must use the differences that appear on the forewings. These differences may seem imperceptible at first, but they're there. You just have to make extremely fine distinctions of a kind you're rarely called upon to make in ordinary life. For example:

On the forewings of most underwing moths is a small kidney-shaped mark called the *reniform spot*. At first these marks look alike, but a closer inspection reveals differences: on some species the tiny spot is white in the center, on others it's brown or black, and the white ring that surrounds it (if there happens to *be* one) may be complete or broken. If the moth declines to help you out by opening its wings even the tiniest bit (as is often the case), the reniform spot may be the only way to identify the species with certainty.

There's also a zigzaggy white line, called the postmedial (p.m.) line, running about an inch above the fringe of the moth's forewings. Is it straight and regular, or is it irregular? Is it white or buffy or yellow? Moving toward the moth's head, you see another white zigzag line—the median line. Then above that is a dark line called the antemedial (a.m.) line. A distinctive p.m. line or a.m. line provides a big clue to the moth's identity.

If a Catocala moth happens to reveal its secret underwings, the task of pinpointing its identity becomes easier. As a desperation move, you can try to capture the moth and put it in your refrigerator for an hour or so. Usually the cold will make it relax and open its wings without in any way harming it. Then, if you're as scrupulous as the Central Park (*nonmaternal*) Mothers are, you'll have to go right back to the park in the middle of the night to give the moth its freedom.

The enigmatic names of the Catocalas cry out for explanation. What makes one particular species a sweetheart and another a darling? Why is one an old maid and another a bride? Nick suggests that the names reflect the entomologists' dilemma when faced with a group of moths so similar in appearance that the usual distinguishing characteristics cannot be used. In a group of moths called the prominents, for example, you'll find the double-toothed prominent, the white-dotted, the black-spotted, the white-streaked, the mottled, and others. Unable to use a varying physical feature for the names of Catocalas, the founding fathers of mothing (not a founding mother [*maternal*] among them) simply had to let their imaginations take over. One of them came up with a romantic name—the darling, perhaps—and they were off and running. It may be because of the weirdness of the Catocala names that almost all scientifically minded moth enthusiasts call the underwings exclusively by their Latin names. For instance, the mothing big shots always called the clouded underwing "nebulosa," as we were to learn in the future.

In a 1976 book specifically about Catocalas, Theodore Sargent finds the names almost as fascinating as the creatures themselves. "What great sadness could account for the Inconsolable Underwing, the Dejected Underwing and the Tearful Underwing?" he asks. "Might these not be cheered by the company of the Darling, the Sweetheart, or the Bride? Better to avoid, perhaps, the Penitent and the Old Maid."

Over the years the Central Park Mothers (*authors*) could not resist playing with the names either. One evening Jimmy Lewis came up with a fantasy sequence of moth arrivals that had a certain mad logic to it: The Charming breezed in first. The Darling turned up next, followed by the Girlfriend. After that, in order, the Sweetheart, the Betrothed, the Bride, the Married. Then, alas, the False, the Sordid, the Delilah. Before long the Penitent appeared and upon its heels the Once-Married. Naturally, the Dejected showed up next and right after it the Inconsolable. In Frankie and Johnny fashion the Widow ended the procession. Nick proposed a species as yet undiscovered: the Clinically Depressed.

4

The
Moth Tree

T he Moth Tree is an English oak located on Central Park's East Drive, just a little south of the Boathouse Restaurant, a little north of the 72nd Street transverse, and up the hill from the model-boat pond. Noreen discovered it one auspicious July evening on her way to Charles's Garden. A flying insect caught her eye, and as she idly watched it land on the English oak she noticed a collection of insects—ants, flies, butterflies, wasps, and hornets—all greedily feeding on spots of dark, sticky, frothy sap oozing from the tree's rough bark. Fascinated, she stayed for fifteen minutes, watching the butterflies and hornets slurping up the gooey stuff with their long probosces as if they were drinking milk shakes with a straw. Just before sunset the insects departed and so did Noreen, hurrying to report her odd sighting to the gang at the moth light.

Charles Kennedy made the next imaginative leap: If something about that tree attracts a bunch of insects in the daytime, might it not bring in a different bunch at night? We checked it out that very evening and wonder of wonders, there they were. Moths! Underwing moths! It was a gift from the gods. From that day on we needed neither the black light nor Charles's revolting mixture of moth bait. The tree attracted wonderful creatures all by itself.

A moth enthusiast named Bill Oehlke, who runs a Catocala website, remembers a similar tree he'd discovered when he was a boy growing up in Hunterdon County, New Jersey. "It was oozing a foamy white substance about two feet from the ground. Lots of insects were attracted. Some of the smaller Catocala species even visited during the day." Nick remembers a sap-oozing fringe tree in the Shakespeare Garden that once attracted insects during the day. But that was long ago and nobody thought to check it at night then. Now it's gone, downed in a storm perhaps, or cut down, Nick isn't sure.

The Moth Tree gave forth a strong, alcoholic smell. The tree's vital tissue, its phloem, is full of sugar, and fermented sugar was what we were smelling. It must be a sign of disease, Nick concluded gloomily. But that wasn't the way we saw it. Why look a gift horse in the mouth, or a gift tree in its phloem? The sap with its fermented smell was surely the magnet bringing in the moths. The remarkable work of biologists such as Thomas Eisner illustrates that communication requiring sensitive smell receptors is supremely important for insects in general and especially for nocturnal ones.

But moths use other senses besides the olfactory, even in darkness. In some cases it appears that moths' visual sense is even more refined than ours. Humans, for example, as well as many nocturnal mammals and birds, cannot discern colors in the absence of light. In recent years scientists have discovered that moths—at least certain species—can see colors in almost complete darkness. In 2002 Swedish biologists demonstrated that the elephant hawkmoth of Europe, *Deilephila elpenor*, can discriminate colors at illumination intensities corresponding to dim starlight. Writing in the scientific journal *Nature*, the biologists explained that "the possession of three photoreceptor classes reduces the absolute sensitivity of the eye, which indicates that color vision has a high ecological relevance in nocturnal moths." The writers of the paper don't discuss what that relevance might be, but color perception probably enhances sexual selection among these moths just as it does for diurnal birds and mammals.

For underwing moths, the colorful hind wings may indeed play a role in the sexual dramas that take place in darkness. But the flashing colors undoubtedly serve a protective function in the daytime. Say a sweetheart underwing is sleeping on a tree in its normal resting position, wings closed. With the streaky brown forewings completely covering the bright underwings, the moth is perfectly camouflaged on the tree's mottled brown trunk. But suppose a bird heading down the tree, a nuthatch, perhaps, suddenly stops short as it encounters the moth. What's this? Before the bird has a chance to gobble up what appears to be a tasty tidbit, flash! the moth opens its drab forewings to reveal the bright colors beneath. It just might succeed in scaring the bird away, or at least startling it for the few seconds it might take for the moth to make its getaway. It's also likely that the sight of the colorful hind wings deflects the bird's attack from the moth's more essential body parts, the abdomen, for example, attracting it to the more dispensable underwings. The moths with damaged hind wings we often see at the Moth Tree lend credence to this theory.

As for the sense of hearing· Amazingly, moths *do* have ears, consisting of a thin membrane, or tympanum, stretched over an opening. But rarely are moths' ears positioned on their heads. Some moth species have ears on their abdomens, while underwings' ears, and those of other members of the large Noctuid family, are located on the thorax. Moths communicate with each other primarily by means of chemicals called pheromones, which are released by glands in the abdomen and picked up by sensitive receptors in the antennae. What purpose, then, do the ears serve? A defensive one, most likely. A scholarly paper published by the Royal Society of Biological Sciences in 1997 established that moths not only have excellent ultrasonic hearing but are especially sensitive to frequencies emitted by their primary predators, aerial-hawking bats.

Though that study focused specifically on geometrid (or inchworm) moths of the subfamily Ennominae, it appears that many other moth families have good hearing too. In his charming book *Discovering Moths*, John Himmelman explains the common misapprehension about moths' hearing quite simply: "Moths just don't look as though they can hear," he notes. He performed a simple experiment.

> A friend once told me that if you jingle your keys where a moth is resting, it will drop to the ground. Apparently, the high pitch of the keys hitting one another resembles the high-frequency calls of bats . . . [One] night, I approached the moths gathered around the light in my yard, I gave my keys a shake and, sure enough, the moths scattered!

This may mean that the jingling keys produce overtones in frequencies just as high as bat calls. But are they loud enough for moths to hear? I don't know. In any event I should mention that on several occasions when we tried shaking keys at the Moth Tree our insects didn't budge. Perhaps we were using the wrong keys or perhaps our local moths are hard of hearing.

☾

Midsummer is the heyday of Central Park's moth-lovers. Only in July and August, especially when it's as hot and humid as a Turkish bath, do the underwing moths in all their glory come flocking to the Moth Tree. That's why we make an effort to celebrate the summer solstice. Summer at last—moths at the Moth Tree any day now.

One year a small group of us gathered at the park's West 81st Street entrance to see in the summer with proper ceremony. We'd chosen the Hunter's Gate as our portal that night, for though it was a bit too early for underwings, we were hunting nevertheless. Our quarry was night wildlife of any sort, and we hoped to catch a few errant spirits that might happen to be abroad on Midsummer Night's Eve, the shortest night of the year.

At Turtle Pond, the "Scottish Play" was just beginning at the Delacorte Theater, the outdoor stage just west of the pond where New Yorkers enjoy free performances of Shakespeare every summer. The "Scottish Play" is what showbiz people call *Macbeth*: they believe that uttering the name of the Thane of Cawdor brings bad luck. We too avoided saying it, superstition being the name of our game that evening. And how perfect to have the Scottish Play providing an appropriate soundtrack for our hunt. If anything could induce sprites and pixies to make an appearance, it would be three hags intoning, "Double double toil and trouble, fire burn and cauldron bubble" on the banks of Turtle Pond. As daylight faded, the ghostly towers of Belvedere Castle loomed above us. Patiently we sat on the grass and waited for our first spectral visitants.

They came at 8:45, two black skimmers. Members of the same family as gulls and terns, these birds of the night suddenly materialized from the southwest and began skimming back and forth just at the surface of the little pond. First they flew in tandem; then they crisscrossed separately, leaving a silvery wake behind them at each circuit. Occasionally we heard the snap of their beaks as they caught a fish.

The black skimmer, a medium-sized waterbird found on both coasts of the United States, is noted for its unusual feeding behavior. Its bright orange and black knifelike bill, whose lower part (mandible) extends beyond the upper (maxilla), is uniquely adapted to catch small fish in shallow water. A feeding skimmer flies low over the water with its bill open, its mandible slicing the surface. When the mandible touches a fish, the maxilla snaps down instantly to catch it. Although skimmers may be seen throughout the day, they are largely crepuscular and sometimes nocturnal; their particular fishing style lets them feed success-fully in low light or darkness when fish are more likely to be at the surface.

The Turtle Pond skimmers are a mystery. Where do they come from? Where do they go when they leave the park? The source of their attraction to Turtle Pond, however, is far from mysterious: the pond is home to legions of little fish, dumped from innumerable fish tanks as their owners get ready to leave for the summer or move from the city altogether, unloved pets whose owners cannot bear to flush them down the toilet or let them die of starvation. And this is probably the source of those legions of turtles that populate most of the park's water bodies—they are re-jected red-eared sliders, still a popular turtle sold in pet shops.

For the last six or seven years black skimmers have been show-ing up at Turtle Pond in late May or June. They often come around sunset and always leave before dawn. Sometimes they stay only an hour or two, and sometimes they are still skimming the pond at midnight, when their most dedicated observers head for home. That year their first arrival was noted on June 11 by Bob Levy, one of the Night People we often ran into. During the day Bob spent many hours observing the red-winged blackbirds around the Lake and Turtle Pond—we'd heard he was writing a book about them.

We watched the skimmers on Midsummer Night until it was too dark to see much more than their ghostly shapes over the water. Even then we could still hear their slightly nasal cries—*ank, ank, ank.* When we anked back at just the right moment it gave the illusion that we were having a conversation with them.

In the twilight a Canada goose family—two parents and four kids—preened directly in front of our waterside vantage point. Canada geese are unpopular in Central Park for good reason: when great numbers of them congregate on park lawns, they leave droppings the size of dog turds behind. Needless to say, no owner scoops up after them.

Some say that when park maintenance workers come upon a Canada goose nest, they insert a fine needle deep into each egg. This will effectively prevent embryonic development without causing the bird to cease incubation. A pair of geese sitting on "needled" eggs will continue to sit and sit long after the eggs are due to hatch, just as Pale Male and Lola did in the years their eggs failed to hatch. Once they finally abandon the eggs—geese or hawks—it will be too late to start anew. I was happy to see that this particular family had eluded the needle, if indeed the needle is actually used in Central Park.

At about 9:00, a black-crowned night-heron arrived from the direction of Belvedere Castle, stopped a moment, and promptly departed. Though the night-heron is a predatory bird, it may well have been deterred by the sinister-looking skimmers. With their wide-open mandibles gliding over the water's surface, the skimmers looked superpredatory. They looked like pterosaurs. No wonder people thought they were related in some way.*

An eastern kingbird twittered overhead, getting ready to roost for the night. Nobody had found a kingbird nest yet that year, but one would certainly be found before long. Kingbirds have nested in the trees overlooking Turtle Pond for as long as I can remember. The bird's Latin name is *Tyrannus tyrannus*, for good reason: these large flycatchers are the boldest birds in the avian class. You may choose not to believe this, but I once saw a kingbird in Cape Cod escorting a golden eagle out of his territory by pecking at the huge bird while riding on his back.

At a quarter after nine, we saw a small bird flying erratically over the water in an odd zigzagging pattern. Within a minute it

*Scientists long thought that the prehistoric flying reptiles known as pterosaurs fed by skimming too. But in 2007, using models of both black skimmer and pterosaur jaws, a group of researchers conducted drag tests in large water tanks and found that the ancient flyers couldn't have sustained flight while skimming. They didn't have the muscle power and jaw thickness. They probably foraged by swooping down, as gulls do, to pluck their fishy prey out of the water.

was joined by another and yet another. All at once we realized that these were not birds: they were bats. Big brown bats, we thought, though it was too dark to identify them by sight.

Bats were perfect for our Midsummer Night adventure, especially after the witches in the Scottish play had stirred their magic pot and listed its contents: "Eye of newt and toe of frog, wool of bat and tongue of dog." All the ingredients were available in Central Park except for the eye of newt.

We noted these and other manifestations of the mysterious forces of nature abroad on Midsummer's Night and prepared to move on—the Moth Tree was just a short walk away. We found that it had not yet begun to ooze its attractive sap—not a single moth, not a sap beetle, not an ant was in attendance. Then someone discovered a small spider starting to spin a web at the tree's base. Yes! What creature could be more otherworldly than a spider? Without a doubt that spider was the errant spirit we'd been waiting for, a messenger from beyond.

Our high spirits turned into a sort of rapture. Everyone joined hands and danced around the tree, shaking and shimmying while emitting muted yells and hollers and a not-very-convincing screech owl whinny. A group of Wiccans, latter-day witches and warlocks, are said to celebrate Midsummer's Night in the park every year with wild singing and demonic dancing at the Ramble end of Bow Bridge. Perhaps some of the people passing by as we whooped it up that night thought we were the real thing too.

☾

From the day of its discovery, the Moth Tree had become our new center of gravity. Arriving there a little before sunset, we'd see the last of the daytime insects—one or two question mark butterflies, a little squadron of bald-faced hornets, an occasional cicada killer wasp—all attracted to the pungent sap oozing from the oak. But these insects leave as night approaches and the period called civil twilight comes to an end.

Scientists use the term *civil twilight* to define precisely those twenty or thirty minutes before sunrise and after sunset when enough sunlight is reflected from the upper atmosphere to allow the eye to distinguish terrestrial objects. Civil twilight coincides with the timing of certain specific events in the natural world. As civil twilight begins, for instance, most birds finish their last-minute foraging and swiftly enter their night roosts, while owls fly out from their day roosts at the very end of it. Daytime insects such as hoverflies and bumblebees conclude their activities at the start of civil twilight, which is exactly when moths, that shadowy legion of the night, make their first appearance. Of course some moths are daytime fliers too. But most underwings, the objects of our special attention, are nocturnal.

Our most exciting times at the Moth Tree come during the next two stages of twilight, nautical and astronomical. It's getting dark when evening's nautical twilight commences. Now the horizon has become indistinct and only the vague outlines of objects may be seen. Nocturnal creatures are at their most active then, while all diurnal animals (apart from ourselves) are fast asleep. Astronomical twilight, when only the faintest traces of the sun's illumination come over the earth's horizon, is indistinguishable from true night for all but astronomers. For them, even a tiny bit of light obscures the dimmest celestial objects— distant nebulae, for example. For that you need night—dark, black night.

But it's never really dark in Central Park. According to the Bortle dark-sky scale, which classifies areas by their degree of light pollution, Central Park never achieves a better rating than 9—the bottom of the heap. Known as Inner-city sky, class 9 is characterized by highly illuminated skies in which only the brightest planets and stars are visible to the naked eye. Nevertheless, you'd be surprised at how many stars you can see in the middle of a park in the middle of one of the world's biggest and busiest cities. And you may find that some of the human resources available in Central Park compensate for the less than perfect conditions for stargazing. I'm talking about a community of friendly, education-minded young men—no women so far— whose generous purpose in life seems to be sharing their enthusiasm for astronomy with all interested passersby, especially children. I think of them as the star guys. On most clear nights they set up their equipment at the northeast corner of the Great Lawn, one of the largest open expanses in Central Park. It's a short walk from the Moth Tree, and even at the height of moth season, news of a special astronomical event will cause the moth-lovers to abandon their beloved underwings and head for the Great Lawn. Moth-watching may be magical, but it cannot compete with the mysteries of the universe.

One year an e-mail alerted me to an imminent astronomical happening: in a few days Venus and Jupiter would be setting at exactly the same time. This would make them appear like one huge star, so close to each other that they'd span the width of an index finger held at arm's length. A conjunction of planets, as it is called, is exactly the sort of picturesque phenomenon that Central Park's amateur astronomers love to point out to the passing world.

On the first of September, Charlie Ridgway and Tom Clabough, two regular star guys, arrived an hour before sunset to set up a large telescope and a pair of sixteen-power binoculars mounted on a tripod. By 6:30, when a little crowd of spectators had gathered, both instruments were aimed at the southwestern horizon to observe the conjunction. But first the curtain-raiser: by using distinctive tree outlines and skyline buildings as reference points, Tom pointed out to us a pinpoint of light in the southwestern sky—Venus, there in broad daylight. I would never have found it on my own—you have to know precisely where to look. I should add that it's not a once-in-a-lifetime experience to see Venus by day. I'd seen it earlier that year, when Ben Cacace showed me its exact spot in the daytime sky. It was just a small, incandescent dot then, as it was now, but looking up and seeing Venus (or indeed any other heavenly body besides the sun and moon) in the daytime sky is strangely thrilling.

By seven that evening Jupiter had appeared a little to the northwest of Venus. By 7:10, eighteen minutes before sunset, you could see both planets in a single binocular view. The seeming distance between them kept decreasing as each minute passed, and just at the moment when the horizon took on the burning red glow of sunset, I held out my arm with index finger extended. The planets were only 1.2 degrees apart at that moment, Charlie told me, and sure enough, my outstretched finger obscured them completely. Of course this did not mean that they were actually close to earth, as he explained to a couple of kids who'd joined our little group. Venus was 102 million miles away from us that night and Jupiter 580 million miles. It was an optical illusion; the two planets just happened to be in the same line of sight. And since this conjunction occurred before real dark had set in, the light it produced in Central Park was not as wondrous as it would be at midnight on a moonless night in a place with a low Bortle rating.

As we stood there that night with the Pinetum and the Reservoir behind us, we were facing the park's southern border and the enchanted night skyline of Central Park South: appearing from east to west, first the Plaza Hotel (now selling astronomically expensive condominiums as well as renting exorbitantly expensive hotel rooms); the Park Lane; the Ritz-Carlton; the gilded ziggurat of the Trump Parc; the copper mansard roof of the Hampshire House; Essex House with its huge red rooftop sign; and finally, at the western end, the two towers of the Time Warner Center at Columbus Circle. The man-made lights glittered. The planets outshone them that night.

Five days later the planets were joined at sunset by the slenderest of crescent moons. "Imagine the astrological significance that the ancients might have ascribed to a celestial summit meeting such as this," the Hayden Planetarium's Joe Rao wrote on Space.com, a widely read astronomy website. In honor of the special occasion, five amateur astronomers had set up telescopes at the usual place on the Great Lawn: Charlie, Tom, and Peter Tagatac, along with Kin Lee and Tom McIntyre, and Nick and I and some other observers joined them.

As the shadows lengthened, Venus became visible in the southwest. At 7:00 p.m. the setting moon came into sight, a slender D-shaped curve. Jupiter appeared just after sunset, and through a telescope we could see its equatorial bands and four of its moons. But the two planets had separated by a few more degrees since the conjunction. Even an outstretched hand in a baseball glove couldn't have blotted them both out that night. Instead, as dusk set in, Jupiter and Venus flanked the moon, two glowing eyes to the curving nose below.

The sun set at 7:19, the moon at 8:35, Jupiter ten minutes later, and Venus a few minutes after that, all at the western horizon. I used to be fuzzy about where the planets set, but eventually I put it all together. Like the sun, everything rises in the east and sets in the west—the moon, the planets, the comets, the stars, the whole shebang. Of course nothing actually rises or sets at all—it's an illusion. As Galileo demonstrated, it's not the movement of the sun that creates sunrise and sunset; in reality it's earth's rotation on its axis that moves us into and out of the light from the sun.

The planets were setting but still visible when the first stars appeared in the rapidly darkening sky. As each one became visible, the star guys told us its name. Spica was first, then Vega. More followed, popping out at a furious pace—Altair, Deneb, and Antares, a prominent red star in the constellation Scorpius. Arcturus I found by myself, the bright star I'd learned as a child by following the curve of the Big Dipper's handle. After that there were too many to keep naming. They marched around the ancient track, rank upon rank of them, while we mortals below watched with awe and wonder.

A few days later a friend gave me a book called *Myth and Meaning*, by the French anthropologist Claude Lévi-Strauss. "There's something about seeing Venus in the daytime that might interest you," he said.

Here's the passage: "Today we use less . . . of our mental capacity than we did in the past . . . When I was writing my first version of *Mythologiques* [*Introduction to a Science of Mythology*] I was confronted with a problem that to me was extremely mysterious. It seems that there was a particular tribe which was able to see the planet Venus in full daylight, something that to me would be utterly impossible and incredible."

I'm planning to send the father of structural anthropology a letter one of these days describing our daylight activity at the Great Lawn before the Venus-Jupiter conjunction. Lévi-Strauss is almost a hundred years old. It's time he heard about the tribe in Central Park that performs the same utterly impossible and incredible feats of sensory perception quite regularly.

☾

It was 8:30 on a sultry mid-July evening, and I was alone at the Moth Tree. A burning orange glow in the west signaled that the sun had just set. It was three weeks since the summer solstice, and the sun was setting earlier every day now. Longer nights—good! Just in time for moth season.

The nessus sphinx, a hovering, crepuscular moth that resembles a fat hummingbird, had already come and gone. It always arrives a little before sunset, takes a quick drink from one of the small sap reservoirs near the base of the Moth Tree, and then vanishes. The last of five hoverflies and the big hornet I'd been

watching for the last few minutes were taking their final greedy
sips. I remembered the evening Nick was stung by one of the
bald-faced hornets. He didn't cry out, just grimaced and rubbed
the assaulted finger. He seemed almost cheerful, but when I
suggested that he had a masochistic streak he said, "No, but it's
a new experience. It interests me."

A lingering cicada killer wasp was still poking its long black
proboscis into a brown gooey spot just above the hornet. The
proboscis, you probably know, is the insect's hollow feeding tube.
(The last syllable is usually pronounced *sis* rather than *kiss*.)
Suddenly, out of nowhere, a host of tiny sap beetles appeared on
the oak and seethed in the sap spots like maggots. When had
they arrived? Or had they been there all day?

I could see fireflies beginning to flash their greenish tail-
lights at Pilgrim Hill, just a little to the south of the Moth Tree.
According to Brad Klein, that compendium of natural history
knowledge, fireflies are actually beetles belonging to the Lam-
pyridae family—there are more than a hundred different species of them in North America. At least two of them show up
in Central Park, *Photinus pyralis* and *Photuris pennsylvanica*.
The Photinus males flash as they fly, producing J-shaped streaks
of light. The females flicker intermittently from the ground,
each species with its own flashing pattern. The female Photuris,
Brad once told me with fiendish delight, is the infamous "aggressive mimic" who flashes her light deceptively in the Photinus
pattern, thus luring unsuspecting Photinus males to their horrible deaths. (She eats them.) Her appetite sated, she switches to
her own pattern in order to find a mate, not a meal.

Nessus sphinxes and fireflies were all well and good, but I
wanted moths. If only Nick would show up. It wasn't just that we
needed his help in identifying those difficult creatures. Indeed,
we probably made more progress when forced to figure them
out on our own. Going through all the steps, comparing every
small feature with the picture in Covell—this imprinted infor-

mation on our memory more effectively than simply having Nick tell us each moth's name. Every beginning birdwatcher discovers the same principle: if someone identifies a bird for you, you're less likely to remember it next time. You have to go through the arduous process yourself in order to make the name stick.

No, we needed Nick's passion, his cultural breadth—insects and trees and flowers and astronomy and meteorology and architecture and music and art and literature and, my god, you name it, he knows it. Nick's rapture at the various beauties to be found in each of these areas—that's what we all wanted to experience. Nick burns with contagious intensity that inspires and energizes us. "Whatever may be the subject broached, he seems quite at home with it, and showers upon us treasures in profusion from his store of knowledge," Goethe wrote. He was referring to Alexander von Humboldt, the very man whose statue stands outside Central Park's Naturalist's Gate. He might have been talking about Nick.

Nick works as an usher at the Metropolitan Opera House, and in early July when the opera and ballet seasons are over for the summer, Nick's long vacation begins. Our real moth season begins then too, when Nick comes to the Moth Tree every night, a Coke and a sandwich in his battered backpack, binoculars in hand, incredible mind at the ready, waiting for new moths to arrive. Where was he now? Maybe he'd acquired a new set of acolytes somewhere else. What would we do without Nick?

My inner calendar proved faulty. It was July 14 and the ballet season was ending that very evening with *Giselle*. Nick would be at the Moth Tree as usual the next day. Meanwhile we were on our own. Looking back, I see that it was a lucky thing.

At about nine I caught sight of Jimmy Lewis rounding the corner from 72nd Street. A man in his fifties with a boyish build, trim and suntanned from regular beach visits, Jimmy was wearing his usual summer uniform—khaki shorts, a well-ironed denim work shirt, and sneakers with no socks. A blue baseball cap sat slightly askew on a full head of only slightly graying hair. He was walking with a lot of energy considering that the temperature was still in the nineties even after sunset. I was really glad to see him.

Faithfulness is an indispensable virtue in nature studies. By steadily following a subject day after day, year after year, you gain knowledge that cannot be achieved through sporadic attendance. Among the Central Park Mothers (*authors*), Jimmy was the most faithful. He showed up at the Moth Tree every night for the entire moth season. He came in the rain. He came in the middle of a heat wave. He'd been there at the first Bug Night years earlier, when Nick had outshone the museum expert. Jimmy had brought along a pretty red-haired girl that evening— Marny or Mandy, was it? In recent years he generally came alone. Jimmy had survived a life-threatening illness that interrupted a promising career in advertising. He had endured six major surgeries, with chronic pain the lasting residue. We marveled at his singular lack of self-pity.

Jimmy was a cheerful presence at the Moth Tree, smart, sensible, and a little mysterious. But somehow, in spite of his faithfulness, Jimmy hadn't made great headway at identifying moths, the task we pursued so obsessively. Not that this bothered him or anyone else. Perhaps it was a matter of choice, we thought. Some people just don't care about identifying. He was always helpful, shining his flashlight on a moth when someone was trying to take a picture, for example, or fetching the Parks Department trash basket to stand on when one of us wanted a closer look at an out-of-reach moth. Jimmy was also our public relations guy, cheerfully explaining the joys of mothing to tourists who stopped by to see what we were up to with our flashlights and binoculars. But Jimmy couldn't identify moths. He didn't even have a copy of the dread Covell.

As the moths began to arrive that night, an uneasy thought crossed my mind: What if a great new underwing showed up?

Would I be able to identify it? Jimmy wouldn't be much help. Oh dear, where *was* Nick?

But the only underwing species to show up that night seemed to be one I knew well. The ilia underwing, *Catocala ilia*, is a big, beautiful, and relatively easy-to-identify moth, our commonest Catocala in mid-July. That night about eight of them congregated at the Moth Tree. Or were all those ilias really ilias? Some other underwing species look very much like them, and I began to feel less confident. Of course with only Jimmy there, who'd know if I made a wrong call?

Besides *Catocala ilia*, moths of three other species arrived to feed on the sap that night. American idias, ipsilon darts, and armyworm moths, they were common moths that show up just about every evening in July. They weren't the spectacular ones we longed for, but still they were moths, and beautiful in their fashion. We always enjoyed pointing them out to others.

That evening Jimmy seemed to be examining the moths in a different way. Something about his posture had changed, I thought vaguely—he wasn't as relaxed as usual. Then, between the arrival of the fifth armyworm moth and the ninth or tenth ipsilon dart, something extraordinary happened. As a nondescript, yellow-brown moth landed on the sap tree, Jimmy said in a voice that seemed surprised at itself, "That's an ipsilon dart." It was. He looked at a moth that had arrived a minute earlier and said without hesitation or doubt, "And *that's* an armyworm moth." Right again. He proceeded to identify every single moth on the tree, even distinguishing the common idia from the American idia, though they are quite hard to tell apart. Then he looked at one of the big ilias we had watched arriving and said with some excitement, "Wait a minute. Are you sure that's an ilia?" No, I wasn't sure.

The next day I ordered a copy of Covell for Jimmy. The reprint was available and he was going to need it.

Later I spent some time thinking about Jimmy's breakthrough. Had he been gaining skills all along and no one had noticed? Had he been intimidated by Nick's learning or too shy or worried about failure at moth identification? That didn't sound like our straightforward, outgoing friend at all. No, there was something about the way everything seemed to fall into place all at once—click!—that made me look for a more specific answer in the field of brain physiology.

In *Memory: From Mind to Molecules* (a relatively accessible text on neurobiology), Larry Squire and Eric Kandel suggest that through study and many repeated experiences, the process of accumulating knowledge and expertise in a specific subject can produce actual neurological changes. "One possibility is that when we encounter visual items . . . the circuitry of the visual cortex changes. These changes in the cortex are a cumulation of the moment-to-moment synaptic changes laid successively on one another." Subsequently, the authors restate the point in a slightly different way. "It seems likely that perceptual and cognitive skill learning, as well as category learning, are cases in which the sensory processing stations themselves change, so as to benefit from the specific perceptual experiences that have occurred in the recent past."

The idea that accumulated experience can actually change the physical structure of the brain gave me a way to consider Jimmy's breakthrough. He'd been looking at moths for years, accumulating information in spite of his seeming insouciance. Perhaps on July 14 everything had come together: the cortical patterns converged, the neurons lined up, the synapses fired in exactly the right order, and eureka!—Jimmy could tell an ipsilon dart from an armyworm moth.

Continuing on the neurobiological track, I wondered why so much time had gone by before Jimmy got the hang of moth identifying. Squire and Kandel propose an explanation for that too. "Memory is not fixed at the time of learning but takes considerable time to develop its permanent form," they state, noting that the way station on the road to fixing information into a permanent form is a structure of the brain's medial temporal lobe called the hippocampus.

Within recent decades, studies of subjects as diverse as London taxi drivers and black-capped chickadees have confirmed that the hippocampus is the critical structure for creating long-term memory.* It takes data coming in from the visual cortex— a small yellowish moth on the moth tree, for instance—and transforms it into the sort of long-term memory you need to identify it as an ipsilon dart and not an armyworm moth.

Besides offering a possible way to look at Jimmy's breakthrough, Squire and Kandel's book made me reevaluate my thoughts about Nick. Writing about people who are prodigious in some domain, they explain, "Expert knowledge depends not only on the prowess of some general memory talent but also on highly specialized abilities, acquired through experience, to encode and organize particular kinds of information. These abilities give experts the ability to recognize quickly a large number of patterns." But the authors point out that the experts perform prodigious feats only in their particular area of expertise. Having a superb memory in general will not transform someone with no knowledge of chess, for example, into someone who can quickly identify chess patterns on a board.

I began to understand that we diminish Nick's skill when we say, "Oh, he's a genius— that's why he can do what he does and we can't." We fail to factor in the hours Nick spends outdoors studying insect life, peering at bees and wasps and butterflies and moths through a magnifying glass or close-focus binoculars.

*A chickadee's hippocampus increases in size during the fall, when it caches food; it will need extra memory skills to remember the hiding places in winter. During later seasons, when memory skills are no longer crucial for survival, its hippocampus shrinks. Similarly, brain resonance studies have found that London taxi drivers, who must commit the entire complex street map of their city to memory before being licensed, have significantly larger hippocampi than other subjects not required to perform such memory feats.

We overlook the time he spends at home studying his treasure trove of entomological texts, journals, and papers.

To be sure, people differ innately in their learning abilities: in how much their memory retains and how fast they can recall what they've learned. But expertise never comes easy. Even gifted people like Nick must work extremely hard to accumulate the huge quantities of data and experience that make them experts in their field. They must be willing to spend enormous amounts of time at their studies.

After my venture into brain science, do I now understand the neurological complexities of moth identification? Not really. But even the experts aren't sure how learning works on a molecular level, or what exactly happens in the various parts of the brain when memories are imprinted. They often resort to words like "it may be" or "it seems likely" in the course of their explanations. In Kandel's own words: "We do not as yet have a satisfactory biological understanding of any complex mental processes." Contemporary cognitive scientists have indeed made considerable progress in figuring out how the giant sea slug *Aplysia californica* learns and remembers. But its brain has only twenty thousand or so nerve cells. Meanwhile, the mammalian brain has more than one hundred *billion*! Nevertheless I plan to continue studying the subject for as long as it takes, hoping that my own big breakthrough is just around the corner.

☾

It was one of those hopeless days. Not only had my work gone nowhere, I'd also torn up all of the pages I'd written the day before.

To the park—I needed a dose of its restorative magic. But after wandering around aimlessly for more than an hour, I still felt out of sorts. Babies were screaming in their strollers. A couple walking toward me were fighting: "You always . . . well, you never . . ." A black gloom began to descend. What to do with myself . . . it was far too early for the Moth Tree. Well, maybe I'd try Turtle Pond.

As I'd hoped, Nick was stretched out on the grass in his usual spot near the joe-pye-weed, reading a Russian novel. All around him was the familiar paraphernalia—backpack, remnants of lunch, a newspaper, a Coke bottle, two field guides, a sweater. At my greeting he cleared a spot on the grass for me, and we talked about nineteenth-century Russian literature for a while, then about moths. It's amazing how quickly spirits can lift. It was actually quite a beautiful day.

It was still too early for moths, though the light was beginning to fail. Then I remembered that this was one of the evenings when Venus and Jupiter would put on a show a little after sunset. "Let's walk to the north end of the Great Lawn and see if the star guys are there," I suggested.

As Nick gathered up his gear, tucking the books and a brown paper bag into his backpack, I realized that the happy, almost exalted feeling that comes over me when I'm with Nick must be love. Not in the conventional, romantic sense of the word—my long marriage isn't at all threatened. No, this is something different. And yet at heart it's the same feeling, the rationality and irrationality of it, the magnetic attraction, the loss of gravity. Actually I think Central Park's entire nature community is in love with Nick. The notion would probably mortify him, since he doesn't seem to love himself in the smallest way. Maybe that's part of it. A mystery.

We're in luck, I thought as we rounded a corner and I spotted the star guys setting up their telescopes at their usual location. Charlie Ridgway, Tom Clabough, and Peter Tagatac were three of the astronomy collective present that day, and a few others I didn't know.

Venus and Jupiter were indeed very bright in the southwestern sky that evening. As I peered at the planets through Charlie's telescope, I could hardly imagine my earlier desperation. Stargazing always makes life's discontents seem trivial.

Not long after sunset the stars began to come out. First they appeared one by one. Then all at once there were too many to count. We were just about to head for the Moth Tree when Peter asked me quite unexpectedly, "Are you a birdwatcher?"

I suppose my binoculars were a clue. "Yes," I answered.

"I wonder if you know another birder I met just about two years ago, here on the Great Lawn. His name was Nick."

Nick had been standing next to me all this time, quietly listening. Now he exclaimed, "That's me!"

The two of them stared at each other. Then Nick said, "I remember you." He peered at the man for another few seconds and said, "Yes, it was you. You showed me the Owl Nebula a few years ago."

"I'll never forget it," Peter said. "It was October sixth. That was the day I became serious about astronomy. There was something about our conversation that changed everything." I was amazed that Peter had remembered the exact date two years later. He turned back to his telescope and then pointed out something to his fellow astronomers. He seemed more animated than before. He's like the rest of us, I thought without jealousy, he loves Nick. That's the odd thing about this particular form of love. It's not possessive. It's expansive.

We arrived at the Moth Tree a little later than usual. Lee, Noreen, Jimmy, Michael Bonifanti, and Norma Collin were already there. By then everybody had accumulated moth questions for Nick. He was our star, I realized. I had a question too but didn't say it out loud: *Are stars aware that they shine?*

5

Miss Jones, You're Beautiful

Winter was once my favorite season—a nice cold, bracing breeze fills me with energy and makes my mind tingle with ideas. Summer, by the same token, especially a hot, humid summer in New York City, is a season to dread. But those preferences changed completely when I became a moth enthusiast. Summer was suddenly transformed into a time of delight—so what if it was hot as hell! Now it was winter I dreaded—a mothless desert. Then I discovered a treasure trove of nocturnal Lepidoptera available for my study and delight all winter—in cyberspace! Thereafter I whiled away many hours checking out various Internet moth sites. John Himmelman's *Moths in a Connecticut Yard* (*MIACY*) became one of my favorites. (Google "Connecticut Moths" for a link.)

One cold day in early March I saw that Himmelman had posted a picture of a new and exciting moth he'd attracted to his backyard sheet that very week. An exciting moth? Actually it was a tiny little gray thing streaked with brown, looking to be about half an inch long. Lacking flashy features (or an inspired name), it was identified only by its Latin binomial, *Acleris logiana*. Its single distinguishing mark seemed to be a small black line near the top of its forewing—a discal dash, Covell calls it. But it was a moth—that was good enough for a true moth lover. And though winter would not turn to spring for two more weeks, this moth had already come and gone in Connecticut. I felt a panicky urge to get out to Central Park with our sheet and moth light. After all, according to entomologists, moths come to lights year-round, as long as it's warm enough for their muscle activity to allow them to fly. Himmelman's website was proof of it.

It was hard to persuade my usually enthusiastic mothing companions to start as early as March. Too cold, there'd be no moths—that was the consensus. Nick was especially dubious, though I figured he'd show up if we set the date for a Sunday, his night off at the opera. We settled on the twenty-eighth, the last Sunday in March. Lee promised to charge the battery pack the day before— she lives near the park and cheerfully allows her apartment to become the repository of our mothing parapher-nalia.

I was the first to arrive at our meeting place, a rustic bench in the Shakespeare Garden we'd come to call the Moth Bench. It was 5:55 p.m. Sitting next to me as I watched the day begin to fade was a real mother (rhymes with *brother*), baby carriage and all. Robins, robins everywhere, already emitting their bedtime chips and cackles while foraging for a last snack before bedtime: it was the week of a big robin arrival. Though the peak spring explosion was still weeks away, early flowers were blooming all over the garden: dwarf irises, daffodils, and beds of pretty little blue flowers called squill. A saucer magnolia nearby was full of big fat buds about to burst open. Today sunset would be at 6:17. It amazed me to think that in a mere three months (with daylight savings time added to the natural lengthening of days), the sun would be setting at 8:30.

Norma Collin, the next to arrive at the bench, was bearing a sweater for Nick. She'd run into him in the park earlier in the day and thought he looked cold. Norma, one of my earliest Central Park friends, finds an outlet for her maternal instincts by taking care of people in need. She often distributes warm clothes to the park's homeless men and women—she seems to know all of them by name. She also keeps a maternal eye on the birders and mothers (*nonmaternal*). Lee, Noreen, and Jimmy arrived minutes later. Just before sunset Nick sauntered in, looking blue in both color and spirits. Norma's sweater cheered him a bit, and he wrapped it around his neck and shoulders like a scarf.

Our modus operandi at the Shakespeare Garden was much the same as the one we had followed in Charles's Garden in our early mothing days: we spread a white sheet over the back of a bench, draped the black light across the middle, plugged it into the portable battery pack, and flicker, flicker, glow! A minute after the light went on, Jimmy pointed out with excitement that a big moth had already arrived. But it was only the paint stain, a white blotch the sheet had acquired during its drop-cloth years. The paint stain was usually our first moth.

It grew darker. The sky was cloudy, but directly overhead a perfect first-quarter moon was emerging. As we waited for moths to arrive—we'd welcome *any* insect, in fact—we reminisced about the time we'd seen five planets in a row after an evening of moth-watching. That must have been five years earlier, when Charles was perfectly well. We had a past.

First came a battalion of tiny flies. At least *something* was attracted to the light! Among them were at least two different members of the Diptera order, each with its single pair of tiny transparent wings and tiny abdomen. A cold fifteen minutes went by and we began to wander about the garden a bit, looking for spiders or praying-mantis egg cases or anything that could possibly justify our being there on such an unpromising night. Then a couple of cries sent us all running back to the sheet. It was Lee, exclaiming, "A moth! A moth!" Jimmy looked at his watch: it was 6:59 p.m. exactly.

Well, it wasn't much of a moth. About half an inch long, silvery gray, covered with tiny brown dashes and spots, it had the home-plate shape that characterizes a family of difficult little moths called Tortricids. The moth book, the moth book, did anyone bring it? Good old Nick drew his battered copy of Covell out of his backpack. So he hadn't been as pessimistic about our chances of finding a moth as he'd led us to believe. The family Tortricidae covered two pages of plates at the very back of the book, each of which contained twenty-five black-and-white pictures of hopelessly small and confusing moths. Nevertheless, only a glance made Nick say, "What about plate sixty, number fourteen?"

The envelope, please. And the winner is . . . number 14 on plate 60—Himmelman's moth! It had the telltale black dash near the top of its forewings—that was the giveaway. Though *Acleris logiana* didn't have a common name, just a Latin binomial, some of its close relatives had lovely ones: the spotted fireworm moth, for instance, or the oblique-banded leafroller moth, or the tufted apple bud moth. This one was just *Acleris logiana*, nothing more. Still, it was a propitious beginning for what would turn out to be our most spectacular moth season.

☾

Finding a bird you've never seen before, a life bird, is one of the high points of birdwatching. But it pays to be restrained in your joy if you're birding with a group. It can be embarrassing to admit that your life list is so paltry that it's missing this particular sparrow or warbler or vireo everyone else has seen a hundred times. And unless they're visiting Attu or Madagascar or some other exotic outpost, rarely does a group of birders come upon a Group Life Bird—one new to all of them.

The Central Park Mothers (*authors*) don't have to worry about revealing abysmal ignorance. A new species that turns up on the Moth Tree is likely to be new for all of us (except, of course, Nick), since we all began moth-watching at about the same time. Thus we're free to get excited. Sometimes we go berserk.

If you'd been strolling in Central Park at around 9:30 on a certain July evening a few years ago, you might have seen seven apparent lunatics dancing around a scraggly oak tree near the East Drive just past 72nd Street, performing exuberant high kicks and pumping their arms in the air. And if you'd passed that way again an hour later, you might have heard a rare performance of the Central Park Mothers' ancient anthem (well, it goes back at least seven years), sung to a tune from *HMS Pinafore*. It begins, "We worship Thoth and the Moth as well," and concludes, "For we are Egyptian Druids," which is hardly accurate, since the group is composed of two residents of the Upper West Side, one East Sider, one lifetime inhabitant of the Bronx, and one longtime SoHo dweller now transplanted to Kew Gardens, Queens, as well as a family that once lived in the city but left after 9/11 for a hilltop in Rupert, Vermont.

The song makes more sense if you know that it was written by Davie Rolnick, one of the group's founding members, when he was barely seven. A passionate G&S fan as well as a prodigious young entomologist, Davie explained with perfect seven-year-old logic that the Egyptian deity Thoth was featured in the anthem for the sole reason that his name rhymes with *moth*.

From the start Davie had had an extraordinary interest in insects, especially those he could deftly capture and place in his collecting jar. He caught fifty-six click beetles one night, making each one produce its little click before thrusting it into the increasingly crowded prison. Of course Davie always released his little captives at the end of the evening, none the worse for wear. His mother, Julia, a brilliant and beautiful former teacher and present writer, saw to that. She encouraged him to bid each of the little black beetles a nice farewell before sending it on its way. The Rolnicks were an invigorating addition to our group.

Alas, they are the ones who moved to Vermont. Now Davie is

on the cusp of adulthood. Still as enthusiastic about entomology as ever, he has added other passions to his repertory: ornithology, music, mathematics, science fiction, history. It would probably be easier to list the few subjects he isn't fascinated by. I still get excited calls or e-mails from him when a new moth arrives at his light or bait in Vermont. (There are many, many more moth species in rural Vermont than in Central Park.) And by lucky chance he and Julia, an avid mother in both senses of the homograph, were visiting town the week of our high-kicking celebration. Instead of taking in the shows, they had spent every evening of their stay at the Moth Tree.

We were deliriously happy that night because we'd added two new underwing moths to our Central Park list: the oldwife underwing (*Catocala palaeogama*) and the clouded underwing (*Catocala nebulosa*). Lee and I had recently bought digital cameras and were still learning how to use them, but we took many pictures of the two new moths and a few of them came out perfectly.

One night a few weeks later the weather was so hot and humid that only Nick and Jimmy made their way to the park at all. Their faithfulness was richly rewarded, for that was the night a cosmic mindbender moth swooped out of the velvety dark and onto the Moth Tree.

I had spent much of the previous night on a rocky promontory at Cedar Hill trying (and failing) to see the annual Perseid meteor shower. Sleep-deprived, heat-crazed, I'd gone to bed early the next night with the air conditioner on high. I was half asleep at 10:30 when the telephone rang. Jimmy seemed to be shouting—I had to hold the phone away from my ear: "Get right over here! We've got the most unbelievable moth!"

If I hopped in a cab, I could be there in fifteen minutes. I threw some clothes over my nightgown. Where's my pocketbook? Flashlight. Close-focus binoculars. I was still racing around the house grabbing things when the phone rang again.

Jimmy, his voice at a normal level now: "Don't bother coming. She's gone." *Aaargh*, as they say in the comic strips.

Only Nick had been there when the Gargantua of moths made its dramatic appearance. Jimmy arrived a few minutes later, startled to find Nick almost completely unhinged. But when Jimmy laid eyes on the creature Nick was pointing to, he became unhinged himself. As Nick described it to me the next day: "I was sitting here on the fence, and then I saw something big coming in. I saw a tremendous fluttering near the tree. Inside me I'm thinking, there's only one thing it could be because I've seen the picture in the moth book hundreds of times—a black witch. Then I thought, Well, maybe it's a bat. But it didn't look at all like a bat. I waited. I didn't want to turn on my light because that might spook it. My heart was thumping. Then I turned on the light, and there it was, a black witch for sure. Spread out absolutely flat. Huge."

The black witch, *Ascalapha odorata*, is the largest moth, indeed the largest insect, in North America. Its wingspan can be up to six inches—the biggest underwing moths are barely half that size. It's normally found in Florida, Texas, and points south, but every so often, for unknown reasons, individuals migrate north. On occasion they even end up in Newfoundland or Alaska. Now one of them had found her way to Central Park. I use the feminine pronoun confidently because the species is dimorphic: the females look markedly different from the males. The moth Nick and Jimmy were gaping at was brown and had a conspicuous white band. The male of the species is black and lacks that white band. Both males and females are enormous.

The next evening Noreen, Jimmy, Nick, and I stood at the Moth Tree and waited. It was still miserably hot—even after sunset the temperature was in the upper nineties. Meanwhile, it was twenty degrees cooler in Tuscany, where Lee was on her annual sketching tour. Lucky Lee. I was in a grizzly mood. So I'd

missed the black witch—big deal. I'd studied its picture in Covell that morning, and sure it was big. But big the way Nick and
Jimmy were describing? I couldn't imagine it—they must be ex-
aggerating. Anyhow, it didn't matter. I *knew* the moth wasn't
coming again.

As Nick rehearsed yesterday's experience, a mean spirit came
over me. He kept saying, "It was enormous, it was awesome, it
was so big it didn't seem real, it was gigantic." When he paused
for breath, I said, "Tell me something, Nick. Was it big?" I enjoyed the split-second response—"Oh yes, it was huge!"—
before he did a double take and laughed at my tease.

At a little after ten that night some tourists from Australia on
their way to the Boathouse stopped to ask the usual question:
"What are you looking at?"

We gave them our spiel about underwing moths. They
looked a bit dubious, and were about to climb over the low rail
to see for themselves when Nick rushed up, his baseball cap
gone, his hair in complete disarray. He was pointing, gesticulat-
ing, shouting like a madman: "It's here! It's here! Hurry, it's
on the tree!" Who knows what the four well-dressed visitors
thought when we dashed back to the tree without giving them
another look. That was the last we saw of them.

Something happened to my perception of time that evening.
I remember photographing the moth a hundred times, once
with Nick holding Covell's field guide next to it to give an indication of size—the book is five by seven inches and the moth was
almost as big. I remember thinking with a pang, *Oh, poor Lee,
she'll be so sorry she missed this.* I remember watching it feed at
the sap, its long proboscis darting greedily in and out of the dark
goo. The next thing I remember is looking at my watch and seeing that it was after midnight and the black witch was still there.

We left before the moth did—the park has a curfew of 1:00
a.m. Nick's last words: "This is actually a brown witch. Tomorrow
we need a male—we need a black witch."

Word about our monster moth got around. Could it be because I e-mailed photos of it to almost everyone I knew, and many others I didn't know but wanted to make jealous? Soon our names and photos were on a website devoted entirely to the black witch moth. Run by a Texas biologist named Mike Quinn, it includes everything you always wanted to know about this extraordinary insect—photographs, taxonomy, distribution, migration timetables, and behavior.

Quinn's site even has a section dealing with black witch mythology. In Mexico, it appears, the beast is known to the Indians as *mariposa de la muerte*, butterfly of death. If a black witch crosses your path, you've had it, buddy, your wife's about to be a widow. In Hawaii the moth is seen as an embodiment of the soul of one who has died—she's returning to say goodbye, the legend has it. If a black witch flies over a man's head, another myth declares, he'll lose his hair. There may be something to it. Nick's cap has been hiding an increasing bald spot in the years since his sighting of the black witch. According to yet another legend, a person who sees a black witch is sure to win the lottery. Jimmy's been buying tickets ever since.

Quinn's site includes a comprehensive list of black witch records in the United States. When we saw Central Park, New York, listed as the only New York State sighting authenticated with photos, we thought we had reached the height of fame and glory. Instead, our real Hollywood moment came from a different moth entirely.

☾

If you're a fan of movie comedies of the 1940s and 1950s, you'll remember this scene: The humble but plucky secretary is in love with her handsome boss. Unfortunately he ignores her, fancying he's in love with a Social Register beauty his mother has picked out for him. One day he discovers the girlfriend is two-timing him with his caddish former roommate. Back in the office, lashing out at anyone at hand, he is unspeakably rude to the poor secretary. She bursts into tears. Taken aback, he sits her down and offers her his pocket handkerchief. She takes off her glasses to wipe her eyes, and somehow a mass of luxuriant black curls comes loose from the severe bun that usually restrains them. The handsome boss takes a long, hard look at her. Then comes the line we've been waiting for: "Why, Miss Jones, you're beautiful!"

In the "Miss Jones, you're beautiful" moment we were to experience that summer, the humble but plucky Central Park Mothers (*authors*) played the part of the lovelorn secretary. Hugh McGuinness, a moth expert from Long Island, costarred as the boss.

I received my first letter from McGuinness on a late summer day not long after our momentous visitation by the black witch.

Hi Marie,

Someone forwarded your post about the Black Witch in Central Park. What a great find! Could you send me the exact dates it was seen? I try to keep track of moth records on Long Island & the NYC area.

Also, I was curious, how did it come to pass that people found a Black Witch at night? Is somebody setting up a black light in Central Park?

Hugh

I was excited to hear from Hugh McGuinness, a real moth expert. I was a little wary, though. I'd had an unsettling encounter with another mothing eminence many years earlier, not long after our discovery of the Moth Tree. I was interviewing Eric Quinter, then on the staff of the American Museum of Natural History, for an article I was writing and mentioned that we had found 105 different species of moths in Central Park. I said it with pride—after all, a list of that many species of *birds* in Central Park would be something to boast about. Quinter's response stunningly demonstrates the difference between bird-watching and moth-watching. "What?" he asked in surprise. "Only 105?"

Would McGuinness be equally disdainful?

Cautiously I answered McGuinness's question about our mothing activities in Central Park, telling him about the Moth Tree and our years of observation there. I didn't boast this time, just invited him to come to Central Park someday and see our Catocalas. I added at the end of my note, "If you want, I'll e-mail you our list of all the moths we've identified in Central Park so far."

He politely declined the invitation to come mothing in Central Park and said nothing about the list I'd offered to send. But I sent it anyway. To my surprise McGuinness wrote back within the hour:

A very interesting list indeed. I have only had time to take a quick glance, but one record stands out above the rest: *Catocala nebulosa*. Did anyone take the specimen or take a photo? If there is a photo, I'd love to examine it. This species is quite rare in NY (in bird terms I'd say it's comparable to Long-billed Curlew).

A moth as rare as the long-billed curlew, one of the most threatened shorebird species in North America! Thank goodness one of my pictures of the clouded underwing had turned out sharp and clear. I e-mailed it to McGuinness without delay. "Here's *Catocala nebulosa*. Please let me know if it comes out okay."

McGuinness answered almost immediately:

Yes, it came out very well. And it appears to be nebulosa, which would perhaps only be the second record in the last 50 years. (I found one last year in Montauk.) I am writing an article on nebulosa and perhaps would like to use the photo. Do you have it in larger format? Very, very exciting.

Very exciting indeed. Though he'd started out skeptical—it *appears* to be nebulosa—McGuinness seemed to see us in a new light now. Like Miss Jones, we were beautiful. It changed our own view too, for only after the moth expert marveled at our *Catocala nebulosa* did we begin to suspect that we had a special treasure trove of these magical moths in Central Park.

I checked out various Internet websites devoted to moths. To my surprise, some of the Catocala species we had seen at the Moth Tree were missing from the photo pages of a large, popular site run by a moth-lover in Maryland, one that included images of several thousand North American moths. Since I was a photography novice, I was a bit apologetic about the photos of two underwings I sent in. A week later my photos of the sad and the widow underwings appeared on the site's Catocala pages— "M. Winn, Central Park," read the credit. A Pulitzer Prize would not have been more thrilling.*

Why did we have so many underwings right in the heart of New York City? Nick would know if anyone did. When I called with the question, he answered without hesitation: "It must be the trees," he said cheerfully.

I didn't get it immediately, and Nick elaborated. "Look at all the Catocala food plants we have growing in Central Park: hickories, black walnuts, oaks, poplars, maples, willows, apples, cherries, hawthorns, black locusts, honey locusts. You never find such a collection in nature. They're here because they were all planted in the park either when it was created in 1886, or later.

---

*The Moths of Maryland website, started by Robert Patterson, eventually metamorphosed into the ambitious Moth Photographers' Group site run by the University of Mississippi. There are no more gaps among the Catocalas there, though my photographs of the oldwife, habilis, darling, and clouded underwings still appear on its pages, among those of many others.

That's why I'm always so interested in Covell's listing of each species' preferred food plants. Moths are very specific in their choice of food plants, and if Covell says a certain moth only uses hickories and walnuts, as he does for the oldwife underwing, for instance, you won't find that moth in an area that only has oaks and maples. It must have hickories or walnuts. Well, we've got almost every kind of tree here. We even have waxmyrtle growing in the park, but we're not likely to find the bay underwing—it's definitely a seaside moth."

We've never seen a bay underwing in Central Park, and the odds are we never will.

After all our excitement came a lull: for three nights the Moth Tree seemed to attract only ilia underwings, and a general restlessness prevailed among the moth-watchers. *Catocala ilia* provided beauty, to be sure—it's a big, spectacular moth, generously inclined to open its bark-patterned forewings to reveal the red-orange and black-banded underwings beneath—but beauty wasn't enough. We wanted diversity.

And so we found ourselves wandering about. Toward the bottom of the hill between the Moth Tree and the model-boat pond, near the gnarly maple that Pale Male often used as a night roost during nesting season, Noreen stopped to point out an odd . . . well . . . an odd *thing* on the trunk of an old black oak. It was chocolate colored and furry. A pure white powdery mass lay at its base. "A fungus?" Lee asked. But it didn't look like a fungus. Indeed, it didn't resemble anything I'd ever seen.

As Nick walked up to it, I could see the cloud of gloom that had enveloped him all evening lifting. It was happening, the transformation Nick undergoes when he's fully engaged in some natural history pursuit, when he finds a new damselfly at Turtle Pond, for instance, or an interesting caterpillar at the Shakespeare Garden, or when a new underwing moth appears at the Moth Tree. It's something everyone in the Central Park nature community looks forward to.

Nick seemed to radiate pleasure. Pursing his lips, he gently blew on the thing. A little white smoky cloud appeared, then dispersed in the breeze. Spores, said Nick. Then he peeled off a chunk of the furry stuff and peered at it through the magnifying loupe that always hangs around his neck.

Finally he was ready to give his verdict. "Chocolate tube slime," he announced happily. "It's a slime mold." His disappointment at finding no new moths that night was gone, gone like a little white smoky cloud in the wind.

The next day I sent an e-mail to Brad Klein, our fellow night explorer. I must have boasted a bit about our find, for instead of admiration I got my comeuppance: "Marie, don't you think you're slumming a bit down there on the evolutionary tree?" he wrote. "There's no shame at gazing at a plant from time to time, but slime mold's not even in one of the respectable Kingdoms!"

I knew Brad was kidding—still I felt I had to defend the humble slime mold and its grabbag kingdom—the Protista.* I sent back a quotation from Thoreau: "The humblest fungus betrays a life akin to our own. It is a successful poem of its kind."

☽

It had been our best moth season ever, with seven new species of underwing moth to add to our Catocala list, bringing the total to nineteen, not to mention the once-in-a-lifetime black witch. Now the sap oozes were drying up. Moths were few and far between at the Moth Tree.

It was time to set up the sheet and black light in the Shake-

---

*While Carolus Linnaeus, the father of modern taxonomy, divided living things into only two kingdoms—animal and vegetable—modern science has expanded the list to six or more, with Protista usually among them.

speare Garden. On most summer nights insects start landing on the sheet and often right on the bulb itself the instant you turn it on. First come small gnats, then flies, often followed by the tiny micromoths we can almost never identify. Once in a while a big green katydid will land on the sheet, as well as a beetle or two. And eventually a good-sized moth will appear, a respectable moth, a moth we can find in Covell. Our pulses race and our addiction stays alive.

The light sends a signal to vertebrates as well. Often we were visited by a posse of brazen raccoons, and on one occasion an enterprising youngster managed to make off with both halves of Jimmy's roast-beef sandwich.

On August 27 things were pretty uninspiring at the Moth Bench—not a single new moth and almost no old ones either. We would have welcomed a beetle or a lacewing—any insect at all. But the pickings were slim that night—not even a raccoon. We decided to pack it in earlier than usual, a little after 10:00. The moth light was already off and stowed in the wheelie when Jimmy called out, "What's this?"

We pointed our flashlights at the wooden leg of the Moth Bench, and holy moly, there was a moth of a gemlike green, with two zigzag white lines on each wing which it obligingly displayed. We knew our identifying task would be a piece of cake, for Covell has only one page with emerald green moths. And there it was: the wavy-lined emerald, a member of the Geometrid family. They're the ones that are likely to open up all four wings, so they resemble the pinned moths in Covell. Not only was it a stunningly beautiful creature, but it was a new species for our Central Park moth list. Our total was inching ever upward.

☾

The long, hot summer was coming to an end. Underwing moths continued to appear at the Moth Tree through September—longer than we expected—but by the beginning of October things were winding down. One night our only customers were a common idia (the nondescript moth Jimmy now easily identified) and two micromoths too small for Covell. That was it. Yet Nick was taking this miserable tally with equanimity, because something else was keeping his spirits up. It was a black swallowtail caterpillar he'd discovered in the Shakespeare Garden two days earlier. The stunning pale green, yellow, and black creature looked exactly like its portrait on page 80 of *Caterpillars of Eastern North America*, David Wagner's new caterpillar field guide which we had all just acquired.

"It was right in front of the Moth Bench, near the top of the latticed fence," Nick related while we waited for the moths that never arrived. There was a new nip in the air. Cold weather made Nick gloomy and taciturn—it happened every winter. But now he continued to be in a talkative mood. "The caterpillar was wandering back and forth on top of the fence, not on its food plant. That's what made me think it was getting ready to pupate. I had a feeling it was about to attach itself to a slat on the fence."

"What will happen after that?" I asked.

"It will become a pupa and spend the winter there.* If it survives the winter it will emerge as a butterfly sometime next spring."

A few weeks earlier, as it happened, I had witnessed the climax of a butterfly's four-act drama of metamorphosis, and it remains among the most enthralling experiences of my life. It began when Aidan Smith, a precocious four-year-old, discovered an odd little sea-green cylinder attached to a milkweed plant at the model-boat pond. Aidan was by far the most fervent of the

---

*The word *pupa* is broadly used to describe the resting stage of the life cycle during which the caterpillar transforms into an adult. Both terms *cocoon* and *chrysalis* are often used instead of *pupa*, but more specifically, *cocoon* is the name for the silky structure created by some caterpillars just before pupation, while *chrysalis* is the name for a smooth case hanging from a plant or attached to a twig or fence or the like.

Central Park Mothers (*authors*), inclined to jump up and down and cry "A new moth! A new moth!" at every single arrival at the Moth Tree. His little brother, James, was waiting in the wings for full-fledged membership in our mothing band, but that wouldn't happen until he learned to walk. James was only one and a half on the day sharp-eyed Aidan made his discovery.

Aidan's chrysalis was about an inch long, a little cylinder with a row of glittering gold dots near its conical top. The host plant was about three feet tall and so, approximately, was Aidan that summer, which may be why he spotted it so easily. He pointed it out to his parents and even woke his little brother, who'd been fast asleep in his stroller. The Smith family had been on their way home from the Moth Tree that evening, but they promptly returned to ask Nick what the little green thing was. Nick easily identified it as a monarch butterfly-to-be. He had even seen the yellow, white, and black banded monarch caterpillar in that same patch of milkweed a few weeks earlier.

At the Moth Tree on that moth-deprived October day, Nick's description of the black swallowtail caterpillar on the fence in the Shakespeare Garden made me lose interest in the obviously minuscule chance that any good moths might still arrive. Here was an opportunity to see another act of the incredible lepidopteran drama: the caterpillar-into-pupa transformation. "Do you think the caterpillar is still on the fence? Couldn't we go and see it right now?" I could hear my voice take on a wheedling tone like Aidan's when begging to stay at the Moth Tree just five minutes more on a school night. "Why not?" Nick said agreeably after casting a look around the tree and seeing that nothing remotely mothlike was arriving from any direction.

It's an easy walk from the Moth Tree to the Shakespeare Garden, where we found the brightly colored caterpillar easily. But between the time Nick had seen it going back and forth on the fence earlier in the day and our arrival at the spot, something had changed. Though the real transformation had not begun—it still looked like a caterpillar—it had begun the pupation process by attaching itself to the latticework fence. Conveniently for viewers, the caterpillar had chosen a spot directly in front of a bench, and not just any old bench. It was our Moth Bench! But the immobilized creature wasn't dangling from a plant as the monarch chrysalis had done, for the black swallowtail attaches itself to a stalk—or in this case, a bamboo slat—by means of a "girdle" encircling its body. Even without a magnifying glass, we could easily see the thin thread going from the caterpillar to the slat.

Early the next afternoon I met Nick at the Shakespeare Garden. The caterpillar seemed unchanged, although the threads attaching it to the slat seemed a bit firmer. We stayed for more than an hour, hoping to see the moment of transformation. Finally Nick headed for Turtle Pond to check out the day's dragonflies. I lingered another few moments and then left too. It was about 4:00.

About an hour later Nick returned to the garden for a last look—Turtle Pond is just a few minutes away. He brought along Lloyd Spitalnik, one of Central Park's best birders and nature photographers, and that's how it happened that Lloyd captured the penultimate act of butterfly metamorphosis on his digital camera. He sent me the photos by e-mail that evening. The last photo showed a dull brownish, woody-looking object—the pupa. I couldn't see the smallest visual connection between the woody thing and the bright-colored caterpillar that had preceded it on the bamboo slat. An unbelievable change. I ate my heart out that I'd missed the actual show, but having the photographs almost made up for it.

Then began the long wait. The pupa would survive the winter, if all went well—if a bird didn't find it and eat its contents, for example. A beautiful black swallowtail butterfly would emerge the following April or May. Perhaps I'd be lucky enough to see it happen.

All winter I made frequent pilgrimages to the Shakespeare Garden to check on the pupa, and so did many others. Regina Alvarez, the park's Woodlands Manager, made it a regular stop on her rounds all winter. The Night People often looked in on the pupa before beginning their owl prowls.

One late winter day my visit to the pupa coincided with Nick's. It was bitterly cold, and I wasn't surprised to find Nick in a particularly wretched mood. "Even if the pupa gets through the next few months without being eaten by a bird," he remarked glumly, "it still might not end up as a black swallowtail butterfly."

"Why's that?"

Nick explained that shortly after the pupa is formed it is often invaded by a parasitoid—a smaller insect whose larvae feed on the caterpillar, eventually killing it. For black swallowtails the invader is often an ichneumon wasp. If that had happened here, then a wasp or some other little killer would emerge next spring, not a lovely butterfly. I looked up ichneumons in Marshall's big insect guide, and though they are handsome creatures, they began to seem evil.

That bitter winter was followed by a spectacular spring. During the first two weeks of May the park was full of vireos, orioles, and warblers—twenty-five warbler species in a single day. Songbirds may be on their way out, done in by global warming or logging in the rainforest, but you'd never know it from the bird scene in Central Park every May.

There was a driving rainstorm on the morning of May 11. At a little after noon I got a call from Lee: "It's gone."

"What's gone?" Was she talking about the Philadelphia vireo, yesterday's star bird?

"The black swallowtail butterfly," she said. "It must have emerged this morning."

I was stunned. "Are you sure?" I asked.

"Of course I'm sure. Nick checked the pupa yesterday and said it had changed a little. But it was still there. So today I headed for the garden as soon as I could. I got there about noon, and the pupa was empty."

I grabbed my camera and dashed to the park. I raced up the steps of the Shakespeare Garden and ran straight to the Moth Bench. It was a little after 1:00. It took me a while to locate the woody little thing, but when I found it, I breathed a sigh of relief. There it was, with its weird little girdle intact. It looked exactly the same.

Then I saw an inconspicuous but telling difference: a neat little opening at the top, just a tiny slit in the woody shell. The exit door. Damn! First I had missed the caterpillar-to-pupa transformation, and now I'd missed seeing the glorious butterfly takeoff.

But something didn't jibe. Nick had seen the pupa intact the day before. Surely the butterfly hadn't made its exit in the rain— butterflies' wings need to dry upon emerging. The monarch I'd watched at the model-boat pond had hung there drying its wings for five or six hours. How could the black swallowtail have managed to be ready for fly-out in the brief time between that morning's rainstorm and Lee's phone call?

A few weeks earlier at a meeting of the New York Chapter of the North American Butterfly Association, I'd met David Wagner, the author of the recently published caterpillar field guide. He'd seemed a friendly sort and had given me his e-mail address. Now I took advantage of the meeting to send him a few photos of our black swallowtail caterpillar and its pupa.

"Here's my question," I wrote. "On May 10, Nick Wagerik saw the pupa we've been following since last October, and it was intact. When someone arrived on May 11 at about noon, it was empty. Yet it was raining hard that morning until about 10:00. Could the butterfly have completed emergence, wing drying etc., between 10:00 and noon?"

He answered succinctly but unequivocally: "Yep, easily . . . only takes an hour . . . once the decision is made things happen fast."

Well, that was that. But a more disturbing question suddenly popped into my mind: How could we be sure a black swallowtail butterfly had emerged through the little exit door? Maybe it was the evil ichneumon wasp!

Early the next day I called Nick.

"Good morning," I said routinely.

"It's not. It's raining." His response was promising. Though glum, he was still playful.

"I'm calling about the black swallowtail. I guess we'll never know whether it was really a black swallowtail that emerged and not an ichneumon wasp, will we?"

"Oh, it was definitely a butterfly that came out," Nick answered without hesitation. He was beginning to sound more cheerful as he focused on natural science.

"How do you know?" I asked.

"When I checked the pupa the day before, the shell had become semitranslucent. You could see the patterns of the butterfly's wings through the shell. You could even see the black swallowtail spots. It was definitely a butterfly in there, not a wasp."

Early one morning a few weeks later, as I was standing at Belvedere Castle watching the last warblers of the spring migration feeding in a big, sun-dappled oak, I saw a small something landing on a rosebush just inside the Shakespeare Garden wall. I can't tell you why, but even before I focused my binoculars on it, I knew with absolute certainty that it would be a black swallowtail butterfly.

Oh, I knew it was unlikely—there are hundreds of butterflies in Central Park in May—but I couldn't help thinking that the swallowtail fluttering near the wall of the Shakespeare Garden was the very one I'd met back in October when it was still a caterpillar. I missed seeing it turn into a pupa and then I missed its emergence as a butterfly. Now the obliging creature was giving me another chance to end my metamorphosis story on a happy note.

6

Slug Sex

In August and September, crickets and katydids come to life in Central Park. Nights that were once quiet are now full of calls and chirps, clicks and tinkles, buzzes and trills, rhythmic pulses, throbs and rattles. But where are the little music-makers? You sweep the bushes and trees with your most powerful flashlight and find nothing. It's hard to believe that you can't find the source of sounds so loud and persistent. But members of Orthoptera, the order of crickets and katydids, are notoriously elusive—many say they practice ventriloquism. Grigologists, people who study singing insects, will confirm that without a lot of trapping equipment you'd better be contented with the sound and not the sight of them.

Some crickets and katydids are attracted to light, however, and give you a better chance at a real sighting. The Central Park Mothers (*authors*) have identified one cricket and two katydids that landed on their sheet during one or another of their Moth Nights: the four-spotted tree cricket (*Oecanthus quadripunctatus*); the drumming katydid (*Meconema thalassinum*), a tiny nonnative insect that has recently expanded its range to the New York area; and the greater angle-wing (*Microcentrum rhombifolium*), a leaf-green, perfectly camouflaged katydid.

One evening in late September I went for a walk in the park

with Jay Holmes, a personable young scientist in the education department of the American Museum of Natural History. Our mission: to find singing insects. The weather was balmy, and as we strolled through Strawberry Fields, the Hernshead area, and the Ramble, we heard five distinct insect songs. I thought I recognized some of them, but I needed confirmation from an expert. It turned out that my companion's subject of specialization was geology, not entomology, and like a true scientist, he didn't care to make positive identifications without absolute certainty. That's why I'm forced to use an onomatopoeic form of description for the singing insects we heard that night:

1. In the barberry bushes at Strawberry Fields, just at West Drive: the melodious tinkler (a high-pitched *ding-a-ling-a-ling-a-ling*)
2. At the Polish statue on the east end of Turtle Pond: the rapid treeper (eight *treeps* in a row, pause, then again eight *treeps*, and so on)
3. On the west side of the Lake, south of Hernshead: the faint lisper (*tsp, tsp, tsp*)
4. In the ground cover outside the ladies' room near the Delacorte Theater: the buzzy triller (*trrrrrrrrrrrrr*)
5. Near the Moth Tree: the quiet single ticker (*tick*, long pause, *tick*, long pause, *tick*)

Since I am somewhat less scrupulous than a scientist about making identifications, I'd say with fair confidence that the rapid treeper was a snowy tree cricket, known as the weatherman (weatherbug?) of the insect world because its chirp rate can accurately tell you the ambient temperature. You count the number of chirps in a thirteen-second interval and add forty. This will give you a number somewhere in the ballpark of the Fahrenheit temperature at the moment. Named "snowy" because it looks white when seen at night, it's actually a pale green color.

I'm pretty sure the quiet single ticker was the bush katydid (*Scudderia texensis*). We've often heard that unsettling tick near the Moth Tree, and that's what Nick said it was. Why unsettling? It sounds a bit like a lurker clicking his tongue in the bushes nearby. And the faint lisper may have been the greater angle-wing katydid, the one we've seen on our mothing sheet more than once and managed to identify. I feel more confident about that guess because my cricket and katydid field guide uses the word *lisp* to describe the angle-wing's song. As for the tinkler, I'll go out on a limb and say it was the tinkling ground cricket (*Allonemobius tinnulus*). One identification I'm sure of: the common true katydid (*Pterophylla camellifolia*). I've heard its unmistakable song twice in Central Park, once near the Zoo and once in the Pinetum. This is the only katydid that actually sings the "Katy did, Katy didn't" song.

There's one orthopteran that never sings along in Central Park's noisy late summer chorus: the restless bush cricket (*Hapithus agitator*). One of the park's most common crickets, this one doesn't sing in most geographic locations. A small light-brown insect with forewings that cover at least three-quarters of its abdomen, the restless bush cricket looks a bit like a small cockroach, which is not surprising since crickets and cockroaches were once considered members of the same order. Cockroaches now have their own order, the Blattodea. The restless bush cricket is not a native species; it's one of those exotics, like Japanese knotweed or the European starling, that have few enemies in their new environment and thus take over.

The local restless bush crickets are silent. No one seems to know how the sexes find each other without singing—maybe they emit pheromones as so many other insects do. But once they proceed to the next stage of romance, the male of this species certainly knows how to keep his mate happy.

Jimmy was the first to alert us to the unwholesome habits of the restless bush cricket. In the days before he broke the moth-identifying code, he was likely to wander off from our moth observation post in the Shakespeare Garden to look for action elsewhere. He was especially interested in spiders and praying mantises. In the old days, he and Charles were always on the lookout for oothecas—praying-mantis egg cases that would over-winter in the garden. Charles loved the word *ootheca* and en-joyed dropping it into ordinary conversation. He also loved the savagery of mantid life and took some dramatic photographs of praying mantises preying.

One evening in early September, when nothing much was happening at the moth light, Jimmy began to watch a funnel spider lurking in a dense web visible in the latticework fence nearby. Suddenly he called out, "He's got a cricket!"

We ran over just in time to see the spider use his fangs to in-ject his prey with paralyzing venom. Actually, the spider was al-most certainly a she—they're the ones that make the webs. We recognized the victim—a restless bush cricket, now perhaps suf-fering the wages of restlessness. But one thing Jimmy wanted to know about the poor cricket: Was it a male or a female? He had done some research about *Hapithus agitator* and proceeded to give us the scoop.

According to Jimmy, you can't really tell male bush crickets from females. They're the same size. The male has an inconspic-uous yellow band around his middle that the female lacks, but it's often hard to see. But if you happen to see them during the sex act, a particular, somewhat gruesome behavior will clearly reveal which one's the male and which the female.

After the male attaches his little packet of sperm—a sper-matophore, as it is called—to the female's genitalia during copu-lation, he has to make sure that enough time elapses for a successful transfer of genetic material. Another male cricket, af-ter all, might come along and substitute his own spermatophore. And so, over evolutionary time, the male bush cricket has developed a strategy to keep his line alive: he allows the female to nibble at his forewings while they mate. Given this opportunity, the female seems inclined to linger. Thus the male's genes have an excellent chance of making it to the next generation. But at what a cost! During a single copulation, the female may consume a quarter of his wings. By the time he has mated with several females, a male *Hapithus agitator* may have nothing left but stubs where his forewings used to be.

Restless bush cricket sex sounds macabre to most people, perhaps more so to men than to women. "I hope that cricket is a female," Jimmy said with feeling as he watched the spider devour its victim in the web. "That would serve her right," he said firmly.

Yet the restless bush cricket's mating peculiarities seem positively benign when compared to others in the insect class—praying mantises, for example. The female mantis does not limit her nibbling to her partner's wings: as the sex act proceeds she devours the male's entire head and thorax, chomping away even as the male's other end is delivering the sperm to fertilize her eggs. Needless to say, he does not survive the process. But his genetic material does. And that's the name of the game in the insect class, and every other class as well.

C

Crickets have a pretty song, variously tinkling or chirpy or thinly peeping. Cicadas, on the other hand, produce sounds that can never be described as pretty or musical. They produce the loud, mechanical screech that periodically rends the air in backyards, parks, and wooded areas from late July into the early days of autumn. Starting with a low buzz, the sound quickly crescendos into an almost deafening din, then recedes again into silence. Bzzzzzz**ZZZZZZ**zzzzzzzz. Imagine a rasp running across the teeth of a saw in front of a microphone, with someone turning the volume up quickly from low to very, *very* high and then back down and off—that's what cicadas sound like. They repeat that ear-splitting song again and again, all day long. Loud as it is, however, few passersby take note of it. Like other regular sounds of nature (the incessant chirps of house sparrows, for example), the cicada's buzz does not imprint itself on the conscious mind. People simply don't hear it. Only when someone points it out— *Do you hear that loud cicada buzzing?*—does one flick on some attention switch and suddenly hear it in all its volume. Then one often exclaims: *Unbelievable! How did I not notice that deafening sound?*

Because cicadas produce audible sounds, many people think they're in the same order as crickets and katydids, the Orthoptera. But cicadas are in Hemiptera, together with aphids, leafhoppers, and spittlebugs. All these insects have tymbals, complex membranes they rapidly vibrate to produce sounds, while their entire bodies serve as resonance chambers. Meanwhile, crickets produce sound by stridulation, a process in which two structures—the wings, for example—are rubbed against each other. Some cicadas' songs are louder than 106 decibels, the loudest of all insect-produced sounds. They modulate the noise by wiggling their abdomens toward and away from the tree they are on. Only the males sing, but both sexes have membranous structures called tympana, the cicadas' equivalent of ears. It makes sense: if one of them sings, the other must be able to hear it.

Central Park's cicadas are not the sort that make news every seventeen years by appearing at various predictable places in enormous plaguelike infestations. That species is the periodic cicada, *Magicicada septendecim*. Ours is the annual or dog-day cicada, *Tibicen pruinosa*. Though its cycle actually requires a two-year period, cohorts of dog-day cicadas hatch in alternate years and thus may appear to be annual.

In 1854 Thoreau noted in his journal that for many years in succession the dog-day cicadas began to be heard on July 25.

That was in Concord, Massachusetts. In Central Park more than a century and a half later the same insect arrives with the same regularity, though about two weeks earlier, New York City being at a lower latitude than Thoreau's cabin in the woods. Around July 8 or 9 the cicadas' loud buzz begins to ring out from the treetops in scattered parts of Central Park.

Central Park's dog-day cicadas always emerge during the hottest weeks of summer. But neither the hot spell nor the insect is named for the other: both derive their name from a bright heavenly body—Sirius the Dog Star. Since this star is invisible to the human eye in July and August when it rises and sets at the same time as the sun, the ancients believed that it adds its heat to the sun's then. Thus, they concluded, the star itself causes temperatures to rise. They named the hottest period after the star and hoped that once it became visible again, the weather would cool off. Of course it often did, reinforcing their belief.

Though cicadas are daytime creatures, one part of their life cycle takes place in the dark of night. That was what brought our little band of night watchers to the northeast corner of Cedar Hill one sultry summer evening a few years ago. We had come to witness the last stage of cicada metamorphosis.

There were six in the audience that night. Nick, Jimmy, Lee, Noreen, and I had seen the cicada show before. But we had a new observer among us, the violist and composer Jean Dane. An appealing woman in her early fifties, Jean had found her way into Central Park's nature community during the Pale Male crisis and became a regular part of our little band shortly thereafter.

We were as eager to show Jean the cicada spectacle as we were to see it ourselves. This was not out of generosity and kindness, in truth, but because sharing our adventures increased our own enjoyment of them. That's why we welcomed passersby at the Moth Tree and encouraged evening strollers to wait at owl fly-outs. We were showing off a bit, of course, but our urge to include others had a deeper reason: we were in on an amazing secret and we couldn't bear to keep it to ourselves. That desire to share extraordinary experiences with others must be universal—I've never met anyone who doesn't feel it to some extent. Maybe it's part of our evolutionary heritage, to be explained by neurobiologists one of these days.

Noreen, as ever, was the first to spot the homely brown bug making its way along the ground toward a large London plane tree. The rest of us came running. This particular cicada's journey to adulthood had started two years earlier, high in a nearby pin oak. There, using a sawlike egg-laying structure, the ovipositor, a female cicada inserted a fertilized egg cluster into the tip of a young branch. Six or seven weeks later tiny larvae, the nymphs, hatched, fell to the ground below, and immediately burrowed several inches into the soil. Safely out of reach of birds, mice, and other predators, they spent the next two years feeding off roots while performing a service for the tree in exchange: aerating the soil.

After its long underground sojourn of sleeping, feeding, and growing, our cicada nymph—an unprepossessing insect with short, stubby antennae, six brown crablike legs, and dull, protruding black eyes—has made its way to the base of a chosen tree.

The preordained moment has come at last. All flashlights are focused on the insect as it begins its slow ascent of the tree. Undisturbed by our lights, it climbs painstakingly, one leg at a time, about four feet up the trunk—eye level for the rapt observers. There it stops and waits. "Here we go," someone whispers. "It's happening." We quickly get out our extra flashlight batteries: the drama about to begin will be a long one.

The transformation begins slowly, with a barely perceptible hairlike split in the center of the brown nymph case. Then the pace accelerates. In its various stages the emerging cicada looks like an alien in a science fiction movie. With its dark, bulgy outer-space eyes, its ridged higher-intelligence brow, and what seem to be two transparent, needlelike fangs poking out of a hard yellow thing—is it a nose?—the weird creature slowly, slowly oozes out of its dull brown shell. Eventually the fangs become antennae. The yellow nose turns out to be part of the head.

Almost an hour and a half has gone by—is it possible? Time seems to have stopped for us. When the entire cicada has emerged, the extraterrestrial look-alike defies gravity for almost a minute, suspended horizontally from the end of the case with no visible means of support. Then it bends over unhurriedly and catches hold of its newly empty nymph case with each of its six tripartite legs—did I mention that they're bright green? This is when we notice two stumpy protuberances sticking out in the area where wings might be located. They're green too. But they don't look like wings at all, not yet.

There is a pause. Then, so quickly that we hardly believe it's happening, the stumps begin to grow. Within less than ten seconds they've metamorphosed into two large gauzy green wings, each covered with a network of transparent veins. If you're watching the transformation for the first time, you are unprepared for what comes next. If you've seen it before, now is when you hold your breath.

Suddenly fluid begins to throb through the veins. At first the wings take on a golden, glittery color that sparkles in our flashlight beams. Then, almost immediately, they turn as bright green as the legs. Let there be life! The rapt audience lets out a collective exhalation—*ah!*

Now the cicada, successfully emerged, must hang there for several dangerous hours while the wings dry, a glowing jewel that would certainly make a tasty meal for a hungry bird. But it is night! The birds are asleep. By bird wake-up, long after we've departed, the cicada will be gone too, off to obey its life imperative—Be fruitful, multiply.

☾

Some spectacles of nature are ravishing to behold. Others are unnerving. Every year Central Park presents a drama that frankly gives us the creeps: the nest-building ritual of the cicada killer wasp. The insect's very name has a horrible fascination.

The cicada killer, *Sphecius speciosus*, is the largest wasp to be found in the eastern United States. One and half inches in length with a wingspan of nearly three inches, this huge, yellow- and-black-striped insect makes people scream and run for their lives when they first encounter it. In reality, cicada killers are highly unlikely to sting people. In this they differ from wasps in the Vespidae family, those hornets, yellowjackets, and others we properly fear. Only cicadas need fear the cicada killer wasp.

Cicada killers don't make paper nests or hives like many of their relatives. Instead, they construct nests consisting of long underground tunnels in dry, sandy, or slightly elevated soil. The burrow has a gentle sloping entrance about six inches long. The tunnel always takes a right-angle turn on the way to the nest, probably for protection against other predators. It then contin- ues another six to eight inches and ends in one or several globu- lar cells about one and a half inches in diameter. Needless to say I've never seen the underground part of the cicada killer's nest, only the entrance and exit hole.

When the tunnel is completed, the cicada killer will lay her eggs in the carefully prepared underground cells. Then she'll go out hunting for a cicada. No other insect will do—it has to be one of the green-winged beauties. Sometimes the wasp will catch a victim on a tree trunk. More often she'll nab one in flight and plummet to the ground with it. In either case the stinger is her weapon—one jab with it, and the cicada is at her mercy, par- alyzed. The cicada is dragged, alive but not kicking, down the tunnel to the nest. When the wasp larvae emerge from the eggs, they'll literally eat the immobilized cicada alive.

One hot August evening a few minutes after 10:00, we made our way to an ancient rock outcrop on Cedar Hill. We always find nests of cicada killer wasps in that same spot—perhaps these insects have been making nests there for millennia. (According to Louis Sorkin, an entomologist at the American Museum of Natural History, a colony of cicada killers was discovered nesting on the lawn outside the museum in the early 1900s and has been seen there ever since.) With us that night were our favorite children from the Moth Tree, Aidan and James Smith, now six and (almost) three years old, accompanied as ever by their young and patient parents, Paula and David. Everyone was delighted with the distribution of labor we had organized: the grown-ups sat near the rocks with cameras, close-focus binoculars, and flashlights at the ready, resting their weary feet, while the children joyfully raced around, noses to the ground like terriers, looking for the telltale mounds of earth that signify cicada killer nests.

Everyone rejoiced when Aidan discovered a promising mound with a dark stain at its small opening. An active nest! Usually the digging wasp makes an appearance within a minute or two to toss out the excavated soil. This time, six long minutes passed and the mound didn't move. It must be an abandoned nest, we thought with disappointment, not so much on our account as the children's. Their excitement is contagious, and so is their unhappiness when things don't go as expected.

At a little after 11:00 we were about to call it a day, when both boys began yelping with excitement. We rushed over and indeed a few grains of sand were moving just outside the opening. Everybody froze, even the children, who (for once) heeded their father's command: "Don't move." A second later, the huge yellow and black cicada killer appeared. Backing out of her tunnel-in-progress, digging, tossing out sand and dirt, she was carefully preparing the scene for the unthinkable crime to come.

From the gauzy green adult emerging from its drab nymph case, a birth as lovely as Botticelli's goddess rising from the sea, to a fate worse than death—all in the course of two nights.

It's politically incorrect to use words like *lovely* and *grisly* and phrases like *unthinkable crime* when describing the facts of natural history. People still look down on anthropomorphism in this scientific age. But we're part of nature too; the behavioral vagaries of classes and orders and families other than our own affect us in our own singularly human way.

☾

W ho was there on the August night we discovered the wonders of slug sex? Noreen, Lee, Charles, Nick, Jimmy, and I: the Mothers (*authors*). A pretty, slender, extremely enthusiastic young woman named Carol, last name unknown. Norma Collin was there—she showed up at the Moth Tree now and then, and so did Sylvia Cohen. A few others: it was a bigger group than usual, I remember. We were heading for Cedar Hill to catch the last of the cicadas emerging from their nymph cases. Their season had begun in early July, and by the end of August it was almost over. We made our way to Cedar Hill a little after ten, when things were at a standstill at the oozing English oak. The evening was cool, not too cool for us vertebrates recovering from a recent heat wave, perhaps, but too cool for the spineless ones, moths and cicadas and other summer insects. For the first time in a month there was not a cicada to be seen on any of the usual trees.

Noreen made the discovery. She had wandered over to one of the European beeches near the park wall at Fifth Avenue and 77th Street. Still looking for cicadas, she scanned the tree trunk with her flashlight, but all she found were two big slugs moving around on the smooth grayish bark. As she idly watched them, she sensed that their movements were not entirely random. After a few minutes it became clear that they were doing something purposeful, for they had formed a sort of ring. Slowly—sluggishly, one might say—they circled around, occasionally stroking and nuzzling one another's end parts in a languorous way. That's when she called to the rest of us to come and watch. And that's how we first came to see the riveting drama of slug sex.

By day the slug is not a beautiful creature. For one thing it's covered with a moist, oozy substance resembling the stuff that comes out of your nose when you have a cold. For another it's drab and warty-looking, oddly toadlike under its slimy veneer. In fact, slugs produce two kinds of slime—one a free-flowing, runny-nose kind of liquid, the other an extraviscous, mucilaginous secretion that serves to defend them from would-be predators—snakes or rodents or you, for example. It's hard to remove the gluey kind from your hands; water only makes it cling more tenaciously.

The slug is usually perceived as alien and lowly. Indeed, the only taxonomic feature it shares with us is its kingdom—Animalia. Its phylum is Mollusca, its class Gastropoda, its order Stylommatophora. It belongs to the Limacid family, a good distance, on the systematics map, from us Hominids. Yet slugs are not as removed from *Homo sapiens* as you might imagine. In recent years the neuroscientist Eric Kandel used the large marine slug *Aplysia californica* to illuminate the biochemistry of human memory formation. Kandel's demonstration of what happens to individual cells in the slug's central nervous system as it processes information, and his application of this to human neurology, won him a Nobel Prize.

The chemical ecologist Thomas Eisner did not look down on the lowly slug. Indeed, when writing about the slug's highly evolved defense system he revealed a certain fondness for the unloved creature:

I have always been fascinated by slugs and by their ability to survive under hostile conditions. Living in soil, as so many of them do, entails special risks. Predators alone are a major hazard, in the form of ants, carabid beetles, centipedes and spiders, and there is really no way that you can imagine slugs being spared exposure to such enemies. In particular you wonder how slug eggs manage to survive, given that they are not only immobile, but gelatinous and soft. It seemed to me a foregone conclusion that slug eggs are chemically protected.

When Eisner and a colleague analyzed the chemical contents of slug's eggs, they were not surprised to discover a chemical compound theretofore unknown to science that served as a powerful insect deterrent. Wondering if slugs themselves were somehow protected from potential predators, Eisner discovered that they have a unique defense mechanism for fending off biting creatures such as ants, and he proposed a simple experiment that anyone can do to demonstrate it:

Look for a slug, and when you find it, poke it gently with a toothpick. A pine needle or leaf stalk will do as well. As long as you keep the stick motionless, nothing will happen. But if you wiggle the stick, the slug will set in motion a coagulation mechanism, whereby the slime in the immediate vicinity of the contact point is converted into a rubbery blob that clings to the tip of the stick. The mechanism is wonderfully effective because it keeps an enemy from piercing the body wall of the slug. Ants are literally muzzled when they bite into a slug. They are thwarted the moment they bear down with their mandibles, and as they back away, are left with their mouthparts encased in coagulated slime.

Apart from the occasional neuroscientist or chemical ecologist, the slug is universally scorned, likely to elicit a rhyming expletive from anyone who encounters it: *Ugh!* Nor do slugs endear themselves in their daytime habits. Virtual eating machines, the voracious creatures wreak havoc on many of the flowers and vegetables we plant in our gardens. Young lettuces seem to be particularly enticing.

Everything changes at night. Like our own species, slugs prefer to engage in sex under cover of darkness. Yet people who have managed to observe the arcane rituals of slug sex by lantern or flashlight confirm that what happens when slug embraces slug is ravishingly beautiful.

One who witnessed the joys of slug sex was Charles Darwin. He knew better than to dismiss slugs as unworthy objects of romance. In book 9 of *The Descent of Man* he wrote: "Anyone who has a chance to observe the love-making of slugs cannot doubt that these hermaphrodites use seduction and allure in their movements as they prepare for and accomplish their double embrace."

Hermaphrodites? Yes. Defined as snails without shells, all slugs come equipped with fully functional male and female reproductive organs. They can, in fact, mate with their own selves—a neat trick. Yet they generally seek another slug to mate with, for purposes of genetic diversity, no doubt. Even then their behavior is unorthodox to the extreme.

In their complex mating rituals each individual slug actually functions as both sexes simultaneously. It's not easy to understand how this works—the human reproductive system seems ridiculously simple in comparison. When a pair of slugs mate, each one provides sperm for fertilization. After sexual congress each of the pair lays three to fifty fertilized eggs beneath a piece of debris, in a crevice or in a hole in the ground. (My source for this hard-to-obtain information is *The Western Society of Malacologists' Field Guide to the Slug*, the only book of its kind in existence.)

The Central Park observers watching the two slugs circling on the beech tree were mildly revolted at first, a knee-jerk reaction. Then, as we watched their stately circumambulation, we found ourselves mesmerized, as entranced by what we saw as by a sensuous dance or movie. The pair of garden slugs, *Limax maximus*, slowly circled the smooth gray trunk of the beech tree again and again, nudging, stroking, caressing each other as they went, oozing globs of shiny, sticky slime all the while. They proceeded in their round dance for many minutes. One by one we had to replace the batteries in our flashlights—that gives you an idea of how long we stood there during the preliminary stages of slug sex.

Suddenly, without warning, the pace quickened. Moving more rapidly now, they attached end to front, forming a sort of wheel. The wheel went around for several revolutions, and then like a kaleidoscope it changed shape. The animals twisted around each other, all the while rubbing and nuzzling. Hardly an anthropomorphic observer, Darwin had used the words *seduction and allure* to describe the slugs' double embrace. I would add the word *tenderness*.

All at once the pair, now entwined in a sort of double helix, seemed to lose their footing. They plummeted from the dance floor. An audible inhalation of breath came from the spectators' gallery. *Something had gone wrong!* But the slugs didn't fall to the ground. Still fastened to the tree by a gluey glob, they dangled on a long rubbery slime string, a gastropodal bungee cord of sorts.

While suspended, they proceeded to spin slowly, first in one direction and then the other, writhing and throbbing as they turned. A few moments later, from under a fleshy lobe on top of each slug's back, a long milky-white appendage emerged. The two slowly came together and formed a single lovely flowerlike structure of a pale opalescent blue color. It resembled one of those Georgia O'Keeffe flowers that family publications won't reproduce because they look too much like sexual organs. According to *Terrestrial Slugs*, the authoritative text by N. W. Runham and P. J. Hunter, this is the moment of sperm exchange.

After a while the film seemed to be running backward. Slowly the creatures untwined and retracted the bluish flower appendages back under their mantles. Then they separated completely and one of them fell to the ground. The other, still attached to the rubbery bungee cord, proceeded to eat it as he hoisted himself up to the tree.

For some reason we found ourselves calling the slug that remained on high *he* and the fallen slug *she*. It turns out that we were not alone in our sex typecasting: a scientist writing about slugs in the early 1960s referred to the slug that consumed the bungee cord as "the male-behaving individual" and the fallen slug as "the female-behaving individual."

We were exhilarated when it was all over. We were also a little embarrassed, as if we'd participated in an orgy. Agreeing that slugs are vastly unappreciated animals, we spontaneously gave the pair—and Noreen, the discoverer—a round of applause. But there's no denying that others who have watched the same spectacle, though similarly moved by the beauties of gastropodal sex, remain ambivalent about the creatures themselves. They all seem to have an identical fixation: their lettuces!

In an essay entitled "Unknown Eros," H. L. Grant Watson, a zoologist and nature writer, wrote a rapturous paean to slug sex. Invoking the poems of Donne and Shakespeare, he compared the writhing gastropods on their elastic string to "human lovers apart and yet suspended on some psychic cord of their own making." He wrote, "Surely no physical union between higher animals or humans was ever consummated with such completeness." But when the act was over, Watson came back to earth with a thud: "What was to be done with the two hungry-looking slugs, each a good three inches long, which were making off towards my young lettuces?" He put the postcoital slug pair in a box. The next day he drove out into the country and released them in a distant meadow.

Another writer and slug enthusiast, Robert Michael Pyle, faced a similar dilemma. "They were beautiful," he wrote, "utterly merged—and they were stunning in their sheer physical exuberance." But Pyle was a lettuce lover too. "We make our choice, Limax or lettuce," he wrote. Rationalizing that the slugs would inevitably freeze when the first frost arrived, he decided to simply advance the moment. He put them into a bread bag and placed them in his freezer. "Making slugsicles gave me no pleasure and some sharp misgivings," he admitted, but he consoled himself with the memory of what had immediately preceded his sluggicide: "There are worse ways to go than entering the Big Sleep in a state of utter rapture."

7

Birds Asleep

I've always had a weakness for liturgies that connect, even obliquely, with nature and wildlife. My favorite part of the Passover service, for instance, has always been the recitation of plagues, especially frogs and locusts—the second and ninth plagues of Moses' "Let my people go" campaign.

As the frog plague is announced, I visualize armies of small anurans—the collective group of tailless amphibians Linnaeus considered "foul and loathsome animals"—swarming out of Egypt's rivers and streams to converge on Pharaoh's palace. I see them rushing into his bedchamber and leaving wet frog-prints all over the royal vestments—millions of frogs, all oddly resembling the ones in the *Little Golden Guide to Reptiles and Amphibians* I used to study as a child. Today I find this sort of mental exercise almost as fulfilling as seeing frogs in real life.

A recent exhibit at the American Museum of Natural History displayed twenty-six different species of live frogs and toads from around the world, but it included only one of Central Park's two amphibian species—the American bullfrog (*Rana catesbeiana*). While the bullfrog is active both day and night, our other resident frog species, the green frog (*Lithobates clamitans*), is primarily nocturnal. Even in the dark you can recognize it by its voice, which is said to sound like a plucked banjo string. It also

·gives a sharp yelp when disturbed. A few years ago, I almost stepped on one at the edge of the rowboat lake. It yelped.

When the locust plague comes up at the seder, I imagine great clouds of grasshoppers (once called locusts) covering the face of Egypt's land. Winged insects with elongated hind legs, they chomp away in my fantasy until they have eaten all the grain and stripped every tree, at least every tree that managed to survive Plague #7, the hailstorm. Frogs and grasshoppers happen to be animals I actively seek out in real life, though not, perhaps, in the numbers described in Exodus 8 and 10.

By the same token, elements of the Christmas story (at least as it is told in the Gospel according to St. Matthew) coincide with one of my most fulfilling experiences as a Central Park stargazer—witnessing the planetary conjunction of Jupiter and Venus from the northeast corner of the Great Lawn. Modern astronomers have suggested that the star of Bethlehem was actually a conjunction of these same two planets seen during the darkest part of the night. This created an illusion of a single, spectacularly luminous star, so bright that it surely would have impelled Babylonian astrologers (magi) to travel to Bethlehem to investigate.

Latter-day calculations show that a planetary conjunction of Jupiter and Venus would have been visible in the Bethlehem area on August 12 in 3 B.C.—close enough to the Nativity date, considering the inexactitude of ancient calendars. Within a religion based on belief in the supernatural—most religions are— the ancients would have seen it as a divine portent, evidence that the prophecy in the Book of Isaiah had been fulfilled: *For unto us a child is born, unto us a son is given.*

Above all, I love Easter sunrise services in Central Park. For many years Charles Kennedy and I used to meet at Belvedere Castle on Easter morning to take in whatever sunrise service we might find there. Without being religious, we were moved by the song and story of Easter. But it was sunrise that really drew us in.

The sudden emergence of our own flaming star on the horizon is always a spectacular show, but it carries special promise for bird-watchers in the spring.

Spring is Central Park's most dramatic season, when thousands of songbirds in their bright breeding plumage stop over for food and drink on the way to their nesting grounds. Thousands of birdwatchers, too, flock to the park during May and early June to enjoy the bird spectacle and check out each other's binoculars. Not infrequently, when winds are favorable for northward flight, birders may come upon little groups of songbirds gathering in the dusk, getting ready to resume their journeys. But even the earliest birders rarely witness a songbird arrival, when a host of hungry birds funnels in from the sky for a daybreak landing in Central Park. It was something I had long wanted to see.

One spring as the migration was nearing its peak, Charles proposed an expedition to fulfill my dream—Dawn Patrol, he called it. We persuaded Tom Fiore and Rebekah Creshkoff, two top-notch Central Park birdwatchers, to come too. And since most avian travelers end their nightlong journeys around daybreak, we had to get to the park early—so early, indeed, it hardly seemed worth going to bed the night before. The appointed hour was 5:00 a.m., and Bow Bridge was our chosen vantage point. The bridge offers an unobstructed view to the south—wasn't that where the little travelers were coming from?

It was dark when we met there on May 2. The Big Dipper was still sharply visible overhead, and Jupiter was low on the western horizon. Yet even an hour before sunrise, robins were singing in various parts of the woodlands. During their breeding season robins sing sporadically much of the night, probably to protect their boundaries from next-door neighbors.

As the first faint light of day appeared, we scanned the skies to the south and east. But apart from some mallards flying across the lake and a single night-heron, there were no birds to be seen.

Then two or three minutes later it began: the dawn chorus, springtime's featured concert. At 5:10 a red-winged blackbird sang its *Conk-a-la-reee* song. I heard it as *Honk-at-Marieeee*, while Rebekah heard it clearly as *Pu-ber-teee!* A little before 5:20 a nearby cardinal greeted the day with a loud series of whistles: *Weeet weeet weet weet weet.* At 5:25, give or take a minute, the first song sparrow joined the chorus, starting with the usual three repeated notes. Song sparrows are known to sing different versions in different areas, so this may not be true for your locals. But the ones that nest in Central Park seem to say *PRES-pres-pres-bi-TEA-ri-an-ism.*

At 5:36 exactly, our first warbler, a common yellowthroat, emitted its loud, harsh *witchety, witchety, witchety* song. (In point of fact, American warblers of the family Parulidae don't really warble; the songs of European warblers in the family Sylviidae are more musical.) The chorus grew louder as every bird within earshot seemed to throw in its two cents' worth. At 5:53, the moment of sunrise, Tom alerted us to the call of another loud nonwarbling warbler, a northern waterthrush. The Sibley guide describes its call as "a loud, hard *spwik* rising with a strong *k* sound."

One minute later the chorus stopped abruptly. It was as if the flow had been turned off like a faucet. What you heard now, if you made a special effort to listen, were the ordinary sounds of daytime in the park: house sparrows chirping monotonously, an occasional blue jay calling, a squirrel complaining, the wind rustling in the trees, all of it receding into the back of your consciousness as if it didn't exist.

Well, we didn't see the waterthrush or the yellowthroat or any other warbler arriving. Why had we missed them? Either we were in the wrong spot, or it was still too dark to make them out when they descended, or maybe they'd come in the day before and decided to stay overnight. In fact, we failed to see a single spring migrant that morning. Still, they say a bird heard is a bird seen; that is, even if you fail to actually see a bird, you may check it off on your day list if you hear it sing and recognize its song. So by birdwatchers' rules, we had "seen" two warblers. And it was lovely to be together in the park, looking at stars and listening to birdsong in the dark of the early, the *very* early, morning.

☾

B irdwatchers are often sleep-deprived during the migration seasons. But what about the birds themselves? How do they manage to keep their wits about them during their sleep-deprived travels? After all, there's solid evidence among humans that adequate sleep is needed for optimal performance of daily tasks and that, conversely, sleep deprivation has negative affects on brain activity. Everyone knows the importance of a good night's sleep.

Niels C. Rattenborg and his colleagues at the University of Wisconsin–Madison have done a research study that contradicts these widely believed understandings. When they monitored the brain waves of eight white-crowned sparrows (*Zonotrichia leucophrys*) for a full year, they found that a change in brain activity occurred at two discrete times: in the spring (when the species migrates from winter quarters to breeding grounds), and in the fall (when the birds head south). At the very times when large numbers of white-crowned sparrows throughout the Midwest and West were preparing to start on their long flights, the caged birds in the laboratory showed signs of restlessness. Instead of their usual zonk-out after sunset, they hopped around and flapped their wings and were uncharacteristically active, night after night. *Zugunruhe* is what ornithologists call this pre-migratory restlessness. All songbirds that migrate at night display it. It is triggered by the rise of two hormones in conjunction, prolactin and corticosterone, which are regulated, in turn, by the amount of daylight the bird takes in (the photoperiod).

This much has been known for a long time. The Wisconsin researchers added something new. First they confirmed that during the hours of *Zugunruhe* both hemispheres of the birds' brains were active, thus contradicting a long-held belief that birds were only half-awake during migration, sleepwalking in the air, as it were.

Then they devised an experiment to investigate the effects of sleep deprivation on the birds' ability to learn. During the *Zugunruhe* period, when the birds would normally be migrating, the researchers gave the birds lessons in pecking buttons in a certain order. If sleep deprivation decreased their ability to learn, you'd imagine that at the end of the three weeks with little sleep the birds wouldn't learn as well as they did at the beginning. But in fact they learned just as well.

Could a study of sleep-deprived birds be in any way applicable to humans? Why not? After all, birds and mammals show very similar sleep patterns. They both experience rapid eye movement (REM) and non-REM sleep in the course of the night. (Since REM sleep is strongly associated with dreams, birds probably dream, though not in a form they could easily relate to each other at breakfast or, for that matter, to their shrinks.)

The results of the Wisconsin experiment looked like good news for bad sleepers like me. By demonstrating that sleep deprivation did not lead to mental incapacity in at least this one particular case, the study allowed me to hope that it might not lead to brain rot in my case either.

Unfortunately for me, the results seem to apply only during birds' two very specific, hormonally driven migration periods. When the researchers repeated the experiment during the non-migrating winter months, they found that after even a single night of sleep disturbance, the birds' performance declined significantly. So I guess I'd better keep up the hot milk, the white-noise machine, and the occasional Ambien. I try to look on the bright side: though my brain may be suffering, I have the chance to see a glorious sunrise much more often than my well-rested friends.

❨

As the first Easter Sunday without Charles approached, I was determined to be at Belvedere for the sunrise service—I didn't want to concede that life would be diminished from then on—but I needed company. Two candidates for an early rendezvous came immediately to mind: Jean Dane, a regular owl-watcher and a poor sleeper, was one. Naomi Machado, who teaches English to foreign students at the Borough of Manhattan Community College, was the other; she's always up for odd Central Park happenings. I sent off e-mail invitations and they each replied enthusiastically. Jean added an enigmatic postscript: "Maybe we'll even see the vernal lagomorph."

My husband was the fourth of the group that met at 5:30 on Sunday, April 16, at the northeast corner of Central Park West and 81st Street. The idea of three small women entering the park in what seemed to him the dead of night made him uneasy enough to abandon his bed at that ungodly hour. Of course I was delighted to have him along, though I'm afraid he didn't really know how many other times I'd been in the park before sunrise or after sunset with similar, or smaller, groups.

Though you might consider 5:30 an early hour, we were late that morning. Even as we walked through the Shakespeare Garden toward the stairs to the Castle, wide-awake birds were singing all around, robins, cardinals, white-throated sparrows, red-winged blackbirds, mourning doves, blue jays, and both kinds of kinglets—the common lot for mid-April. In another two weeks the major songbird migrants would be there—warblers, orioles, vireos, thrushes—and the morning din would be even louder. As we stood at the Castle ramparts and looked eastward, we could see a pinkish glow at the horizon. The sunrise was yet to come, but we had missed the magical moment of bird wake-up. That happens at daybreak, or the start of civil twilight—5:47 that morning, according to the U.S. Naval Observatory website.*

We were the only souls there at 6:17, the official time of sunrise. Where were the Easter worshipers? we wondered, a little disappointed. Naomi rose to the occasion with a hilarious version of an old Beatles song, the one that begins, "Well, she was just seventeen . . ." Her version, composed on the spot and accompanied by a rather irreverent bump and grind, began, "Well, it was six-seventeen. You know what I mean . . ." We sang it several times on the battlements of Belvedere Castle as the sun changed from a mysterious red eruption rising out of the void to its ordinary blinding white presence above the horizon.

At 6:25 a small group of men and women arrived, a bit breathless from the stair climb. Easter celebrants at last! Methodists from both an East Side and a West Side congregation (a twain that rarely meets in Manhattan) distributed booklets of stapled pages entitled "Easter Dawn Service," containing the words for seven hymns and three prayers. Most of the hymns had a morning theme, and we quietly joined in for "When Morning Gilds the Skies" and "All Things Bright and Beautiful."

Then we stole away, down the steps and south to Bank Rock Bridge, where we had a date with a tame red-winged blackbird. His name was Larry, but a more recent Central Park chronicler, Bob Levy, seemed to think it was George and was writing a book about him. Larry aka George was waiting for us impatiently on that Easter morning and gave my outstretched hand an ungrateful little peck as he landed to take his unsalted peanut. He snatched a nut from each of the others and disappeared. I glanced at my watch; it was only 7:15.

*You can find the exact time of civil twilight for any date and location in the United States by going to the One Day page of the observatory's site. The best way to get there is to write "Sun and Moon data for One Day" in the Google search engine.

Just before we dispersed for our various destinations—mine was back to bed—I remembered Jean's enigmatic e-mail. "What's the vernal lagomorph?" I asked.

She beamed. "I'm so glad you asked," she said. "Well, Lagomorpha is an order of the class Mammalia. And guess what animals it includes."

"What animals does it include?" I asked dutifully.

"Rabbits," she answered.

"Rabbits? Oh, of course," I groaned. "The Easter Bunny."

☾

I can always depend on Naomi Machado to join me for adventures at any hour of day or night. One morning in early August, I met Naomi at the park entrance on Fifth Avenue and 79th Street. But why call it morning? It was 4:00 a.m. and as dark as night—my earliest rendezvous in Central Park ever.* Our destination was Cedar Hill, where a spot under one of the cedars offered an unimpeded view of the northwestern sky. That's where the spectacular array of shooting stars known as the Perseids would be most clearly visible, we'd been told.

Tom Clabough and Charlie Ridgway, our mentors at the Venus-Jupiter conjunction a year earlier, were already there when we arrived—don't amateur astronomers ever sleep? Before we got there, they'd seen a few meteors (another name for shooting stars), including one flaming orange streak. Then the weather changed and a light cloud cover obscured most of the sky. While we waited for the clouds to move on (if they ever would), Tom explained what a meteor shower is, and why it appears so predictably year after year. Helping people understand astronomical phenomena, after all, is a star guy's mission.

---

*Since then I've learned that our visit that day, like our Easter visits, was illegal. The park's official hours of operation are from 6:00 a.m. until 1:00 a.m.

First of all, shooting stars are not stars at all but bits of dust or pulverized grit from a comet's tail. In the case of the Perseids, the comet is Swift-Tuttle, which intersects earth's orbit every year in August. The particles of debris hit earth's atmosphere at the speed of 132,000 miles per hour, creating vivid streaks of light—meteors—when they disintegrate. The meteors known as the Perseids are so called because the intense stream of them appears to be emanating from the constellation Perseus. Comet Swift-Tuttle, by the way, is scheduled for a "near miss" with earth one of these days. But not to worry, it won't happen before the year 3044, when it will pass within a million miles of our planet. That's called "near" in the world of astronomy.

According to the star guys, the cloud cover had been predicted. But expectations of spectacular shooting stars had lured Naomi and me from our cozy beds that morning, and we hadn't even noticed the absence of stars on our way to the park. But flying objects of other kinds were to make our morning unexpectedly thrilling.

The first of these arrived at 4:45 a.m., just as we were beginning to face the reality of a meteor no-show. A small patch of starry sky appeared between the shifting clouds in the southwest sky, and with some excitement the astronomers pointed out a bright object briefly visible there, moving northeast. It was the International Space Station, two hundred miles above the earth and moving at a speed of eighteen thousand miles per hour. Manned by an American and a Russian, it was an example of peaceful coexistence unthinkable during my Cold War childhood.

At 5:00, as the faintest beginnings of day began to appear, an unexpected flying object made an appearance, one that didn't require clear skies for visibility. A large owl swooped right over our heads, probably just as startled to see us directly in its flight path as we were to see it. Then it disappeared into a pine tree to our east. It looked bigger than a long-eared owl—a barred owl, I guessed, or even a great horned. We watched the trees where the bird had landed, and ten minutes later we could just make out a dark shape moving from the pines westward, toward the Great Lawn.

At 5:20, as sunrise approached, we were startled to see three chunky-bodied bats circling directly over our heads—more flying objects! I'd never seen early-morning bats in Central Park before, only the ones that appear at dusk. But why shouldn't bats be out hunting in the twilight of dawn just as they do after sunset? It makes perfect sense—the light level is identical.

A moment later the cloud cover began to break up. Alas, the constellation Perseus with its fiery showers of meteors was in the northern part of the sky, which was still obscured. By the time the clouds finally drifted off, it was three minutes before sunrise. There was too much light to see any heavenly objects at all except, of course, the sun.

So we didn't see any shooting stars at our Perseid watch. No matter, we'd seen owls and bats, and a space station circling the earth just like the ones in science fiction movies. We had another sighting that proved to be important, though we didn't know it at the time. As Naomi and I headed for home, we saw a juvenile robin landing on the Great Lawn a few feet away from our path. Then we noticed four or five other robins arriving at the same place. We became dimly aware of a bird commotion coming from the direction of the nearby Pinetum, but we were busy chatting and didn't stop to investigate. The following spring we remembered those robins when we discovered the Robin Boys' Dormitory at the northwest corner of Cedar Hill.

☾

For years I'd watch small birds disappearing into a tree or bush at dusk. They'd chirp for a few minutes and then fall silent. Well, I knew they were there—I'd seen them go in. But somehow I could never find a single one, not even with my best flashlight playing over the foliage like a searchlight at a film premiere. Under cover of darkness birds seemed to blend into the background and become invisible.

Over the years finding one of these disappearing birds became something of an obsession. Surely *someone* had uncovered the secret of how birds managed to stay invisible at night. When that rich compendium of up-to-date bird knowledge, *The Birds of North America*, was completed in 2003, I hoped it would contain helpful facts about birds' sleep. But while the *BNA* provides information about migration, habitat, behavior, breeding, and more, and though it includes data on the sleeping habits of nocturnal birds that can be seen sleeping during the day, owls, for example, it gives few clues about how and where birds active in the daytime sleep at night. In its thorough account of the American robin, for instance, the category entitled "Sleeping Behavior" contains only two words: *not documented*. Few ornithologists or field biologists, it appears, study this issue. I wondered whether they too had trouble finding sleeping birds in the darkness.

Then I heard about a book dedicated entirely to that neglected subject. Its promising title was *Birds Asleep*, and its author was Alexander Skutch, a highly regarded American ornithologist. Though out of print, it was listed by several Internet used-book sellers, and my eagerly awaited copy soon arrived.

At first I was disappointed. I wanted to learn about birds that sleep in Central Park, but Skutch seemed more interested in the black-legged kittiwake, a pelagic bird that sleeps facing the wind while floating on the stormy seas off the Grand Banks of Newfoundland. The writer had much to say about bedtime among the long-tailed tits of northern Eurasia, which sleep nine to twelve in a bunch, clumped into a compact ball with their tails sticking out in all directions. I marveled at Skutch's ability to ferret out these facts. But it wasn't what I wanted to know. Then, out of the blue, he offered me a startling piece of information about a very familiar bird:

Among thrushes, American Robins often roost in large aggregations . . . These roosts are at first occupied, as early as May, by
adult males, apparently including paired birds, whose mates still
incubate or brood nestlings. After the young fledge, the male
robins are joined by females and juveniles, sometimes swelling the
roosts to an estimated twenty-five thousand robins.

Twenty-five thousand robins! Sleeping in sex-segregated dor-
mitories! The idea seemed outlandish. Had anyone else ever noticed this phenomenon? Thanks to an Internet database called
SORA (Searchable Ornithological Research Archives) it took me
only minutes to find articles and papers that would have required weeks or even months of searching in the days before
computers. The two most interesting ones were more than a
century old, but that didn't matter to me in the least. Though
language and nomenclature may change over time, and perhaps
the timetables are beginning to shift because of global warming,
I'm confident that the facts of natural history will be the same
over the years represented in SORA.

One of the old articles was written by a noted ornithologist of
the late nineteenth century, Bradford Torrey. In it he described
his discovery of a robins' night roost near Cambridge, Massachusetts. For a few months he'd noticed a good number of robins
flying past his house every evening, always in the same direction.
Finally, on the evening of July 25, 1889, he decided to see where
they were going. He followed them through woods and swampy
underbrush and ended up in front of a certain tree at the edge of
a narrow field. He wrote:

> It was too dark for me to see what was going on, but as I brushed
> against the close branches the robins set up a lively cackling, and
> presently commenced flying from tree to tree before me as I ad-
> vanced, though plainly with no intention of deserting their quar-

ters. The place was full of them, but I could form no estimate of their number.

Torrey returned the next night and took a stand on a nearby knoll from which his robin tree was plainly visible. Counting the birds flying directly past him and into the tree, he figured that his total would account for a quarter of all the birds roosting in the tree. By that calculation the grand total of roosting robins was twelve hundred.

When I searched further on the SORA website, I found several other papers describing gigantic aggregations of American robins in a single roost. One of these, by Torrey's contemporary William Brewster, reported twenty-five thousand robins in a roost he monitored on August 4, 1875. The number rang a bell. It was the same number Skutch had mentioned and I had doubted. I doubted no more.

The American robin is Central Park's most prolific nester. By midsummer there are extraordinary numbers—thousands, perhaps—of these large, red-breasted birds to be found within the park's 840 acres. Indeed, Central Park's robins may set some sort of record: during a breeding-bird census undertaken in the mid-1990s, the number of active robins' nests per square acre exceeded any known breeding-density statistics for the species recorded anywhere.

Though a few hardy robins overwinter in the park, the bird's scientific name, *Turdus migratorius*, defines its migratory nature. The great majority of them head south in late October and return toward the end of April. After a few weeks of settling in and jostling for territory, Central Park robins begin nest-building in May. By June the speckle-breasted young of the first broods can be seen throughout the park. A robin pair often has two more broods, so with an average of four eggs per brood, each robin couple may produce up to twelve fledglings a season. Of course the number of surviving chicks is usually far lower.

This was especially true after Pale Male settled into the park and developed a taste for robin nestlings. Nevertheless the robin population in Central Park never seems to diminish.

Where do robins sleep at night? With so many of them in the park, it shouldn't be hard to find out. Yet no one seemed to have a clue. We knew that during incubation the females sleep in the nests to keep the eggs warm and safe from predators. And even after the eggs hatch, the robin moms continue to brood the hatchlings at night, keeping them toasty until their thermoregulatory systems kick in. But where do the fathers sleep all that time? Alexander Skutch's book, as well as the two papers from the SORA database eventually led to an answer.

☾

It was a few minutes after sunset on a mild day in early June and the park was bathed with that warm glow filmmakers and photographers call golden light. As I walked along the path beside the Pinetum on the north side of the Great Lawn, I became aware of an odd din. It sounded vaguely familiar—I had probably gone by there hundreds of times before without paying attention to it. I might have passed right by it again that day. But I had just read Skutch's description of communal roosts and that might have made the familiar racket finally penetrate my conscious mind.

I stopped and looked around for a few moments to check out the sound. Nothing special going on, just a small group of robins feeding on the edge of the Great Lawn. Then I noticed more robins on the Pinetum side of the path and a few perched on low branches of nearby trees. A minute or two later I looked up. Holy mackerel, a huge stream of robins, like a plume of smoke, was funneling into a big linden tree on the south side of the path. Hundreds and hundreds of robins!

You can tell male robins from females by their breast color:

the males' are a rich, deep red color, while the females' are paler and drabber. I scanned the breasts of those birds still feeding on the lawn and those coming in for a landing, and saw that they were all the same sex, not a washed-out breast among them. And suddenly everything fell into place. I had stumbled on the Robin Boys' Dormitory.

That night I called Naomi Machado—I knew it was her kind of thing—and we began systematic observations of the Dormitory Tree the very next day. Our vigil went on for almost four months. Donna Browne often joined the robin-monitoring team, along with Eleanor Tauber, a nature photographer and former actress.

After a few weeks we began to see a pattern in the robin bed-time ritual that rarely varied: Though groups of birds from all directions arrived in the vicinity of the Dormitory Tree well before sunset, the moment of mass fly-in for the night occurred about fifteen minutes after the sun went down. Until then robins flew back and forth from the roost tree to the Pinetum across the path and then back again. All the while many continued to feed on the Great Lawn near the base of the linden. And then suddenly, almost as if someone had blown a whistle, the birds took wing and swooped into the tree all at once.

On clear days the dramatic influx could be predicted by the color of the sky: the robins were likely to take their positions for the night at the moment when the post-sunset sky was at its rosiest. Thomas Hardy once coined a perfect name for that stage of twilight: "pinking time." On June 28, for example, Naomi and I observed that the greatest mass of birds flew into the tree at 8:45, fourteen minutes after sunset, and the exact moment of pinking time.

As in any boy's dormitory, there was considerable pushing, shoving, and roughhousing just before bedtime. In the rapidly fading light we could see little skirmishes breaking out as the birds jostled for position: *That's my spot! No way, I was here first!* A hundred years earlier, William Brewster observed similar behavior at his monster roost in Cambridge, Massachusetts, and in his 1906 paper he described their aggressive posturing in detail:

> I have been interested to learn that a sound resembling the pattering of hail, which is heard when they are fluttering among the foliage and which I had formerly supposed to be caused by their wings striking the leaves, is really made, at least in part, by their bills. When two or more of them are contesting for possession of the same perch they first threaten one another with wide-opened beaks and then bring their mandibles rapidly and forcibly together, thereby producing the sound above described.

After nightrise—for why in the world must night fall?—our observations moved from the visual to the audial. We watched the birds go into the tree—so many of them! We swept the branches with our flashlights, but failed to locate a single sleeping bird; they just seemed to blend into the woodwork. Yet we continued to hear them for quite a while before silence descended on the Boys' Dormitory. Soon we developed a discriminating ear for the many different calls and songs robins can make—sounds they produce throughout the day but seem to briefly rehearse just before going to sleep.

To give you an idea of how much variety there is in robin patois, here's an annotated list of the ten common notes of the American robin, compiled by Arthur Cleveland Bent in his multivolume work *Life Histories of North American Birds* (the illustrious predecessor of *The Birds of North America*):

1. *Seech-ook*
2. *Pleent tut-tut-tut* (sort of a gasp, accented, higher in pitch)
3. *Sss tut-tut-tut* (a tremulous, sibilant sound, followed by troubled sobbing)
4. *Skeet, skeet* (two or three high screams, uttered as if in haste)
5. *Seech, each-each-each* (a common note, suggesting unrest)

6. *He-he-he-he-he* (a rapid laughing giggle)
7. *Chill-ill-ill-ill* (the rhythm suggests the kind of bell formerly used on ambulances and police wagons)
8. *Hisselly-hisselly* (a sibilant, whispered phrase; associated with courtship)
9. *Sssp* (a faint trembling hiss; refinement of the shriek)
10. *Tut* or *huh* (a low sobbing note with a deep undertone; a note of trouble, given when a cat is prowling near)

We recognized many of the notes Bent had translated so well from Robinese into English. But one day we heard a call from the dorm that resembled none of the songs we'd ever heard robins make. It went *secret-secret-secret-secret-secret-secret* (pause), *pitti-sing, pitti-sing, pitti-sing, pitti-sing, pitti-sing*. We finally located the singer on a low branch—it was a mockingbird.

On any given day, according to my records, our Central Park redbreasts went from *Chill-ill-ill-ill* to *he-he-he-he-he* (we called that the whinny) to *pleent tut-tut-tut*, to *Seech, each-each-each*, finally ending with the little *tut-tuts* I'd been noticing for years at the time of owl fly-out. These are the final robin night-night sounds heard throughout the park as darkness descends. What happens next? As light fades at the Boys' Dormitory, the birds gradually settle down. The calls become intermittent. Fifteen minutes after the last stragglers have arrived, not a sound can be heard. Utter silence.

The breakthrough in our quest to see an actual bird asleep arrived in the form of a flashlight, the Surefire. Powered by two lithium batteries, this small and extremely light device (about five inches long and four ounces in weight) produces a stronger, more focused beam than any of our conventional flashlights. Finally, the Surefire's superpowerful illumination revealed a sleeping bird. I had expected the sleeper to have his head tucked under his wing as in the old rhyme that begins: "The north wind doth blow, and we shall have snow, and what will poor robin do then, poor thing?" But that's not the way my robin looked. His head was scrunched down into his neck, and his bill was pointing straight upward. His eyes were closed.°

To be sure, the robin I saw sleeping merely shared a name with the one in the poem; it was a different species of bird. Our large, red-breasted, worm-digger-upper is officially known as the American robin, to distinguish it from the much smaller European bird that is called simply the robin (*Erithacus rubecula*). For all I know, the European robin tucks rather than scrunches.

When we began observing the Boys' Dormitory in early June, it was an all-male club; the females were still occupied with nest duties. As time went by, the speckled young of the first and then second broods began showing up along with the dads. In September the lighter-breasted females finally made their appearance. It was a co-ed dorm at last.

After Naomi and I had spent so many hours monitoring the robins' bedtime rituals at evening fly-in time, we thought we should see what happened when the birds got up in the morning. What would robin fly-out be like?

We knew we'd have to get there early, but it took us a while to understand just how early. On August 10 we paid our first morning fly-out visit to the Dormitory, arriving at sunrise. Too late—the tree was already deserted. Two days later we came fifteen minutes before sunrise and again found it empty. We began to see that robins really *are* early birds.

On August 16 we wanted to be sure we wouldn't miss the morning departure yet again, and so we met at the robin roost in

---

°I still don't know what makes sleeping birds so hard to find without the help of a superbright flashlight. They seem to have evolved some way of positioning themselves on their night roosts that keeps them safe from owls or wolves or coyotes or other possible predators. I know I've just revealed the secret of finding sleeping birds to members of the most predatory species of all, the one with access to superbright flashlights. Please proceed with caution.

the middle of the night. Actually it was 5:00 a.m., but the sky was dark and stars were shining brightly. Only the faint drone of a plane overhead gave a preview of the roar of morning traffic still to come. A series of gentle, evenly spaced chirps came from the direction of the Pinetum—crickets. I couldn't possibly have heard them if the ambient sound level had been any louder. And not a sign of life in the Boys' Dorm. Was it possible they'd already gone? I directed my Surefire beam to a branch where I'd seen a robin sleeping the night before and there he was, still asleep, bill pointing upward.

At 5:35, we heard a soft *kwick-kwick-kwick* from somewhere in the tree—a new sound not on Bent's list. One bird was singing quietly but obviously with authority. Less than a minute later, *whoooosh!* A huge black wave of robinhood surged out into the morning's gloom. Two minutes later, accompanied by a few more *kwicks* and sharp *cheeps*, an even bigger squadron sailed out of the tree. In 1906 William Brewster had reported that "on several occasions I have seen practically the entire body of birds leave simultaneously in the morning twilight, in one immense flock."

Naomi and I stared at the disappearing mass of robins. Had we really seen it or had we dreamed it? But they didn't all disappear. Many of the robins from the second flight descended on the wet, dewy grass of the Great Lawn just in front of us and began to feed hungrily, doing the odd hop-hop-run dance that no other bird does in quite the same way. I saw one capture a fat worm at about 5:45; he slurped it down the way a kid slurps down spaghetti.

At 5:50 the sky was taking on the flat white color that precedes the first visible signs of an impending sunrise. Nevertheless, just minutes before our star was scheduled to break out at the horizon, Naomi and I felt the same magnetic pull. Coffee! We headed for an all-night Greek coffee shop on 86th Street and Columbus Avenue—they say it's the one where Isaac Bashevis

Singer used to write the stories and novels that won him a Nobel Prize. We found it inspiring too.

☾

One summer, Ben Cacace, a meticulous nature observer, decided to keep track of all the birds flying across the Great Lawn at the end of the day. Belvedere Castle, the fanciful structure at the lawn's south end, afforded a perfect view of its entire grassy expanse, and every evening from dusk to darkness the young man stood on the Castle's parapet and counted birds. He posted these reports on *e-birds*, a Listerv from local birders. Since that was the year Naomi and I had discovered the robin roost at the lawn's north end, we were especially interested in his robin count. One night he counted 675 robins heading north between 6:22 and 7:47 p.m. That total, of course, included only the ones Ben saw streaming in from the south. There might have been an equal number that he couldn't see, heading for the same location from the north. We had estimated that more than a thousand birds were converging on the roost tree every night, so Ben's total was on the button.

In September Ben began to report large numbers of grackles flying across the lawn at the same time as the robins. But these shiny black birds were all heading in the opposite direction. Where were they going? he wondered idly. On September 30 he followed the birds and made a staggering discovery. His report on *e-birds* that day made the numbers of birds at the Boys' Dormitory look like chump change:

> A Common Grackle roost was found near the south end of Central Park. While birding in the area around Gapstow Bridge, south of Wollman Skating Rink, I watched grackles & starlings flying towards the southeast corner of the park.

The birds were heading out of the park towards a group of ten trees surrounding a water fountain just east of the Plaza Hotel. I started watching the stream around 6:20 p.m. The number of birds reduced to a trickle shortly after sunset (6:45 p.m.). The last bird seen entering the roost was around 6:54 p.m.

The number was close to uncountable. They were flying in so densely that only an estimate could be given of the groups, and multiple observers would be needed to come close to separating the starlings from the grackles. The number of roosting birds is huge but the difficulty in counting them is huger. My estimate for the short time I spent on the plaza in front of the Plaza is a few thousand. The ability for this many birds to settle in such a small number of trees with plenty of room for many more is simply amazing.

On the first day of October I skipped my daily rendezvous with the robins at the Dorm. Instead, I made my way to the area Ben had described. Nobody calls it by its fancy moniker, the Grand Army Plaza.* Named after the Civil War's Union army and inspired by the design of the Place de la Concorde in Paris, this public space is universally called the plaza in front of the Plaza. Over the years I'd passed through it hundreds of times, on the way to one of the department stores on its periphery, or to the Paris movie theater diagonally across from the hotel's entrance, or to some periodontist, endodontist, or oral surgeon in the vicinity—for some reason a lot of people who fix gums or pull teeth seem to have their offices within a few blocks of the Plaza. It is a two-block-long rectangle of sorts, bisected in the middle by Central Park South—59th Street to most locals.

Every New Yorker knows the fountain at the plaza—it's a midtown landmark, though nobody calls it by its official name, the Pulitzer Fountain, either. At its center stands Pomona, the Roman goddess of abundance. She is carrying a large bowl of

---

*The plaza at the main entrance to Brooklyn's Prospect Park, also named the Grand Army Plaza, is usually called by its real name.

fruit in token of her bailiwick, but all she wears is a flimsy sash draped over one shapely leg. She is surrounded by five stepped granite basins, and when the fountain is on, the water spills from one tier to the next in a soothing, rather hypnotic way. A semicircle of ten slender trees around the fountain forms a border.

At the north end of the plaza stands an imposing gold-plated bronze man on horseback: General William Tecumseh Sherman, Civil War hero. In contrast to Pomona, the general is fully clothed. He too is surrounded by a semicircle of ten trees. These trees—Bradford Callery pear trees—are the most important feature of my story.

That day I arrived at 5:30, an hour before sunset. Planting myself on one of the backless stone benches between the naked goddess and the gilded general, I waited for Ben's multitudes to arrive. But there wasn't a grackle or a starling to be seen, only some house sparrows chirping monotonously in one of Pomona's pear trees and a bunch of pigeons milling around near the fountain. Five or six were bathing in the bottom two basins.

At a little before 6:00, I noticed that all the sparrows were gone, and most of the pigeons too: only a couple were still splashing in the second tier. A minute later they also flew off and I watched them landing on the scaffolding surrounding the Plaza Hotel. The historic landmark was beginning a multiyear conversion to condos that year and the pigeons were happily taking advantage. That's when I noticed a group of large, long-tailed birds perched on the trees at the southeastern edge of Central Park. I don't know how long they'd been sitting there. Grackles!

At 6:05 black birds began streaming into the plaza, some from the staging area along Central Park South and others coming from the depths of the park proper. Some flew straight to the fountain, landing on the basins around Pomona to splash around and take long drinks. Others flew directly into three of Pomona's ten pear trees, the ones closest to Fifth Avenue. Still others landed in the general's trees.

At 6:10 another stream of birds arrived, about a hundred, I estimated. Now I could clearly see that some of them were smaller and shorter-tailed—starlings. More than half the birds flying in were big, beautiful grackles. They alone availed themselves of the fountain; not a single starling landed there to drink or bathe during the months I monitored the plaza fly-in.

At 6:15 the light was fading and the western horizon took on a peachy glow. Now the number of birds arriving to take their places in the Pomona trees increased dramatically. Hundreds upon hundreds of birds were flying into the plaza. Though some first landed in the Sherman trees, none of them stayed there long. Eventually they all made for Pomona.

At 6:25 the sky was almost blotted out by a solid stream of black birds heading for the trees around the fountain. There were more than a thousand, beyond any doubt. But don't imagine that the birds divided themselves among all ten of the Pomona trees. This grand army of grackles and starlings was crowding into only three of the ten, the ones closest to Fifth Avenue.

The Grand Army Plaza is one of New York's most popular tourist attractions. Tour buses always stop there, disgorging visitors who want to see the hotel where Eloise lived, to gaze at Tiffany's down the street, where Audrey Hepburn breakfasted, and to take pictures of one another in front of the fountain. Tour guides lead the way, listing the heroic deeds of William Tecumseh Sherman and relating the sad history of Audrey Munson, the young model who posed for Pomona because her mother insisted and who eventually ended her long sad life in an insane asylum. At the end of the afternoon the plaza is full of New Yorkers hurrying home from work or on their way to a last-minute shopping spree or a late dental appointment.

Here's the most confounding part of this story: every night as the birds settled into their roost trees, the starlings rattling, hissing, and emitting slurred whistles that sound like human cat calls, the grackles uttering their harsh, toneless *gree-kle* calls, *none* of those passersby noticed the avian drama going on all around them. I scanned the crowd, looking for reactions, but found not one head raised, not one jaw dropped in wonder. Nobody paid the birds the slightest attention, not a single, solitary person!

Birds were still arriving at 6:37, the moment of sunset, but in smaller numbers. Ten minutes later the last stragglers zipped into the roost trees as streetlights up and down Fifth Avenue began to come on. The large, decorative fixtures outside Bergdorf Goodman, the Sherry Netherland, and A La Vieille Russie were aglow. For another fifteen or twenty minutes a chorus of loud squeaks, calls, and cackles resounded in the vicinity of the trees, but still no one seemed to hear it. No one stopped to see who was making such a racket.

Not until the middle of December when the pear trees had lost their final leaves did I hear a boy say to his mother, "Hey, look at all the birds on top of that tree." The grackles and starlings were now completely exposed on the bare branches, and in the wintry twilight the trees seemed to be heavily laden with hundreds of small black apples or plums. In the early twentieth century the poet Amy Lowell must have been describing a similar sight when she wrote, "I am persuaded that grackles are birds; / But when they are settled in the trees, I am inclined to declare them fruits . . ."

Without the leaves, the birds' pre-bedtime din of calls and cackles was louder than ever. Every night as I listened, I wondered what they were saying. For all I know they were wishing each other good night and pleasant dreams. A mystery.

A greater mystery remained: Why would this flock of birds choose to spend its nights roosting in a brightly illuminated city plaza when Central Park's dark woodlands were available nearby? In *Winter World*, the biologist Bernd Heinrich describes a similar mystery. For more than twenty years he had been observing a huge flock of crows congregating nightly at a communal sleeping roost in Burlington, Vermont. As he describes it:

> One evening I watched them again as they came into the heart of the commercial district on Church Street. Round and round they flew in swirling clouds above the evening town crowd going to restaurants and theaters. It seemed as though they were looking for a place to land. I watched them fly over patches of trees at the edge of town that looked to me like ideal roosting sites, yet the birds still kept coming back into the center of town. Eventually they settled in several young cottonwoods next to Bove's restaurant. The birds were soon closely packed upon the branches, as ever more continued to stream in.

There must be a reason why these birds chose those few available trees downtown instead of heading for the woods nearby, Heinrich thought. Perhaps there was something to be gained by avoiding the woods and choosing the town lights. Then he had a sudden insight: of course, there *was* something to be gained. A nocturnal predator would be much less likely to be out marauding in a well-lighted, noisy public place than in a quiet woodland. In the case of the Vermont crows, the most dangerous predator was the great horned owl. For the Plaza grackles, an atavistic memory of the same predator might still govern their behavior, even in a place where great horned owls are only an occasional aberration.

Heinrich's theory would also explain why the Plaza grackles all crowded into the three trees nearest to Fifth Avenue. If you visit the spot at night you'll see that those are the only ones completely illuminated by streetlights. And the same is true for the trees around General Sherman's statue: they are all in the dark when compared with the three easternmost pear trees by the Pulitzer Fountain.

I met Veronica Goodrich (and Molly and Emma, her two basset hounds) two years after the nest-removal crisis that ended Pale Male's long run on Fifth Avenue. That year a new pair of redtails had built a nest on the thirty-fifth floor of a Central Park South high-rise, the Trump Parc, and Veronica became one of their most ardent followers. The hawk nest was just around the corner from her apartment, and she could even peek into it if she stood on a chair in her kitchen. On a day when the female hawk was still sitting on the nest, I'd joined a group of Trump Park hawkwatchers who gathered regularly at the park's south end. There wasn't much hawk action to attend to that day, but I learned from Veronica that she too was a devotee of the Plaza grackles. Soon I discovered that she watched the grackle spectacle under very different circumstances from mine.

Veronica is a personal shopper at Bergdorf Goodman, the department store across the street from the Plaza fountain. Her job (in case you're as unfamiliar with the concept of personal shopper as I was then) is to present her wealthy customers with a variety of possible outfits from the store's various departments. They make their selection—sometimes they'll buy *all* of Veronica's choices—and a seamstress arrives to adjust each garment so that it fits perfectly, regardless of figure imperfections. What an enviable way of life! Then Veronica realized she could make personal shopping even more delightful: she added the grackle show. She sent me a detailed report:

> My observation of the flock of grackles takes place on the fourth floor of Bergdorf Goodman, in my dressing room. The times they arrive these days are around five to 5:30. That's usually when I have one of my last clients in for the day, trying on clothes.

Here's how it goes: First a few grackles swoop around the plaza and perch on the very top of the plaza fountain trees closest to my store. Then about thirty follow this swooping and settle into the trees. All of a sudden hundreds and hundreds turn the corner of the plaza, rolling and swooping, a perfect ballet of sorts, until the very last one rests on top of the plaza trees. This drama takes all of about 5 seconds total. There they perch for the eve and could be mistaken for the very last leaves of the season except for their loud chatter.

I always keep an eye out for this happening to share with the fitters, husbands, clients, and whoever else is in the room at the time. It happens every night . . . quite a show for my clients!!!

One day in February, Veronica invited me to watch the grackle show from her dressing room, an invitation I eagerly accepted. I wasn't sure what to expect. I knew that the room was bound to be more luxurious than the small cubicles for trying on clothes in Macy's or Bloomingdale's, but I was unprepared for the spectacular view her two large windows afforded. From the fourth floor, looking north, you could see all the way up Fifth Avenue; the view resembled a Childe Hassam painting but without the flags. On the left was the Plaza Hotel, covered with scaffolding. "When the conversion is complete, a studio there will cost six million dollars," Veronica said.

The windows also looked directly out at Pomona. Surely on a cold February day the underdressed goddess needed a personal shopper! Most thrilling of all, the windows looked directly into the grackles' pear trees that surround the fountain. And across the plaza you could see the statue of William Tecumseh Sherman on his gilded horse, surrounded by *his* ten pear trees. It was a stunning sight.

At a little after five, Veronica and I went to the window to watch for the grackles. For about ten minutes we saw nothing. Veronica looked at her watch and said, "Well, it's a bit early. Their

ETA is between 5:10 and 5:20." About ten minutes later she exclaimed, "There's the flock!"

It took me some seconds to spot a black mass far off, circling over the park. It disappeared to the west, and then, after another minute or two, it appeared again, rounding the corner from the north side of the Plaza and zooming around the ex-hotel's eastern façade. The birds headed straight for Pomona's pear trees and roosted, as usual, in the three easternmost trees. I could plainly see them jostling for position on the bare branches. Even without binoculars I could see the grackles' yellow eyes and the starlings' beady black ones.

Watching them from a new angle was deeply engrossing and I didn't notice the passage of time. Suddenly, a loudspeaker crackled and a well-modulated voice announced: "Veronica, your 5:30 client is here."

I jammed my binoculars into my backpack, grabbed my ski jacket, and tore out of there, but not before running into a slender, elegant, perfectly coiffed woman of about fifty at the door. She was wearing an understated coat—yet anyone could see it was lined with mink. For some reason I particularly noticed her shoes, lovely black, soft leather pumps with tapered heels. She gave my shoes a reciprocal glance, and I became acutely aware of my comfortable old walking boots still spotted with mud from my early-morning bird walk. She looked puzzled as she walked into the dressing room and I could hardly blame her.

The grackles roosted in the pear trees around Pomona all winter. Long after I'd expected them to depart for their winter roost down south, they kept coming, night after night. Clearly this *was* their winter roost down south. Then, at the beginning of May, I received an e-mail from Veronica: "I should tell you that the 'ballet of the grackles' no longer performs outside my window at Bergdorf's. Alas, they have all moved on to find their own new nesting sites. It was wonderful while it lasted."

8

PALE MALE
ASLEEP

S uccess without a hitch for ten years: courtship in January, mating and nest-building in February, incubation in March, hatching in April, and fledging in early June. Hawk nursery school was in session all July, with flying and hunting lessons squeezed in between frequent feedings. Finally, toward the end of August, the hawk kids dispersed, first to outlying sections of the park and then to parts unknown. Vacation time at last for Pale Male and his mate. From their vantage point at the model-boat pond, the hawkwatchers followed the glorious show year after year. They marked the exact dates of each reproductive stage on a large comparative chart entitled "The Pale Male Dynasty," which Jimmy Lewis painstakingly created and then updated annually for as long as there was something to record.

The show ended its long run on a rainy December morning, when by order of the board of directors of the elegant co-op on the corner of Fifth Avenue and 74th Street—the Hawk Building, as we called it—two workmen on a window-washers' platform ascended to the twelfth floor and shoved the whole messy accumulation of twigs, ten years' worth, into a big black plastic bag. Destination: trash bin. They also took pains to remove the antipigeon spikes that had served to hold the twigs in place.

Without the spikes to anchor them, any twigs the birds had deposited on the ledge would have blown away within minutes. When the nest was removed the entire Central Park nature community—hawkwatchers, bird-lovers, mothers (*authors*)—was united in sorrow.

The emotional roller coaster of the following weeks took a toll. We went from despair to anger, to solidarity as we marched with placards and chanted in protest: *Bring back the nest! Bring back the spikes!* The emotional loop-the-loop reached its pinnacle—triumph!—when the Hawk Building's board of directors hired an Italian architect to design a new structure (it was dubbed the Cradle) to hold new nesting material on the ledge. Our joy knew no bounds as we watched it installed at a public ceremony. Then down, down, down went our spirits as new anxiety set in.

Though the powers that be at the Hawk Building had spared no expense in making the ledge suitable for re-nesting, we wondered if Pale Male and Lola would accept the high-tech stainless-steel structure now bolted down on the former nest site. Wouldn't they reject something so *unnatural*? And even if they were to rebuild the nest there, we worried that the sticks they brought might not stay put. And what about the eggs? Would Lola lay any at all in the new environment? And if she did, would they hatch? Perhaps the stainless-steel Cradle would conduct cold to the delicate embryos.

An unexpected resource helped us weather those difficult months, a man who came to our aid like a beneficent angel. Shortly after the first reports of the nest removal began appearing in newspapers and on TV, I received an e-mail letter from a hawk expert and falconer in Ohio named John Blakeman.

> Dear Ms. Winn:
>   I am a licensed falconer and raptor biologist with over 30 years of personal experiences with the majestic red-tailed hawk. Please

understand the shared concerns Ohio falconers have concerning the destruction of the famous Central Park nest.

It's bad enough that any active red-tail nest would be so cavalierly struck down. But for all of us, Pale Male's nest was special. As a biologist specializing in red-tails, I recognize both the pair's urban rarity and unique success. The fact that the pair fledged a trio of eyasses (the proper name for baby hawks) last year testifies that the pair was extremely successful. Three eyasses is the maximum the species can possibly raise in a year, and it can only be done under the most ideal circumstances.*

Out here in the distant countryside, we especially delight that urban New Yorkers can now merely step into Central Park with a pair of binoculars and see this great red-tail spectacle. Formerly, these delights were reserved to those of us out in wild red-tail country. Now, these great birds have come into New York for everyone to enjoy.

I regard Pale Male as a typically representative new American. New York City has been the fertile ground of American innovation from newcomers for two centuries. The characteristic American traits of overcoming difficulties, seeing new personal opportunities, and following through with successes against all odds is what Pale Male and his consorts have done. Pale Male ain't just a bird. He's an American, sharing the traits of all of us, rural or urban

---

*Many of us disliked the word *eyass* and resisted using it, perhaps because of its echo of *jackass*. We might have felt less resistant if we had understood a linguistic process called false splitting. This occurs mainly with words that begin with the letter *n*. When preceded by the indefinite article *a*, it becomes unclear whether the *n* belongs to the word or to the article. For example, the word *orange* derives from the Sanskrit word *naranga*. By the time it reached English, the initial letter *n* joined the article *a*, making it *an orange* rather than *a norange*. Similarly with *eyass*. The original word was *nyas*—derived from the Latin word for nest, *nidus*—which over time transmuted into *an eyass*. False splitting can also occur with words that begin with a vowel, which then acquire the *n* of the preceding article *an*. Thus *an uncle* became *a nuncle* in Shakespeare's time.

Thanks for telling his story, it's a portion of each of our own. Pale
Male will be back!

> Sincerely,
> John A, Blakeman
> Ohio Falconry Association

That was the beginning of an extraordinary relationship—I
might even call it a friendship—between a man in Ohio and a
community in New York. During the critical weeks after the
nest's removal, Blakeman wrote frequent letters to all parties in
the crisis—the experts at Audubon and various public agencies,
as well as the hawkwatching public—and I posted them all on
my website. For Pale Male fans who were fearful about the hawk
pair's future, Blakeman's long essays about red-tailed hawk psy-
chology and physiology were hugely reassuring.

Even after the immediate crisis was resolved, he remained a
valuable source of information about hawks in general and red-
tails in particular: what they eat, how they fly, how they hunt,
how they sleep, and many other subjects. And his experience
with redtails was personal as well as academic, for his falconry
bird was a female red-tailed hawk named Savanna.

As we sat on the Hawk Bench on cold post-crisis February af-
ternoons watching the hawks rebuilding the nest, Blakeman's
frequent dispatches gave us hope. In nature, redtails lose their
nests regularly, he wrote, and they're hard-wired to build new
nests when old ones are destroyed in storms or natural disasters.
Indeed, he explained, the necessity of rebuilding a nest has positive value—it strengthens the pair bond. What a perfect silver
lining he'd provided for a perfectly terrible cloud.

Starting at that anxious time, we found ourselves determined
to say good night to Pale Male and Lola at the end of every
hawkwatching day. As the light faded each afternoon, we'd
watch intently to see the direction of flight each bird took. Then
we'd search and search for the building or tree that the hawks

had chosen for night roosts. Sweeping the rooftops with binoculars, we scanned ledges and niches, balconies and chimneys. We searched the various trees between Pilgrim Hill at the 72nd Street transverse and the Great Lawn's northern border near the Metropolitan Museum of Art.

Why did we search for their night roosts so fervently? Maybe without knowing it we were seeking the relief parents feel when they tuck their children into bed at night. Nothing bad can possibly happen to them now. They're safe for another day.

Donna Browne, my frequent companion at the Robin Tree, was one of the most energetic (and successful) of the night-roost searchers. Even before Roostwatch became a real project, Donna had made some important discoveries about the pair's bedtime routines. She was the first to realize that the couple, whose sex life on rooftops and TV antennas up and down Fifth Avenue was a model of marital closeness, actually maintained separate bedrooms. And she was the first to figure out that their separate sleeping trees were not chosen at random: the hawks picked roosts that gave each a clear line of sight to the other's tree. Even when the trees were quite a distance apart, Pale Male and Lola could wave good night to each other if they wanted. In addition, each hawk had a perfect sightline from its sleeping tree to the twelfth-floor nest site at 927 Fifth Avenue.

During the last week of February, Donna discovered the hawks' favorite night roosts: Pale Male's was a pin oak ten or fifteen yards from the Hawk Bench, and Lola's was a large shingle oak up the hill toward the Pilgrim statue and just steps from the Moth Tree. From their separate roosts, each hawk could see the other plain as day. And each could see their freshly completed nest inside the Cradle.

Pale Male and Lola slept in those favorite trees often, perhaps once or twice a week. Finding their other roosts was the challenge of Roostwatch. We'd begin following the hawks at dusk, splitting into groups and communicating by cell phone to keep one another abreast of the birds' itineraries. "Pale Male heading for the Pinetum," the message would go out, and everyone would hurry in that direction, only to find the hawk had stopped there just briefly and was now on his way to Turtle Pond.

On one occasion, at least, the hawks changed their nighttime routine. Donna sent me a report: "Found Pale Male and Lola's roost tree last night on the path from the model-boat pond to Trefoil Arch. It's the first time I've seen them both roosting in the same tree, although on branches rather far from each other. It's quite a distance from the Hawk Bench, but I do believe their position in the tree, which is on a small hill, still allows them to have a sightline to the nest."

Of course once incubation began on March 8, Lola spent her nights on the nest keeping the eggs warm. It eased our minds to know that whenever we found Pale Male's night roost thereafter, it was in a spot where he could keep an eye on the nest.

One night when Pale Male slept in his favorite pin oak, Lincoln Karim, a daily presence at the Hawk Bench, swiveled his gigantic telescope away from its usual view of the nest to the hawk in the tree. On that lucky occasion I was able to observe His Guyness (as Charles Kennedy used to call Pale Male) making the transition from wakefulness to sleep. The presleep ritual began, as usual, with a thorough grooming of what seemed to be every single feather on his body. Then he went over them all again. After more than half an hour of meticulous preening, the light-colored bird grew still. Though his eyes seemed wide open, I could see that the nictitating membrane—the thin, translucent structure that acts as a "third eyelid" for all avian species—had closed. Slowly, slowly his head descended into his neck until he seemed to have no head, just a neck and body. You've heard of the headless horseman. Well, now we had a headless hawk. He always falls asleep that way, Lincoln said.

The next day I sent a description to John Blakeman, who

replied: "Your note prompted memories of Savanna [his falconry hawk] doing the same thing. Often she would just begin to nod off. Slowly her eyes would begin to close. Like a little child doing the same thing, she would often catch herself falling asleep, and quickly pop open her eyes and begin to look around. But a few minutes later, she'd be out. How wonderfully human that was."

Blakeman sent several more letters about Savanna's sleeping patterns.

You wondered where my falconry red-tail Savanna spends her nights. She stays outdoors year round, especially in the winter. Red-tails are a bit put off with room temperature warmth in the cold seasons. After all, they wear a remarkably effective down coat year-round. Beneath the outer covert feathers, the ones we see, is a thick layer of the finest insulating down. This is what keeps the birds warm. The outer covert feathers are oiled daily by diligent preening, and this repels water rather well. The down feathers retain heat. To be kept indoors all winter is somewhat like wearing a thick winter coat indoors.

Actually, the bird can be parked indoors at room temperature with little problem. Red-tails, along with other similar hawks, have a remarkable way of coping with temperature changes, which also often relate to food availability.

Red-tailed hawks are "homeotherms," otherwise known as "warm-blooded," like all mammals and birds. But unlike humans, who tend to keep body temperatures narrowly near 37 degrees Celsius (the classic 98.6 degrees Fahrenheit), red-tail body temperature can vary greatly, which allows them to sleep as they do, changing body temperatures with the weather and body food reserves.

It was great to have an expert at the ready to answer our questions about redtails. The Internet had not proved helpful on the subject of sleep. Typically, the only information about red-tails' sleep offered by one website in the Dallas–Fort Worth area was: "Sleeps at night."

But when I asked Blakeman questions about wild hawks like Pale Male and not falconry hawks like Savanna, his answer echoed that of the other hawk experts: information not available. Apparently we Central Park hawkwatchers had opportunities to see hawk behaviors that neither Blakeman nor, perhaps, any of his fellow experts had witnessed: "Just where and how do these wild birds spend their nights? I don't know. I have never seen a wild red-tail roosting as you people so frequently have done in Central Park. I always presumed that the hawks I see during the day fly into a woodlot and park themselves on the downwind side of a tree trunk. For me, your Central Park observations are new and helpful."

All the roost-searchers were curious to know how hawks manage to stay upright on their night roosts without falling off. I asked Blakeman and received a quick reply:

Red-tails will use a locking grip when sleeping. They have a rasp-engaging set of circular muscles and tendons that wrap around the vertical tendons that extend between the leg muscles and the toes. When the bird goes to sleep on a windy night, she takes her perch and then locks the encircling muscles and tendons around the leg tendons. She falls asleep with a firm grip on the branch or other perch.

I've seen red-tails just at dawn's first light sitting on a large, flat surface, where they couldn't have gripped anything. They slept the night through merely standing on the flat ledge. Any wind gust would have knocked them down. But it appears that red-tails are rather able to discern the night's weather before they retire. If it's going to be a windy night, the bird will almost always select a branch perch around which they can lock their feet. Just how they know if a night will be windy or not is not clear, but they seem to be very accurate in these predictions.

Lastly, however, we know that if weather changes, the birds can and do fly around at night to new or better perches. Having watched my trained red-tails for several decades, I believe that they can see at night just about as well as we can, so they can stumble upon a new branch if they have to.

After Pale Male and Lola's eggs failed to hatch for the second year in a row—nobody knows why—we lost our intense focus on Roostwatch. The game—for it *was* a game of sorts—had filled us with the sense of purpose we had once felt while watching the Fifth Avenue hawks nest-building, incubating, and taking care of two or three chicks. And it had made us realize how little is known about the nighttime activities of diurnal birds. But eventually a certain predictability about the pair's choices of night roosts set in. Lola spent most of her nights on the southeast tower of the Beresford, a palazzo of an apartment house on Central Park West and 81st Street and by sunset Pale Male could usually be found somewhere in the neighborhood of the Great Lawn—at Turtle Pond, or the Pinetum, or anywhere in between. From any of his chosen trees he could see Lola on her handsome tower bedroom twenty-two stories above Central Park.

Then another redtail pair at the park's southern end began to deflect attention from the uptown couple. Since the male was unusually light in color, he was dubbed Pale Male Junior by a crew of new hawkwatchers. His mate was called Charlotte, in memory of Charles Kennedy. The pair made a nest on the thirty fifth floor of the Trump Parc on Central Park South, between Sixth and Seventh avenues, and successfully raised two chicks there.

The new hawkwatchers caught our fascination with redtail sleeping habits—maybe it's contagious—and considerably expanded our small store of knowledge. One who passionately followed the first Trump Parc nest was a young woman named Kelley Harrison. Just after Junior and Charlotte's two nestlings fledged that spring, she noticed that the youngsters slept in the park in certain favorite roost trees near the Columbus Circle entrance while the parents spent the night on high building ledges or signs in the vicinity of the nest. The second *S* of the Essex sign due west of the Trump Parc was one of Junior's favorite roosts.

One evening I went with Kelley and Irene Payne, another Trump Parc regular, to watch the juveniles falling asleep in a tree near the Heckscher playground. We returned the next morning to find the kids still asleep in the spots where we'd left them. They woke early. By 6:00 a.m. both kids were emitting the standard redtail begging cries—*kleek, kleek, kleek.* Around 6:30 the cries became louder as they spotted Junior arriving from the southeast. Long before he landed, we could see something dangling from his lowered talons. Rat for breakfast that day.

Wondering whether our observations were in any way typical, Kelley asked me to ask John Blakeman what time redtails generally get up in the morning. The Ohio biologist answered:

> These big hawks are famous for lounging on their perches in the morning. They are not by any account early starters. When everyone else in Manhattan is rushing to get busy each morning, the red-tails are sitting up on their perches calmly preening or just sitting in a quiet attitude of contemplation watching the inexplicable mayhem below.
>
> In the morning, the air is generally cold and heavy, making flight more difficult. So red-tails tend to sit around for most of the early morning before venturing out for real hunting. In summer, many red-tails will still be perched at 9:00 a.m. or later. Of course, there are always exceptions, with a hawk on the wing going about the day's business just after sunup. But by and large, don't get up to be in Central Park before eight or nine o'clock expecting some good hawk flights or hunts. There won't be many.

Even when we factored in the difference in longitude between New York City and Huron, Ohio (where sunrise is about thirty-two minutes later than in New York), our Central Park redtails were obviously much earlier risers than their country cousins. A day later Kelley sent in another report:

> Pale Male Junior was already on his roost at 8:30 when I went to Columbus Circle last night. This morning I was determined not to miss fly-out and went to the roost building at 4:40 a.m. As dawn approached I could see a dark shadow of wing movement. A hawk. He flew out at 5:18 a.m. and headed straight for the park.

How extraordinary, I thought, that this young first-time bird-watcher could confound the expectations of an expert like John Blakeman. Far from being a slug-a-bed, Junior started his day at 5:18 a.m.! But even more extraordinary, I thought, was Kelley Harrison herself, out there monitoring hawks at 4:40 in the morning. It was love, or insomnia, or both.

Two years later the Trump Parc hawks moved three blocks south to 888 Seventh Avenue, a big office building, where they successfully raised a single chick on the thirty-sixth floor. Bruce Yolton, a publishing executive and the principal blogographer of Charlotte and Junior's Trump Parc family, continued his coverage of the urban hawks on his popular blog.*

That year Bruce became a grandmaster at a new version of our old "find their night roost" game. We had once searched for hawks in Central Park's sheltering trees; now the game was played in a very different habitat. Not only had these ultra-urban hawks perfected a highly successful hunting mode that used 58th Street as a canyon for pursuing pigeons, but they adapted rapidly to the opportunities presented by the West Side's burgeoning

---

*Bruce's blog gradually expanded to cover a wide range of wildlife not only in Central Park but throughout the city. His photograph of a Central Park screech owl is on this book's jacket. (See the bibliography for his and other URLs.)

construction boom. Day after day Bruce reported the hawks' ever higher nighttime roosts:

> On Sunday evening, I found the 888 fledgling high atop the new Zeckendorf building at 15 Central Park West. She looked quite majestic that high up. I think she's sitting on a 45-million-dollar condo! The building's 201 units sold for over $2 billion. The 888 Seventh Avenue hawks have expensive tastes!

Not to be outdone, the next evening the parent hawks chose the same building for *their* night roost. Though it was dark by then, Bruce managed to get shots of both birds settling in for the night on adjacent window ledges. Thanks to his camera's long exposure mechanism, his photos were as clear as day. The following morning he posted the photos and a comment: "These are the highest windows on the building. This may be the highest roost we've seen a red-tailed hawk use."

☾

I knew how Bruce felt when he discovered the hawks' extraordinary night roost. I had experienced the same exultation years earlier when I came upon the night roost of a very different bird. It was a ring-necked pheasant. This handsome large game bird has a long pointed tail and short rounded wings. The male of the species is marked by iridescent plumage and fleshy red wattles, while the female is a warm brown all over. Unfairly, it seems to me, only the male sports the white neck ring for which the species is named. The bird is a native of Asia, introduced into the United States in the mid-1850s to provide sport for gentlemen hunters. By the end of the nineteenth century the pheasant had become naturalized in many parts of the country, perhaps by spreading out into areas not frequented by sportsmen with guns—Central Park in the heart of New York City, for example.

There may have been pheasants in Central Park in its earliest years: an 1878 article in *Harper's Monthly* mentions a pheasant "scurrying through the shrubbery" of the Ramble. But an 1886 survey of Central Park bird life did not include pheasants among the 121 species it listed. Perhaps during that period of eight years they had all ended up on dinner tables, victims not of sportsmen but of the poor who lived on the park's outskirts in those days.

Subsequent Central Park bird lists fail to include any sightings of the ring-necked pheasant. According to those sources, the pheasant was absent from Central Park until April 30, 1972, when a number of birdwatchers ran into one in the Ramble. Even then the bird, a flashy male, did not rate more than a footnote in the Linnaean Society's 1974 update of its official list, "The Birds of Central Park." The publication dismissed the 1972 sighting as an "escaped bird," not to be officially counted in the tally.

On a day in early June during Pale Male's second year of successful fatherhood, when the Bird Register was still the park birdwatchers' communications center, a serious birder named Bruce Rickenbacker reported a highly unusual sighting: "In the thicket at the southern edge of the lawn between the Castle and the Shakespeare Garden I observed a female ring-necked pheasant with at least three chicks."

A pheasant with chicks in Central Park? Could this be believed? An hour later Norma Collin and Annabella Cannarella, two dependable birdwatchers, confirmed the sighting by adding a note to the original entry: "We counted FOUR pheasant chicks." The next day Tom Fiore, the register's most faithful correspondent, reported a sighting of the ever-enlarging family— *five* chicks watched over by one very attentive mother bird. That proved to be the final number.

All that summer the pheasant family was the highlight of every birding expedition—between the spring and fall migrations bird action is scarce in Central Park. But there were good reasons to fear for the exotic creatures. On several occasions we'd seen dogs chasing the young pheasants as they grazed in their usual little meadow below the stairs to Belvedere Castle. Mostly we worried about the night. That's when most dog-owners who work all day come into the park to exercise their pets, usually off the leash. What if one of those uncontrolled canines discovered a baby pheasant tucked in for the night behind some bush or shrub? An awful thought.

One evening in early September, when the young pheasants had almost attained their adult plumage, eight members of the Woodlands Advisory Board met at six o'clock to walk through the Ramble and inspect some of its troubled areas. Composed of Central Park Conservancy officials and members of the park's nature community, the group is involved in all decisions made about the park's wildlife habitats. Present that day were the park's Woodlands Manager, the Conservancy's director of horticulture, a Parks Department field biologist, a forestry expert from the state's Department of Environmental Conservation, and three Central Park birdwatching regulars. I was one of them.

Our goal that day was to begin planning for an eventual restoration of the Ramble, always Central Park's most important wildlife area. For years the Conservancy had been improving neglected parts of the park, section by section—and to much public acclaim. Only the Ramble remained in its original unimproved condition. Why?

A brouhaha in the early 1980s over cutting down trees at a favorite birdwatching location had brought a planned Ramble restoration to a halt. The episode had left many park regulars bitter and suspicious about the Conservancy. It took years to reestablish good relations between the birdwatchers and the organization entrusted with bringing Vaux and Olmsted's design back to its original splendor. The Woodlands Advisory Board had been established for the specific purpose of repairing this great divide.

Fifteen years later, the Conservancy took its first cautious step toward a Ramble restoration. At a regular monthly meeting of the WAB, now a close partner rather than an adversary, the group chose a desolate, badly eroded hillside in the Ramble for the first experimental site. It had been taken over by dirt bikers, and the relentless two-wheeled traffic over the years had left roots exposed. Many trees were dead or moribund.

The group worked out a simple plan for this devastated enclave. The entire hilly site was fenced in, and work began. Park workers and volunteers inserted hundreds of small cherry stakes into the compacted ground on the steepest slopes, thus breaking up the subsoil and allowing air and nutrients to reach the tree roots. They added organic matter and a jute mesh cover—a trauma blanket, they called it—to hold the earth in place. Then they planted hundreds of hardy native plants— wood asters and goldenrods and others. Signs were posted throughout the area explaining the purpose of the project—a crucial move that helped win back the nature lovers.

A year passed. How had the recuperation site fared? We set off on an official site inspection. Entering the Ramble at Bank Rock Bridge,* we walked under the Stone Arch, a narrow vaulted structure half hidden in the cleft between two rock outcrops. When we arrived at the snow fence where the site began, we could hardly believe it was the same place.

"Hallelujah!" said Charles. "The sick child is on the mend." And indeed, last year's plantings were still alive. New seedlings of Virginia knotweed, pokeweed, oak, and hickory were sprouting everywhere on the formerly barren soil. Even the cherry stakes had sprouted! Most amazing of all, no one had broken

---

*It was partially restored in 2008 under its original name, Oak Bridge.

down the fragile fencing. Not a single irate dirt biker had wreaked vengeance. It was a clear success, one that would be repeated on a much larger scale in future years.

During the visit the birdwatchers occasionally turned their attention from the subject at hand to a bird in the bush. That evening we looked up to see a red-eyed vireo scolding a blue jay. Several times we were distracted by groups of thrushes that were feasting on cork-tree berries just ripening that week. Wasn't that one a gray-cheeked thrush? No, look at the buffy eye-ring!

The Woodlands Advisory Board does not take votes; it seeks consensus, a time-consuming but gratifying process. That night consensus was reached on the thrushes—they were Swainson's. As for the question of whether a particularly confusing fall warbler was a blackpoll or a bay-breasted, the consensus was that it was getting too dark to tell.

Time to head home. As we made our way back to the 79th Street maintenance yard, the visit's beginning and ending point, it was getting dark. Near the Evodia Field we saw three juvenile raccoons and their mom climbing out of a tree to begin their night scavenging.

We were walking through a little wooded glade just south of the 79th Street transverse and a little east of the Humming Tombstone, when the forestry expert stopped abruptly and said, "Wait. There's something big in that tree." Binoculars went up and one of the birdwatchers exclaimed, "Look, there's a bunch of them! What in the world are they?"

A closer look provided the answer, which filled us with wonder and, better still, with peace of mind. For the dark shapes proved to be five big pheasant babies settling in for the night in a spot where their most determined four-footed enemies couldn't reach them: the leafy branches of a London plane tree in the center of Central Park in the heart of New York City.

9

THE OWLS
AND THE
PUSSYCAT

I've been a member of the Woodlands Advisory Board from its earliest years. Over time many other birdwatchers, most of the Central Park mothers (*authors*), and various nature lovers in general have joined too. Quite a few of us were there at a long-ago meeting that marked the beginning of the screech owl saga. Oddly enough, neither screech owls nor any other owls were on the agenda that day. Only frogs.

An Urban Park Ranger took the floor to inform us that a few weeks earlier he had released a number of spring peepers at the Loch, a pretty stream in the northern part of the park. Spring peepers? They're a species of tiny tree frogs that . . . well, that peep in the spring. We were taken aback at the news—introducing a new species could have serious consequences for the ecosystem. Look at what happened with starlings: a misguided anglophile had introduced fifty pairs of this nonnative species into Central Park. Their North American population has burgeoned to more than 200 million. Though spring peepers, unlike starlings, are native to North America, they had never been seen in Central Park. Maybe it was the wrong place for these tiny creatures. In any case, this seemed precisely the sort of venture the Woodlands Advisory Board should have been consulted about. Now it was a done deal.

At the end of his presentation the ranger explained that the peeper release was part of a larger, more ambitious enterprise: the reintroduction of ten plant and ten animal species into New York City parks—Project X, it was called. Informally we learned that it was a pet project of the parks commissioner and was to be managed by the Urban Park Rangers. Now we understood why the WAB hadn't been consulted! Neither the commissioner nor the rangers are under the jurisdiction of the Central Park Conservancy, our parent organization.

Next came the luna moths, beautiful, large, pale green insects in the Saturniidae, or giant silkworm, family. More than a hundred of these dramatic creatures were released in Central Park on a date coinciding with the twenty-ninth anniversary of the first U.S. lunar landing. This wildly pie-in-the-sky idea seemed to have nothing more than a tenuous verbal connection—*luna, lunar*—to recommend it. Nevertheless the event focused attention on Project X and attracted media coverage—the name of the game was Photo Op, we thought bitterly.

The release of these moths provoked a negative response among scientists. Dale Schweitzer, a notable entomologist, observed to a *New York Times* reporter that "if an area does not have Luna Moths now, it's probably because it's not capable of sustaining a population. At best it's a waste, or it could be something a lot worse." The moths released in Central Park had been purchased from a Pennsylvania dealer, he pointed out. If the out-of-state moths interbred with a genetically different local population, it might weaken the species. Fortunately that danger never materialized, for the released moths, like the peepers, disappeared without a trace.

The eastern screech owl was the featured presentation on the Project X list for Central Park. The second-smallest owl species in the Northeast, it is about 8.5 inches in length and has a wingspan of 20 inches. Not a rare bird, the screech owl nests in other city parks and had indeed once flourished in Central Park.

In 1869, a few years after the park first opened its gates to the
public, a report to its board of commissioners stated that the
eastern screech owl was "a permanent resident; abundant," noting that the owls "build their nest in the crevices of rocks in the
Ramble." It appears on numerous other lists of Central Park
birds through the first half of the twentieth century. But according to Peter Post, a present-day birdwatcher whose careful
records go back to the 1940s, screech owls had been absent from
the park for more than fifty years. Now Project X proposed to
bring them back.

Screech owls in Central Park! An enticing prospect. But it
raised a troubling question: Why had Central Park's original
screech owls, once a thriving species, disappeared completely?
What adverse circumstance had led to their demise? Was it the
increased use of anticoagulant rodenticides that began in the
1950s? Or was it a growing housing shortage? Perhaps the growing populations of raccoons and squirrels had taken over the
cavities that screech owls need for nesting sites. Was it the ever-
increasing number of people who tromp through the park day
and night? Or could the increased car traffic on the park drives
have been the decisive factor? Nobody had an answer. After
some discussion the Woodlands Advisory Board reached a consensus and the screech owl project was rejected.

But in spite of our objection, the project advanced. Though
we were only advisory, this was the first time our advice had
been ignored. Unfortunately, the commission and the rangers
were outside our sphere of influence.

☽

Five of Central Park's first six screech owls had been orphaned when their mother died protecting them from a
chain saw. As their nest tree fell, the little white fluffballs floated
to the ground uninjured. Later that day a good Samaritan found

them and took them to the Raptor Trust, a bird rehab center in Millington, New Jersey. There Len Soucy, its founder and director, raised them as wild birds, protecting them from unnecessary contacts with humans and allowing them to acquire hunting skills from screech owl "surrogates." Only under such circumstances would they retain a proper fear of that dangerous predator *Homo sapiens* and be ready for release in the wild.

Well, why not the wilds of Central Park? Soucy thought when a ranger requested some first-year owls. The idea pleased him. Central Park had red-tailed hawks but it didn't have any owls. His owl orphans could found a great dynasty right in the heart of New York City. He threw in another first-year owlet (no shortage of orphans at that time of year) to even out the number.

Soucy was well known to Central Park birdwatchers. Years earlier, when one of Pale Male's consorts had collided with a truck on the New Jersey Turnpike, Soucy had fixed her broken wing, nursed her back to health, banded her, and released her over the Great Swamp of New Jersey. Eventually she made her way back to Central Park. A few years later, amazingly enough another Soucy-banded redtail found her way to Central Park and Pale Male's heart.

During the nesting hawks' long reign on Fifth Avenue, their loyal admirers often called on Soucy for advice, information, and sometimes, when the story took an unhappy turn, solace. Many devoted hawkwatchers paid visits—you might say pilgrimages—to the Raptor Trust to see the mythic place for themselves. Now Soucy had embarked on another Central Park wildlife drama. Driving his six little owls to New York City on a hot August evening, each wearing a numbered aluminum band from the U.S. Geological Survey Bird Banding Lab on its ankle, Soucy couldn't have known that ten years later Central Park's birdwatchers would be needing his help again.

The launching of the first Project X screech owl release was well covered by the media, not because the commissioner of parks was present, or even the redoubtable Len Soucy, but because it featured the lovely Isabella Rossellini. Wearing a falconer's glove for protection (screech owl claws are razor sharp), the actress stretched out her beautiful bare arm and tossed a somewhat bewildered creature into the night. Soucy's band number was recorded for posterity: 70527460. After that, with less fanfare, the Urban Park Rangers released the five other owls. Cameras clicked and flashed and videotape rolled for a documentary on Central Park's wildlife to be narrated by Isabella herself.

One year after the release, three of the six owls were gone: two were casualties of car collisions and the third just disappeared. On the second anniversary of the release, two more were missing and presumed dead. Now only one of the six remained. Occasionally we'd catch sight of this sole survivor, most often at the Upper Lobe. We didn't know if it was a male or a female, though occasionally we'd catch sight of a band.

For most of us, having five of the six owls perish was ample confirmation of our pessimistic prognostications for Project X. But the rangers pointed out that one survivor out of six means a 16 percent survival rate, close to the survival rate of screech owl fledglings in the wild. The Project X organizers began preparations for a second influx of owls.

☾

If you can't beat 'em, join 'em. Our little band of night explorers—Charles, Lee, Noreen, Jimmy, and I—adopted this unprincipled philosophy as soon as the screech owls arrived in the park. Now that we knew they were there, nothing else mattered. We wandered the park at random, looking for owls. For we had to find a daytime hangout in order to fulfill our dream of a regular owl fly-out at day's end. We needed an owl to follow.

One warm, clear February day Charles struck pay dirt. As he

was trying to locate a noisy woodpecker drumming somewhere near Warbler Rock, his binoculars lighted on a little screech owl sunning itself at the entrance of a cavity about fifteen feet up in a black locust. The bird was perfectly camouflaged, detectable only by sheer serendipity—Charles's specialty. At sunset on that very day he led us back to the spot—four midsummer moth-watchers transformed into winter owl prowlers.

We found the cavity easily enough, but it seemed to be empty. Then when it was almost too dark to distinguish the hole from the trunk, an owl popped out like a jack-in-the-box. Poised at the entrance, his body blocked the hole completely—it must have been a tight squeeze down there. *Time of appearance at entrance: 5:55 p.m.*, Charles wrote in his notebook. The bird preened dreamily, then more alertly. Five minutes later it flew out into the darkness.

We followed. That is, we followed Noreen, for she seemed to know exactly where to go. She walked ahead confidently, unhesitatingly, pursuing the owl as the Indians of yore may have done back in the old days, when people called them Indians and not Native Americans. Noreen once told me that as a child—one of six children in an Irish-American family—she had fantasized about tracking animals in the woods. Her father had studied Greek and Latin at a Jesuit seminary back in County Kerry. (In the old country only the smartest boys were slated for the priest-hood.) But he immigrated to the New World before finishing his studies, the attractions of marriage and family life outweighing his mother's ambitions. He became a New York City policeman. At home in the Bronx he spent his free time unsnarling the tangles of *Finnegans Wake*. He enjoyed reading poetry, and often read Longfellow's verses from "Hiawatha's Childhood" to his children at bedtime. Noreen especially remembered the part about owls. "What's that?" the boy Hiawatha cried in terror when he heard owls calling in the forest. His mother answered in resonant trochees:

"That is but the owl and owlet,
Talking in their native language,
Talking, scolding at each other."
Then the little Hiawatha
Learned their names and all their secrets.

Noreen too wanted to learn the owls' secret ways—that was how she put it.

We were approaching the Rustic Summerhouse area, one of the few places in the Ramble I still found frightening then, day or night. As we neared the large faux-rustic shelter in the heart of the birders' paradise, dark shapes loomed on the benches within—and not imaginary shapes. Tough-looking homeless men hung out there in the daytime, and we usually gave them wide berth on our birdwatching walks. Now I could see they were there at night too. To add to the creepiness of the spot, the bulbs of the decorative lamp-posts near the Summerhouse always seemed to be broken. I followed the others meekly, reluctant to admit fear. Noreen didn't go right up to the Summerhouse, I was glad to see, but headed for the Swampy Pin Oak area, a favorite birdwatching location during spring and fall migration. A bit tensely we followed. Jimmy held his large flashlight securely—he always said that in case of trouble the best thing to do is to shine a bright light directly into a bad guy's eyes.

All at once Noreen spotted an owl. Though it was sitting right out in the open on a horizontal branch of a tree near our path, and though all of us must have looked directly at that branch as we scanned the tree, only Noreen found it. She had indeed discovered some of the owls' secret ways. A minute later the bird began to sing: Hu-hu-hu-hu-hu-hu in a downward glissando. It was the first time I ever heard a screech owl singing. My earlier qualms completely vanished.

In spite of their name, screech owls produce the most musical and haunting song of all owldom. It has two distinct versions, each characterized by the same quality of sound but differing in direction and volume. The first is a rolling trill on one pitch, accelerating and getting louder at the end. This is sometimes called the monotonic trill, the adjective signifying that it is one-toned, not that it is boring. Paired owls use the trill song to keep in touch with each other or with the family. Males and females sing trilling duets in mating season, with the male's voice lower than the female's. The trill song doesn't travel far—studies have shown that sounds consisting of rapid repetitions of one frequency tend to degrade quickly in forest environments as a result of reverberation. But the song doesn't have to travel far to reach family members—they are likely to be near at hand.

The other version of the screech owl song is composed of a series of descending notes that resemble the whinny of a very musical horse. This is the bird's primary territorial song. It tells other screech owls, *Keep out! I'm master here now*. The whinny song transmits better over long distances; for that reason it is far more effective for staking out territory and keeping potential intruders informed of the singer's boundaries.

In addition to songs, screech owls give off various hoots, the most familiar of which is a soft, low-pitched note sounding like a moan. Sometimes they bark. And yes, on occasion they'll emit a single loud piercing cry that deserves to be called a screech. They'll screech when the nest or the young are threatened. As the owl expert Julio de la Torre once wrote, "Screech owls do, albeit rarely, screech, or more precisely, go vocally berserk."

In his journal entry for August 6, 1845, Henry David Thoreau wrote a deeply felt, if slightly overwrought passage about the screech owl song:

> It is no honest and blunt tu-whit, tu-who of the poets, but, without jesting, a most solemn graveyard ditty, the mutual consolations of suicide lovers remembering the pangs and delights of supernal love in the infernal groves. And yet I love to hear their wailing,

their doleful responses, trilled along the woodside, reminding me sometimes of music and singing birds, as if it were the dark and tearful side of music, the regrets and sighs that would fain be sung. The spirits, the *low* spirits and melancholy forebodings of fallen spirits who once in human shape night-walked the earth and did the deeds of darkness, now expiating with their wailing hymns, *threnodiai*, their sins in the very scenery of their transgressions. They give me a new sense of that nature which is the common dwelling of us both. "Oh-o-o-o-o that I never had been bor-or-or-or-orn!" sighs one on this side of the pond, and circles in the restlessness of despair to some new perch in the gray oaks. Then "That I never had been bor-or-or-or-orn!" echoes one on the further side, with a tremulous sincerity, and "Bor-or-or-or-orn" comes faintly from far in the Lincoln woods.

That February night we heard the graveyard ditty coming from deep in the Central Park woods. Charles loved to note exact details of time and space. (Once he measured every stick in Pale Male's Fifth Avenue nest, the one I'd retrieved in a black plastic bag the first time the building tried to evict the pair. Eleven inches was the average length of all the sticks in that conglomeration.)

Now Charles began to time the intervals between screech owl song phrases. The first owl refrain was 4.83 seconds long, followed by a 40-second pause. The song resumed for 4.62 seconds, then a 39.4-second pause, and so on, for about five minutes. Finally the owl flew to another tree across the path. It paused there for exactly 96 seconds before flying eastward and out of eye- and earshot.

A few minutes later we heard the owl whinnying again not far from the Heartbreak Hotel—our name for a large, hole-ridden tree where we'd witnessed starlings taking over woodpecker nests time and time again. That night I sat on the bench at the top of that hill and listened to owl music.

There's a poem by Shelley that begins, "Music, when soft voices die, vibrates in the memory." So too the screech owl's song. Its tones hang on tenaciously in the mind, an aural version of a camera flash that stays in the eye long after the picture has been taken. *Do you hear that?* we kept asking each other as we strolled homeward through the Ramble. *Is it a siren? Or is it the owl again?* We heard it in our mind's ear long after we were out of the park, a phantom song vibrating in the memory.

☾

Three years went by. Though the introduced screech owls had brought us many hours of happy owling, we grieved for the five owls that didn't make it. We knew Project X was alive and well in other city parks—it continued to provide photo ops for park officials or local celebrities—but we thought its day was over in Central Park. Then one Tuesday evening at the monthly meeting of the Woodlands Advisory Board we learned that the next phase of the project was soon to begin, and this time it would bring thirty-two new screech owls into the park. Thirty-two! At the 16 percent success rate, we calculated that twenty-seven beautiful young screech owls were soon to be martyrs to public relations. Our indignation grew.

But Phase 2 proposed to be different. In response to critics of the first round, new and more scientific protocols were established for the next batch of owls. In the past, the only way to reliably tell a male screech owl from a female was by internal examination, a task often requiring the bird to be anesthetized. Sex determination of the Phase 2 owls would be far easier, though more expensive. By plucking three feathers from each owl's breast or back and submitting them for DNA analysis, the girls could be told from the boys with ease. (A Florida lab eventually provided the sex breakdown: thirteen males, eighteen females, and one whose sex, for some reason, could not be determined.)

Like Soucy's birds, each of the thirty-two new owls was to be marked with a standard band from the Bird Banding Lab. But when the time came, the rangers chose a slightly different method of locking the ends of the thin metal strip. As a result, the Phase 2 birds could be distinguished from the six Soucy-banded owls by the presence or absence of a little raised crimp, though only through binoculars or on an enlarged photo.

The greatest advance in Phase 2 was in the crucial area of monitoring. Checking to see which of the released owls were still in the park and where they were roosting had been a hap-hazard undertaking in the first round: a ranger simply walked through the park with playback tapes once a week, hoping a bird would respond. For Phase 2 a scientist with experience in the high-tech field of telemetry monitoring, William Giuliano of Fordham University's Ecology Department, was hired to keep track of the birds.

Under Giuliano's direction, each owl was to be equipped with a miniaturized radio transmitter (not much bigger than a nickel) contained in a mini backpack attached to the bird by Teflon ribbons. The transmitters could broadcast a signal for al-most a mile. Now, presumably, each owl's location could be dis-covered at all times.* Of course telemetry works only if the batteries don't wear out and the subjects continue to wear the equipment. Batteries do wear out, however, and screech owls are not fond of wearing equipment they were not born with. Consequently the researchers planned to use a bal-chatri trap to capture the owls and retransmitterize them when necessary.†

But before any owl tracking could be done there had to be owls to track. Unfortunately for the planners, Len Soucy de-

---

*In the event, only thirty-one owls were equipped with transmitters. One bird was deemed too small to manage the gear.
†The bal-chatri, a widely employed trap, is an adaptation of an ancient east Indian device that uses a horsehair noose to trap raptors. The Indian name is said to mean "boy's umbrella."

clined to send more owls this time. Central Park had been sprayed with strong chemicals against West Nile disease that year and Soucy deemed it no longer a suitable habitat for raptors in his trust. "I'm not going to put my owls at risk for someone's entertainment," he declared. Other rehabilitators—one in Michigan, one in upstate New York, and one on Long Island—were found to supply the additional birds, but at greater expense this time; Soucy's services had been gratis.

E. J. McAdams was the Urban Park Ranger assigned to direct Project X the year Phase 2 began. (Three years later, as executive director of NYC Audubon, he played a major role in the Fifth Avenue nest-removal drama.) Chris Nagy, then working for a master's degree at Fordham University, was hired as head owl tracker. And as fall approached that year, both young men were worried. They knew that inexperienced first-year owls need plenty of time to adjust to a new environment before the harsh realities of winter set in. Now time was running out. Finally the good news came: the first two owls were being flown in from Michigan on September 10. The other thirty birds would be sent thereafter in several installments.

The owls arrived on time, but their release was fatefully delayed, for on the next day all Urban Park Rangers were given a far more urgent assignment: to transport medical supplies to the wounded at Ground Zero. Alas, the victims at the World Trade Center were beyond medical help. Then the rangers found another way to serve: for the rest of the week they helped thousands of distraught pet owners rescue their stranded pets from apartments evacuated because of the terrorist attacks.

One week after their arrival, the two Michigan owls had a quiet sendoff in Central Park. The eastern screech owl comes in one of two colors, red or gray, and the carrier E.J. and Chris brought to a clearing in the woods near Belvedere Castle contained one of each. After banding the birds and attaching their transmitters, the rangers unlatched the cases and let the birds walk out on their own. They'd get their bearings better that way, the men figured.

At first the birds refused to leave their enclosures. Then E.J. tilted the carrier and they gingerly stepped out. For a moment one of them looked back at the men. Then, all at once, they both flew out in different directions. Gone.

One year later New York was an altogether different city from the one it had been on the day the Michigan owls arrived. American flags waved on every block as if it were Memorial Day or the Fourth of July—they'd been up for a year and would stay up for almost another. New Yorkers had to endure bag searches at the entrance to every office building, hospital, museum, concert hall, or other public institution. Airplanes passing overhead still made many people jumpy.

But Central Park remained unchanged—no security checks there, no ugly concrete barriers protecting important landmarks, no scary announcements on loudspeakers blaring, "If you see a suspicious package, don't keep it to yourself." The park was a haven of peace. Even the Project X controversy was a thing of the past; most of the park's regular bird-lovers now accepted the screech owl's presence cheerfully. To be sure, the radio transmitters were a turnoff for most owl fans. A report distributed at a WAB meeting emphasized how "humane" these devices were, but the sight of an owl rigged up with a backpack and an antenna sticking up was distressing to most of the park's nature community. It seemed to negate the very reason we were there in the first place: to forget civilization and its discontents and immerse ourselves in the natural world.

Fortunately the transmitters didn't stay on long. The tenacious little owls worked diligently to get free of them, and within a month of their arrival more than half of them had wriggled out of their harnesses. Even though a few owls were trapped and their transmitters replaced, it never took them long to get rid of them again. By the time we managed to locate a regular daytime screech owl roost, no backpacking owls were to be seen anywhere in Central Park. It was a setback for the Fordham researchers but a blessing for the tenderhearted birdwatchers.

As much as we'd enjoyed following the Cedar Hill long-eared owls, they were only winter residents of the park, after all. They always left for their breeding grounds just when things began getting interesting. Besides, they'd all turned out to be females. A new excitement stirred us now. These little screech owls were in the park to stay, and they were male and female. *Vive la différence!* All our senses quickened at the thought of owl romance.

☽

Winter had just begun on the dark December day Pale Male's Fifth Avenue nest, so long our special pride and joy, was ripped from its twelfth-floor ledge. And then, on the last day of that dismal season, the winter of our discontent was made glorious summer by a new wildlife story.

On March 19 Malcolm Morris, a neighborhood birdwatcher, was taking an early-afternoon walk around the Pool. A picturesque body of water in the northwestern corner of Central Park, it is sometimes a haven for interesting ducks in the winter. As he passed a stand of sweetgum trees on the pond's north side, an odd sound caught his attention. He looked up and there on a horizontal branch directly over the path were three baby screech owls. They were looking around alertly, bobbing their heads in the peculiar way baby owls do, while above them, sleeping soundly, were two other owls—the parents, no doubt. All five birds were right out in the open, plainly visible, for the sweetgums had not yet come into leaf. But the tree was not bare—scarlet blossoms were hanging from every branch; in the fall these flowers would become the well-known spike-headed sweetgum fruit. Even the flowers looked a bit macelike.

Though the three owlets looked as big as their parents, their fluffy baby down was still visible, and they hadn't developed the ear tufts that give screech owls their characteristic look. Unmistakably babies. And like babies, they were wide awake and demanding attention in the middle of the night, for that's what midafternoon is for an owl. They were in the same tree the next day, and the next and the next.

Every evening after sunset the five owls flew across the path from their sweetgum roost to a little wooded area nearby. One parent, probably Mom, stayed behind to supervise while Dad disappeared into the woods to the east. While he was gone, the owlets faced the direction they'd last seen him and emitted a steady chittering sound. If any of the human observers got too close, the babies hissed and clacked their bills. And when Dad returned with food—mainly moths and other insects—the kids went wild with excitement. One would grab the tidbit, and Dad would fly off into the woods again to fetch a meal for the next. Back and forth he'd go until all three owlets had been fed.

Word spread rapidly, and soon a little crowd gathered every evening to watch the five birds begin their owl day. It was a rare opportunity and everyone knew it. These owls were not in a zoo or a rehab center. This wasn't a nature show on television. These were regular, honest-to-goodness real, live owls flying free in the heart of New York City.

With their huge forward-facing eyes and elegant markings, owls may be the most photogenic of birds. During the weeks the owl family was on display at the Pool, just about every photographer with any connection to Central Park (and many with none) came by to take pictures. But the photographers faced a moral dilemma: the moment when daylight fades and the owls come to life is exactly the moment that a flash attachment is needed. Yet many people believe that the sudden, extra-bright light of a photography flash can damage an owl's eyesight.

The debate occasionally heated up into harsh words between

owl-watchers and flash photographers. Many owl-watchers instinctively felt that a sudden flash would adversely affect a nocturnal animal. Meanwhile the flash-users cited scientific evidence supporting their contention that a camera's flash is harmless to owls' eyes. Graham Martin, a British scientist who has written on nocturnal birds, presents a compelling case against the indiscriminate use of flash in the neighborhood of owls*:

> It seems reasonable always to err on the side of caution in these matters. The scotopic spectral sensitivity and rate of dark adaptation of avian retinas are very similar to those of mammals, including ourselves. Thus if our own dark adapted vision is disrupted by the flash used then it is wise to presume that the bird's dark adaptation will be equally affected. If we are temporarily "blinded" by the flash then so also will be the bird for a similar length of time. For example, if you knock out a fully dark adapted retina assume it will take up to 30 minutes for full sensitivity to be recovered.

Martin adds another observation few of us had thought of: In the human world we often experience sudden transitions when we must wait for our eyes to adapt to a different light level— walking out of a dark movie theater and into the light of day, for instance. But such sudden changes almost never happen to creatures in the natural world, except, perhaps, during a thunder-and-lightning storm. As Martin writes:

> Ambient light levels change through dusk and dawn at a relatively slow rate. Even at the equator, where dusk light levels change most rapidly, the rate of change is more or less in step with the rate of dark adaptation, and so under natural conditions a bird will always

*A majority of the park's best wildlife photographers use long exposure times instead of flash to photograph owls at night. There is usually *some* artificial light available to make this possible.

be well adapted to the ambient. With the exception of entry from a dark roosting site into full day light, there are few, if any, natural situations where marked light level changes are experienced and hence dark adaptation is disrupted.

By mid-April the owl family had moved to a small pine east of the Pool. Spring was finally winning its annual battle with winter; daffodils and lesser celandine were blooming everywhere. Trees were budding and flowering, though none was in leaf yet. The fledglings had begun to take on the narrower, wiser-looking visages of their parents. (Of course "wise" is anthropomorphic here. Owls are not the wisest birds by any means; the crow family wins the intelligence prize.) But in spite of the baby owls' more adult look—they even had the little ear tufts now—their behavior immediately gave them away as juveniles. They were clumsy, they squabbled with each other, and they incessantly begged for food.

The owls' new roost tree stood on a little hill overlooking the park's West Drive, with the deep woods of the Ravine directly below. As I approached it on the owls' second day there, a reflection of the not-quite-setting sun was glowing on the windows of Mount Sinai Hospital's Annenberg Pavilion—about fifteen minutes to fly-out was my reading of that reflection.

But the owls took off earlier than usual that evening, possibly because they were spooked by three photographers using flashes. This time they flew directly to the east, down into the cooler, darker, more peaceful precincts of the Loch. But peaceful is hardly the way people think of those remote North Woods locations. One of the most vicious Central Park crimes occurred just east of the Loch—the Central Park Jogger attack, as it came to be called. Perhaps fear explains why nobody followed the owls that night. But the next evening we screwed up our courage and headed into the deep, dark woods.

☾

When I arrived for the owl show the following evening, I knew at once that I was late and the owls were gone. It wasn't because they weren't immediately visible—birds can be hard to find in an evergreen. No, a sure sign of their absence was the presence of a little flock of house finches chipping and flying in and out of the pine's inner branches. Had there been owls in residence, small birds would never have dared come near.

By seven-thirty that day most of the regular owl crowd had left, but the hard core remained: Bruce Yolton, Jimmy Lewis, Jean Dane, and Chris Karatnytsky, a theater and film librarian at the New York Public Library for the Performing Arts. Accompanying Chris, as ever, was her border collie Fig, the best-behaved dog I've ever met. Chris seems only to think the word *sit*, and the dog sits. As we stood there, not quite ready to call it quits, we saw two other would-be owl-watchers arriving, Donna Browne and her thirteen-year-old daughter, Samantha.

Donna was a new hawkwatcher that year, and everything about the hawks enthralled her. She reminded me of myself ten years earlier, especially her detailed, minute-by-minute notes of the hawks' comings and goings at the nest. "3:27, Pale Male arrives on nest; 3:43, he departs," and so on. Now she and Samantha were coming from the Hawk Bench, where excitement was running high. It was the first spring after the nest-removal crisis and the incubation window had opened. The first batch of eggs might hatch any day. In fact, the eggs didn't hatch that year or the next or the next.

Samantha, an engaging, unaffected child who is generally called Sam, was disappointed to find no owls in the tree; this would have been her first owl fly-out. She's a child actress who seems to play characters who don't end up particularly well. In her first movie role someone ate her. In her second she fell off the Staten Island Ferry. After that she snagged the part of one of the little princes in the Scottish Play. No happy outcome there either.

A few minutes later another Johnny-come-lately showed up—Bill Stifel, a tall, quiet, good-looking man in his forties, whose life seems dedicated to saving Central Park's wild birds and animals. With his first-aid kit always at hand, he has managed to rescue great numbers of birds who get entangled in the monofilament lines that people who fish in the park's lakes and streams use and then abandon. Bill had started recording bird sounds in the park that year and was determined to add screech owl calls to his collection. Now he arrived with his digital recorder, a collapsible parabolic dish, and a fancy-looking microphone.

As the light faded, we could hear the night-night chips of robins about to retire; they were still courting and pairing off. Clearly the Boys' Dormitory hadn't opened for the season. The park was emptying out—a burst of cheering from one of the North Meadow's ballfields signaled the end of a game. A deep orange glow appeared on the horizon—the sun had just finished setting. Without our having noticed it happening, the streetlamp had come on.

We were reluctant to go down to the lonely Ravine until Jimmy came up with a plan. It was similar to a strategy the ornithologist Tim Gallagher described in his book *Parts Unknown*. At the start of a twenty-four-hour birding marathon in New Jersey, Gallagher and four teammates stopped at a certain marsh on the outskirts of Jersey City, where they hoped to find sora and clapper rails and perhaps a few owls. As they walked along some litter-strewn railroad tracks, their flashlight beams suddenly illuminated three or four hulking male figures heading toward them. Any viewer of *The Sopranos* knows that running into a bunch of unknown guys in a northern New Jersey swamp does not bode well. But Gallagher and his team had planned for just such a contingency. They rushed to the edge of the marsh and sent up "a ghastly cacophony of night-bird imitations: ler-wee, ker-wee, kid, kid, kick-kee-do, kick-kee-derr, woc, woc." The men hardly paused a moment before running off into the night.

According to Jimmy's plan, we too would terrorize our would-be terrorizers by transforming Fig into an attack dog. "Don't come nearer," we'd say if someone questionable approached. "Stop! This is a vicious dog trained to attack. One word, and he'll go for the jugular. Please don't make us say the word."

With our canine weapon trotting placidly beside us, we descended the steep bank, headed along a wood-chip path, and made our way toward the rustic bridge that crosses the Loch. Night was rising fast. Earlier, the moon had been palely loitering in the southeast. Now it had become a lustrous half globe. A red-bellied woodpecker uttered a single *chork*, a cardinal gave a last whistle, two or three robins pronounced a final goodnight, and then the silence began.

The complete stillness of the place brought back memories of the weird quiet that settled over Central Park after the 9/11 attacks. In the absence of the usual daily sounds—planes overhead, horns and screeching brakes from the city streets—you could hear the wind rustling in the September-crisp leaves. It was easy to make out the usually inaudible chips of warblers that had stopped in the park to refuel for their southbound journeys—fall migration was in full swing then. For two days of that bleak September, the sounds of nature were heard with unprecedented clarity in Central Park.

Now it seemed almost as quiet. We stopped at the bridge and waited, the dark waters of the Loch below occasionally reflecting the silvery light of a streetlamp or my Surefire flashlight. We'd almost given up on the owls when Bill pointed upward and said in a low but urgent voice, "Look!" There in a tree a few feet ahead was the screech owl family, all five of them. A minute later they flew out, all at the same time. Soon we began to hear soft screech owl trills coming from the stream below. Only the adults make that call; perhaps the parents were trying to round up their kids, we thought. As we strained our ears, we heard the faint chittering of the babies, which seemed to say *Stop worrying. We're here. Where's dinner?* Bill pointed his microphone toward the sounds and quietly pressed the Record button.

At eight-thirty a dog began to bark nearby, but something about it didn't sound quite right. The mysterious barking was followed by a series of catlike utterances coming from the other side of the West Drive. We headed for the sounds, Bill leading the way. As we scrambled up the hillside through brambles and brush, the drive in full sight now, we almost stumbled on the source of the loud meows. It wasn't an animal that *sounded* like a cat. It was the real thing, a huge cat sitting on a log halfway up the hill. As we stared at it, we heard the barking sounds again.

Then we saw them, two gray adult screech owls sitting on a branch almost directly above the cat. With throats vibrating and ear tufts aquiver they were barking like not-quite dogs: *Yip! Yip! Yip!* We had heard a variety of screech owl calls in the past, both in nature and on tapes, but none of us had ever heard one like this. Still, its meaning was clear. In the face of danger—more specifically, in the face of a treacherous feline—the parent owls were issuing an unmistakable command to their owlets: *Freeze!* We couldn't see the fledglings but knew they were nearby. Obedient children, they weren't moving a feather.

Sam went into action immediately. "This is a stray cat," she said. "You can tell by the way it's crying. It's lost and hungry. I'm going to try to rescue it."

Donna befriends birds in distress. She takes them home, nurses them back to health, then releases them in various parks. If they're beyond help and she can't find someone to take them in, she ends up keeping them herself. She had six pigeons in her bathroom that very day, she told me. But besides birds, she and Sam often rescued cats. "Sam's amazingly good at it," said Donna. "Sometimes we have three or four cats in the house that

Sam's rescued." I had a sudden image of the Browne household, pigeons in one bathroom, cats in another, and never the twain shall meet—at least I hoped not.

Sam began a conversation with the cat. "Meow," she said. *Meow*, said the cat. It wasn't clear who was answering whom, but they were obviously speaking the same language. As she me-owed, Sam crept closer toward the cat on the log. Closer, closer, ever closer, inch by inch.

The scene had a Theater of the Absurd air about it—the owls woofing, the cat and Sam chatting. More than half an hour went by—rescuing stray cats evidently requires time and patience. But then, just as the girl was a mere arm's length from the pussy-cat—so close!—it bounded into the woods.

As Sam was stalking the cat I realized that I was starving, and probably everybody else was too. I quietly reached into my back-pack and brought out some bread and a wedge of leftover Brie. We sat on the ground near the top of the hill and ate every last bit, spreading the cheese on pieces of bread with our fingers. All the while Bill recorded the sounds for eternity—girl and cat and owls. I have it all on a CD.

By May 1 the owl family had dispersed. Mission accom-plished. We never saw them together again. Chris and others who regularly walk in the North Woods occasionally reported an owl seen or, especially, heard in the area. But the park rangers moved on to other pursuits and stopped monitoring screech owls in Central Park. And though many of us searched through the entire North Woods the following spring, looking for an-other owl success story, we found no nest or nestlings.

10

Little Red
and the
Big Bad Owl

It was always a special thrill to run into Little Red, one of the two Michigan-born screech owls released in the park soon after 9/11. Her rich color was a big attraction—not the red of a cardinal but the deep, beautiful russet hue of a red fox. Still, we rarely had a chance to feast our eyes on her. There were so many of the gray owls, after all, and only one red.° How, in fact, did we know she was a she? We didn't. But for some reason we always referred to her with the female pronoun. There was something about her . . . that's all I can say. And of course we had a fifty-fifty chance of being right.

Three years after Little Red first set talons in Central Park, she became easier to find. That October, at the end of a long housing search familiar to so many New Yorkers, the red-phase screech owl finally settled into her dream apartment: a cavity in an old, gnarled black locust just up the hill from the Loeb Boathouse. Its bark was reddish brown (almost exactly her color), and its furrows and crevices perfectly matched her mottled plumage. Sitting at the cavity's oval entrance, right out in the open, the owl was invisible to all except those who knew she

°At least one other red-phase owl was among the thirty-two released in the second round of Project X, but it vanished during its first year in the park and was presumed dead.

was there. That soon included the entire Central Park birding community. The obliging bird couldn't have chosen a more convenient roost tree, since the Boathouse is where birdwatchers congregate. It offers relatively inexpensive food and tables where you can eat your own brown bag lunch if you prefer. Its restrooms are relatively ungrungy.

What a gift it was to have a predictable bird, a bird always available for inclusion on your day list, a knockout bird to entice the kids away from television or video games on a nice Saturday or Sunday, a bird to take visitors to see on those winter days when all other bird life in Central Park is quiet (a birders' euphemism for nonexistent), a Good Bird. It was a bird with an asterisk, to be sure, since screech owls hadn't exactly made their way into the park on their own. When the park's best birders, Tom Fiore or Starr Saphir, for example, ran into a screech owl, they wouldn't include it on *their* day list. But photographing it was perfectly acceptable; Lloyd Spitalnik, another top birder, took a photo of Little Red peering out of the cavity entrance and winking flirtatiously—a once-in-a-lifetime shot.

Every evening around sunset a group of five or six of us gathered at the black locust to watch the little owl take off for her night's hunting. On sunny days the owl might appear at the roost entrance several hours early and sit there in full view, though asleep. But the colder the day, the later she appeared. While the bird is out of sight, many of us can't resist taking advantage of the social opportunity. We chat about this or that. But the minute someone makes the announcement, "She's out!" we fall silent. We know the drama is about to begin.

The little owl comes to life when it's almost too dark for human vision. Her eyes, heretofore narrow slits, become huge. Then she proceeds to preen. Moving her beak along her feathers, she gently nibbles along each one from base to tip, cleaning and straightening out the plumes and filoplumes, barbs and barbules. She takes an especially long time to preen her wings, and for good reason. While other birds' flight feathers have a smooth leading edge, those of owls are serrated. This structural modification, a marvel of evolution, allows them to fly in complete silence.

How does it work? According to *The Birder's Handbook*, the feather's serrated edge has the effect of "disrupting the flow of air over the wing in flight, and eliminating the vortex noise created by airflow over a smooth surface." Obviously, flying silently is an advantage for a nocturnal hunter. *Pounce.* The poor mouse or vole is a meal before it even knows it's in danger.

At Little Red's roost tree the twilight deepens and everything is gray—colors have vanished. Night is rising. The owl takes a five-second nap, wakes, stretches, preens for another twenty seconds, then stands erect in her doorway. Now she fills up most of the opening. She looms. Even a tiny owl looks huge as it gets ready for the moment of flight. A second later she's gone—only her image remains, clearly etched on the mind's eye.

Little Red was the first screech owl we could identify with confidence. Then as certain gray owls established regular roosting habits, we came to know them too. We recognized one, for example, by his daytime residence, a cavity in a half-dead London plane tree directly behind a bench in a sunny lakeside area birders call the Riviera. You'll find old-timers basking in the sun there on cold winter mornings.

Soon the Riviera owl enjoyed an audience of fly-out followers who gathered at his roost hole every evening. "His" roost hole? Well, the bird had the rugged, craggy look of a male, another ridiculous assumption, as embarrassing to admit as my hunch about Little Red. But both hunches proved to be right.

Since the Riviera owl's plane tree was not very far from Little Red's black locust, some people tried to make both fly-outs in a single evening. The gallop between roosts was a fine aerobic workout, but by trying to see both fly-outs, one risked seeing neither.

But soon it became possible to take in the two owl shows without running a step. On December 10 a hot item appeared on *e-birds*, the electronic newsletter:

> Today the red screech-owl was not in the black locust where it usually is, but the Riviera gray was present in its London plane tree. While we were watching the gray, who should poke its head out of the hole but the red owl! The gray owl flew out at 4:55 p.m. He perched nearby for a few minutes as though waiting for the red, but then flew away. The red one flew out about ten minutes later.

Was something amiss in Little Red's apartment—leaky pipes or raucous neighbors? Maybe it was loneliness. But sheer expediency was not what had brought the two owls together. The next night we began to hear the pair singing the one-tone trill that signifies screech owl courtship and love. They sang it as they wandered about the Ramble after fly-out, keeping track of each other as they stalked their supper. Or perhaps Little Red was keeping track of *him* as he stalked supper for both, since during the courtship period the male screech owl provides most of the female's meals.

The owls didn't settle down in one apartment or the other; they commuted between the two. Sometimes they slept in separate trees. This seeming indecision brought out the wags among birders who sent in regular reports to *e-birds*. On December 12, for example, Jack Meyer, a year-round Central Park birder who used to lead walks during the migration seasons, sent a communiqué:

> The red screech owl seems to get around. Saturday it had moved in with the Riviera owl. But on Sunday, it was back at its old stand. Then today, it was gone from there again. I looked for it in the plane tree at the Riviera but couldn't find either owl there. Maybe they are both off on their honeymoon.

Bob Levy, whose book *Club George*, featuring the park's red-winged blackbirds, was to be published the next spring, wrote:

Here's an update of the seemingly on-again, off-again relationship between the red-phase and gray-phase eastern screech owls in Central Park. Today the relationship was most definitely on again. After sunset I positioned myself opposite the gray one's tree cavity. At 4:56 p.m. the gray owl popped up into the opening . . . Instead of seeing the gray one bolt out of the hole, I saw a second screech owl pop into view. It was the red owl. It nestled a little below the other bird with its head pressed against its flank. For a few seconds the two owls sat motionlessly in this pose, and I thought to myself, *They really do make a nice couple.*

As the love affair continued, debates among the owl-watchers grew heated—they often do when gender issues are involved. Which of the two owls was male and which female? The controversy was resolved by a call to Chris Nagy, the graduate student who'd been in charge of monitoring the Phase 2 owls. Why hadn't we called him earlier? Little Red was a female. The Riviera gray had to be a male.

On December 17 I missed the fly-out, but a few hours later I received an informative report from Bruce Yolton:

> Tonight was a surprise. Only the red owl flew out of the hole that had been shared by both the red and gray earlier this week. The fly out was at 5:08 p.m., with the bird flying NW.
>
> I wonder if the gray owl is the male. Articles I've read say the male would be responsible for securing a number of possible nest sites. If so, the red must be a female, who's told her mate, "We need a better apartment if we're going to have kids," and sent him off to find a home without squirrels in the attic?

We'd all made jokes about the screech owl pair—just thinking about them made us feel cheerful and optimistic. But on the next day, December 18, a new character joined the cast of our lighthearted romance and turned it into a wild melodrama. Enter the great horned owl.

C

Bubo virginianus, the great horned owl, shows up in Central Park almost every winter, but it rarely stays for more than a day. That's why it generates so much excitement when it appears: you don't have much of a chance to "get" it, as birdwatchers like to say. The birders' various grapevines are activated the moment this biggest of all Central Park raptors is sighted. But no organized telephoning or e-mailing was necessary when the whopping big owl arrived that day. That's because every Central Park birder was already in the park for the Christmas Count, part of the annual census of bird life sponsored by the National Audubon Society throughout the United States.

Central Park's count is always held on a Sunday morning in mid-December. The park's best birdwatchers invariably show up and often bring their family and friends, for the event is a perfect occasion to introduce children and beginners to the pleasures of birdwatching. And that's why everyone was delighted—even the major-league birders like Lloyd Spitalnik, Brian St. Clair, Harry Maas, and Dick Gershon—when the most spectacular bird that year was found by a wet-behind-the-ears birdwatcher. In fact, the young woman who made the discovery that morning, Chris Wood, was already their birding protégée. On many Tuesdays after the bird-feeders were filled, Lloyd and his birding buddies wandered around the Ramble with Chris instructing her in the fine points of birdwatching.

Chris sent me a detailed account of the whole story.

As you know, I'm still relatively new to birdwatching. I started in earnest about a year and a half ago. I don't mean to brag when I say I am a pretty good spotter—I just happen to see birds everywhere. But along with that gift comes a curse: identifying birds is very difficult to me. It must be a left brain/right brain thing. I can't seem to tell one sparrow or warbler from another by their wing bars or whatever. It's as if I cannot see the details that distinguish one bird from another.

As it happens, that inability to see those distinguishing details is not a curse particular to Chris; it's the universal lot of all beginning birdwatchers. For the most part they notice only the gross differences among birds: big versus small, black versus red, a big fat bill (must be a duck, especially if it's swimming) versus a sharp little bill on a tiny little bird (may be a hummingbird if it's also feeding on a red flower). When I started birdwatching, I couldn't tell the difference between a white-breasted nuthatch and a black-capped chickadee. They looked the same to my eye—each was a small bird with a black cap. Obviously my brain zeroed in on their small size and black caps and filtered out everything else. Now they look as unalike to me as an elephant and a giraffe. How did I ever confuse them?

Similarly with birdsong. To a nonbirder, the calls of a crow and a blue jay may sound almost the same. Both give out loud shrieking cries. After a while, especially if the difference is pointed out to you, you begin to hear that the crow's caw is the diphthong *Aw! Aw!* while the blue jay shrieks *Eee, eee.* The volume alone seems to overwhelm the brain of an untrained listener, who hears only *Loud shriek, loud shriek.* But after the listener focuses attention (perhaps laying down new neural patterns), those two calls begin to sound remarkably different. (One of Central Park's most accomplished birders recently confided that she still confuses blue jay and crow calls if she's not really concentrating.)

Chris's letter continued:

Fortunately, I *do* know an owl when I see one. I had been thinking about owls all fall. I was determined to see one, but had not been in the right place at the right time. At the Christmas Count this year—my second one—I had owls on the brain. I picked the Ramble section—Lloyd's group—specifically because I knew that eastern screech owls were roosting in the area.

When the group split in two, I went with Brian instead of Lloyd because Brian was headed toward both known owl roosts.

(I might also mention that Brian St. Clair is young and handsome and an exceptionally good birder. And he's an up-and-coming rock star. His group is called Local H.) Chris went on with the story:

Unfortunately, it was turning out to be an unlucky day. I'd heard there was a pair of owls that lived in a London plane tree right on the West Drive, but when we got there, the owls weren't visible. We canvassed each evergreen in Strawberry Fields looking for saw-whets, but no success. Then we headed back to the feeders to reunite with the other half of the group. We walked along the Riviera, but since the other group was responsible for this section, we were just casually chatting, but not counting.

I had pretty much given up hope of seeing an owl. As we came around the bend, heading to Willow Rock, I looked up and saw a mass in the big willow tree there. At first I thought it must be a squirrel's nest. But then I looked through my binoculars. My not-so-scientific alert to my fellow birders was, "Hey, you guys! There's a huge owl in this tree right here!"

Brian made the identification, but he sweetly let me write it on the list. He said, "Looks like you found the bird of the day, Chris."

At the lunchtime tally at the end of the count, Chris sat with her team and listened as the count leader, Sarah Elliott, called out the names of the fifty-nine regular birds on the official tally sheet one by one, in taxonomical order, from pied-billed grebe to house sparrow. Then she read off the names of ten less common birds that fell in the category "other." Three red-breasted nuthatches were reported and one sharp-shinned hawk. Finally she came to the last category. "Any rare birds that are not on the tally sheet?"

Chris raised her hand. In a voice only slightly too loud she announced, "Great horned owl." Had it been a surprise, it would have been a bombshell, but a great horned owl sighting is impossible to keep secret. Everybody had been buzzing about the bird even before the tally began. When Chris made her announcement, there was no gasp of amazement, only a round of applause. I glanced over and saw that she couldn't stop beaming. She looked dazed when I went over to congratulate her. "It was amazing," she said. "Sitting there with Lloyd and Brian and Harry and the other great birdwatchers was like sitting with the cool kids in the high school cafeteria."

In the recorded history of Central Park birdwatching, no great horned owl had ever visited the park for more than a couple of days. But Chris's owl didn't leave after the first day, or the next. Before long, crowds began gathering every night to see that rare event, a great horned owl fly-out. As the days turned into weeks, some began to worry: What if the bird had moved in to stay, the way Pale Male had done some fifteen years earlier? Would that make trouble for the red-tailed hawk pair?

The hawk expert John Blakeman seemed to know as much about nocturnal raptors as he did about redtails and other hawks. In answer to our questions, he wrote:

> Red-tails and great horneds in the East, South, and Midwest have a remarkable relationship, an ecological détente, as it were. Here's how it usually works.

The crucial fact is that great horned owls don't build nests. They simply expropriate (read that as steal) existing ones. No one—even if they could see at night—will ever observe an owl bringing twigs to a nest site. Owls don't do that. The great horneds just perch themselves on an existing red-tail's nest in December or January and claim it. GHOs [a common abbreviation among birders] are larger and more muscular than red-tails, and at night red-tails can see about as well as we can. Red-tails will intelligently abandon a nest claimed by a great horned owl. The hawks will frequently go just a short distance and build a new nest, sometimes even in the same woodlot, perhaps only a few hundred yards from the old nest.

At night a great horned owl could easily drop down upon an incubating red-tail and have her for a midnight snack. Conversely, in broad daylight, when a female owl is hunkered down over her owlets, a red-tail could do a classic red-tail stoop, dive, and take the head off the owl before it knew what hit her.

But these things seldom happen. There seems to be an understanding between the species that the owls will do their things at night, and the hawks theirs in daylight. By this arrangement, the owls find beautifully formed, existing nests to claim each December (long before the red-tails resume nesting activities). As for the red-tails, they don't get killed by the larger, more aggressive owls. This is a raptorial version of MAD, mutually assured destruction, the tenuous but effective arrangement between American and Soviet thermonuclear powers that used to be talked about during the Cold War.

So far there have been no MAD things in Central Park. So far there has been only one ecological superpower, the red-tailed hawks. But might that change? I think it could. Great horned owls hunt for and kill the same prey as red-tails, rodents. They use exactly the same habitat, only at night instead of in the hawks' day-hunting periods. And clearly there is an abundance of available food in Central Park. Because they are nocturnal hunters, great

horneds aren't going to take many pigeons. But at night there will
be a surfeit of rats that owls could thrive upon, the same population
of rats the red-tails catch by day.

Blakeman's letter allayed our anxieties about the red-tailed
hawks somewhat. Obviously Central Park has more than enough
rats to go around, enough for Pale Male's family *and* for a bunch
of great horned owls as well. But as we studied various accounts
of GHOs and their behavior, we began to understand what
Blakeman meant when he called it a new superpower. This was
one big savage hunter! Maybe the powerful red-tailed hawk had
worked out a cordial détente with the GHO over the centuries.
But what about smaller creatures? What about the screech owls
we had come to be so fond of? According to A. C. Bent's *Life
History of North American Birds*, the great horned owl "is not
particular as to what it kills for food and will take what is most
available and most easily caught." It does on occasion eat birds,
even other owls. Bent's long paragraph about the avian preferences of *Bubo virginianus* itemizes the various owl species on
the big owl's carte du jour—barred owls, saw-whet owls, long-
eared owls, and short-eared owls. But the eastern screech owl
leads the list. It is the great horned's favorite dinner-owl.

☾

During the years the long-eared owls honored us with their
winter presence, we started a tradition of festive New
Year's Eve owl fly-outs. We revived that tradition thirteen days
after the great horned owl arrived in Central Park. At sundown
on December 31 a small group of us gathered at Willow Rock to
make a champagne toast to *le grand duc d'Amérique*, as some
French-Canadians call it. It was lightly snowing at five minutes
before five, the moment the owl chose to take off for the night.
We raised our plastic glasses of Veuve Clicquot, a tradition that

went back to the first year the Fifth Avenue nest produced chicks, and wished one another, the great horned owl, and all other creatures a happy, peaceful new year, especially those that lived within the Grand Duke's sphere of influence. We drank a special toast to the screech owls.

We were worried about them. The budding romance between Little Red and the Riviera gray seemed to have hit a snag—the evening before, they had emerged from separate holes. But during the New Year's Eve champagne revelry Lincoln Karim, moonlighting as an owl-watcher during Pale Male's off season, arrived with the news we'd been hoping for. While we were toasting the Grand Duke, Lincoln had seen both screech owls fly out of the Riviera hole. Reconciliation! Hurray!

After the festive fly-out, with spirits elevated at least in part by the champagne, we started back through the park for a pre-fireworks dinner at Lee's—she's an inspired cook. Instead of maintaining the Hiawatha code of stealth and silence, I was singing a camp song called "Mrs. Murphy's Chowder," when suddenly Noreen shushed us. There on a bare, twisted tree near Bow Bridge sat the Big One. It looked enormous. Its ear tufts were raised. Its head was scrunched forward, alert. Listening. Obviously it too was looking forward to a festive dinner.

For the next few days Little Red slept at her old black locust pad. Where was the Riviera gray? Everyone knew there was one obvious answer, but no one wanted to say it out loud. Bob Levy aired a few optimistic possibilities on *e-birds*: "Maybe the gray morph is scouting for a better tree cavity in which the two will nest? Maybe the owls have divorced? Don't laugh, it happens."

E. J. McAdams, once the ranger in charge of Project X, came to see the great horned owl for the first time on January 3. In addition to running NYC Audubon, he was also the father of two small children—time was at a premium. But McAdams was still emotionally involved with the screech owls that he'd helped to install in the park. As we stood on the overlook at Willow Rock just before the big owl's fly-out, E.J. put our unspoken fear into words: "Gee, I hope the great horned hasn't been feasting on screech kebabs."

The next day Donna Browne found the great horned owl in a new location, an evergreen not far from its original willow roost. Donna, a close observer of animal behavior, had once been Pale Male's daily diarist at the Fifth Avenue nest. Now she was keeping close tabs on the GHO. That afternoon she was the large owl's only monitor. It wasn't that the rest of us had lost interest, but that the weather was abysmal: heavy rain, with wind gusts of up to twenty miles per hour.

Donna watched the bird carefully from 3:30 to 4:50, and she took copious notes—she must have used an indelible pen. The owl spent a good part of that time at feather maintenance—preening— and most observers would have left it at that. But Donna saw subtleties we might have overlooked. For instance: while the bird was working on its outer breast feathers, completely wet and stuck together, she observed that the fluffy underlayers appeared dry.

At 3:53, as the owl moved from preening its back feathers to nibbling its tail, Donna noted that the bird's motion reminded her "of an old-time wringer washing machine. But instead of rollers it's the beak pressing against the feathers and pressing water out and off the tail."

I posted Donna's notes on my website—the great horned owl had been the dominant subject for weeks. In response, John Blakeman sent in more information about preening:

> I'll add that the reason the bird spends an inordinate period of time preening the base of the tail, the rump, is that that is the location of the sebaceous or oil gland. Birds, especially big ones like hawks and owls, are much like turtles in that they carry their houses around with them. They live inside their feathers. The feathers must keep out wind and rain and keep in warmth. The owl's attentions with its rump and tail attend to these essential matters.

Before flying out for a night of hunting, the owl was stropping its beak across the oil gland, loading it with water-repelling feather oil. Then it strokes other feathers, rubbing the oil into the feathers to keep the night's rain out of the soft, downy underfeathers. These are the ones that keep the bird warm. The outer feathers can get sopping wet and the owl will be just fine. But if oil isn't sufficiently kept on all of the body feathers, the bird will die of hypothermia.

Undeterred by a little rain, Lee and Noreen arrived at the owl's evergreen just as Donna was leaving. Jimmy and I came a few minutes later, and the bird rewarded us all for our faithfulness with a solid hour of preening. Finally at 5:01 we saw the huge owl leave its roost and land on a branch just a few feet away. And what did it do there? It sat and preened some more for almost half an hour. By 5:20 it was almost too dark to see, and the bird was still working on its tail feathers.

At 5:30 we heard an eerie sound coming from somewhere nearby, a sound we recognized. It was the screech owl trill song. Without missing a beat the great horned owl continued to preen, though it must have heard the new song too—its hearing is far better than ours. On and on went the trilling, and it made us deeply uneasy.

Five minutes later the huge owl finally took off, but for once we didn't follow—we stayed there listening. The screech's trill is always plaintive, but this time, to our ears, it sounded inconsolably sad, as doleful as Thoreau had described it to be.

Jimmy was the first to make out the shape of a little owl on a low branch. The bird was so close to us we could almost reach out and touch it. It was too dark to see which of the pair it was, and none of us wanted to shine a flashlight on it. When the small owl flew off, heading west, I thought I caught a reddish glint in the light of a streetlamp. Little Red, looking for her mate?

The Riviera gray was never seen again.

T hough it broke our hearts to hear Little Red singing for her
mate during the first weeks of January, we knew we couldn't
blame the great horned owl. He hadn't committed a crime by
eating a little screech owl for dinner, if that's what he'd done. He
was just doing what comes naturally. As he extended his stay, we
followed him after fly-out every night.

Our success at playing Follow the Owl increased when we
discovered a variation of the old axiom *Cherchez la femme*. For
us it was *Cherchez le rat*. We'd head for a certain place at the
lakeside where phragmites and bamboo offer perfect cover for
a colony of rats—we could actually hear them down there in
the darkness squittering and squeaking to one another. The owl
must have heard them too, for we found it on a nearby branch
staring down into the reeds on many occasions. Later, when we
dissected our collection of great horned owl pellets, we found rat
bones in every one.

By mid-January a sizable GHO fan club had formed. At five
o'clock on January 17 more than twenty-five people gathered in
the fading light at the north end of the Azalea Pond to watch the
"strixine Nimrod" (as Julio de la Torre called it in his owl book)
perform its evening toilette. Among the owl regulars were my
mothing companions Lee, Noreen, and Jimmy; Donna Browne
and her daughter Sam; Bruce Yolton with his omnipresent camera; Anne Shanahan, one of the earliest Pale Male devotees;
Martha Marshall, a recent owl addict; James O'Brien, a hawk
and falcon fan who was making a video about the new redtail
nest at the Cathedral of St. John the Divine; Gabriel Molnar,
who regularly fed Danish pastries to a waiting gang of raccoons
at gate 2 of the Delacorte Theater; Barbara Kent, who was a new
convert to hawk- and owl-watching; Ben Cacace, whose website *NovaHunter* includes posts about stargazing as well as

birdwatching; and the violist Jean Dane, who had become one of the most devoted owl prowlers.

"Look, he's about to take off!" someone exclaimed as the great horned owl stretched and extended a long wing.

"No, not yet," said Lee. "He hasn't pooped." It was in the owl's best interest to be as light as possible before setting forth for his night hunting.

A few minutes later the owl lifted its tail and sent forth a stream of whitewash. A second later it was gone. In the Charles Kennedy spirit of precise measurement, Ben recorded the time of fly-out to the second: 5:19:34 p.m.

C

A week later I found myself alone in the woods at fly-out time. Not another soul had shown up to see the great horned owl depart, perhaps because it was pouring again. Normally a little rain wouldn't stand in the way of a die-hard owl prowler, but Lee was in Philadelphia, Noreen was taking Aunt Katie to a family party, and Bruce was home with a cold. I'm sure the other regulars had similar excuses. It felt a little crazy to be there in the rain all alone, owl obsessed. I missed Charles. He would have come in a hurricane.

It was the thirty-second day of that extraordinarily long great horned owl stay. The bird was in the previous day's tree but on a different branch when I arrived. Fly-out might be soon, I thought—the bird was already alert and preening energetically. I looked down at my watch for a split second, and wouldn't you know it? That was the moment the owl chose to take its leave. Damn! Had it gone northwest, toward the Great Lawn? Or southwest, toward Bow Bridge? If you don't see the direction an owl takes at fly-out it's not easy to play Follow the Owl.

I'd never been the one to find an owl first—Lee and Noreen were far and away the best owl-spotters. So this was my big chance. That's what compelled me to venture into the Ramble again that night, though I was soaked to the skin and though I was alone and though I hadn't a clue which way to go.

I decided to head for Bow Bridge. Once we'd found two long-eared owls sitting on an old, misshapen tree near the bridge's north end. We'd watched them take off together and fly slowly and deliberately across the Lake, looking like gigantic moths. But as I made my way through the deepest part of the Ramble I began to regret my decision. Where was everybody? Not even a dog-walker was in sight, not a soul anywhere. I was smack in the middle of the woods between the park's east and west boundaries. Nothing to do but forge ahead.

The huge silhouette of a great horned owl sitting on the branch of a bare tree should be conspicuous, yet it rarely is. At least four times on my lonely walk I was sure I'd found the owl, but closer examination always revealed a large knot on a limb or an odd bend in a branch. Some of these formations were so deceptive that they even seemed to have ears. Once I was taken in by a perfectly owl-shaped squirrel's nest.

When I reached Bow Bridge I breathed more easily. There I could see the comforting city skyline outlined in both directions: the complicated rooftops of the Dakota and the Beresford gleaming on one side, the brightly illuminated tower of the Hotel Carlyle on the other—a breathtaking view. And what's more, it had stopped raining!

Back to owl-hunting. Standing in the middle of the arched span, I moved my binoculars up and down a tree on the Ramble side of the bridge, where the owl prowlers had seen the great horned owl twice last month. Not there. I turned to search the trees on the Cherry Hill side. Not there either. I'd obviously picked the wrong direction. His or Her Royal Highness was probably digesting an appetizer at the Great Lawn right now.

Time to go home, I decided glumly, stopping for another moment to gaze over the Lake. It was preternaturally quiet. Only a faint hum of traffic could be heard, almost like the dull sound of ocean waves at a cottage beyond the dune.

At that moment a bird began to chip somewhere nearby. That's odd, I thought. Birds don't chip in the dark unless something disturbs their sleep. The sound seemed to be coming from the carriage-horse turnaround just up the hill from the bridge, a spot officially named (though never called) Cherry Hill Plaza. What's bothering that bird? Could it possibly be an owl? I decided to investigate.

A white sedan and a black sports car were parked near the ornate fountain that stood in the middle of the turnaround. The bird chips seemed to be coming from a bush just beyond. As I walked past the cars to check out the bush, I saw some shapes within. I quickened my pace and looked straight ahead, turning off my flashlight to avoid attracting attention. Then I focused the light on a low bush. Yes, the chips seemed to be coming from that one. And there it was as plain as day in my flashlight's gleam—a white-throated sparrow on the ground, chip, chip, chipping in alarm. Another sparrow was standing right next to him, also chipping. That clinched it. There must be an owl nearby. I swept the trees above with my Surefire. At that moment I heard a car door open. I swiveled around and saw a man step out of the black sedan while a second guy, a big, hulking fellow, emerged from the other car. *Uh-oh.*

Now both of them were walking toward me. For a moment I felt a sharp, chemical pang in my stomach. Then they revealed their badges: cops.

I quickly switched off the flashlight. The men strolled up to me, and one of them said, "Is something wrong?"

"No, everything's fine," I said brightly.

They stared at me.

"I'm looking for an owl," I explained, even though I knew it would sound preposterous.

They exchanged glances.

"Really, I'm fine," I repeated, thinking, *At least I was fine until you guys scared the daylights out of me.*

"Are you from the city?" one of them asked.

"Yes, why?"

"Don't you know it's dangerous to walk around the park by yourself in the dark? Did you notice our cars?"

"Yes," I assured them. "I thought I saw someone inside as I walked by."

"Well, what did you think?" the cop persisted.

"I thought it was a couple looking for privacy." That thought had actually crossed my mind.

They glanced at each other again.

"A little lady like you should be home, not walking around in the park," the first cop said.

A little lady like you? I didn't like the tone of it. Then an uneasy feeling came over me. *Watch your step*, an inner voice warned. *These cops might take you off in the paddy wagon for observation. Looking for an owl indeed!*

"Okay," I said quickly. "Guess I'll be getting along." Each cop carried a gun in a holster at his side. Power. I started walking toward Central Park West. It was frustrating to know there was an owl nearby but I couldn't search for it.

"Now go straight home!" the second one called after me. "Don't stop and look in any bushes or trees!"

Both of them had addressed me as if I were a wayward child. And like a child being rebuked, I felt a surge of shame.

This was my other scary experience. The first one had involved faux cops. These guys were the real thing.

☾

On January 21 the great horned owl moved to the North Woods. A birder discovered it with the usual assistance of an avian mob, this one including four blue jays, a pair of titmice, a nuthatch, and a downy woodpecker, all screaming their heads off. The big bird was sleeping in a tree at the bottom of the Wildflower Meadow, a unique habitat in Central Park. Ten years earlier Dennis Burton, then the park's Woodlands Manager, had supervised the planting of a variety of tall grasses and open meadow flowers there, intended to attract grassland birds like bobolinks, meadowlarks, and savannah sparrows. Burton had done it right—it had become a great birdwatching spot.

Arriving there at a little after three, I had no trouble finding the owl's roost tree. Bruce Yolton was already there, tripod set up, clicking away. About an hour later the bird flew to another perch directly across the path, spooked by music blaring from a boom box. As the Boys with the Box passed by I was tempted to say, *Look up! Look above you!* I wanted to see their eyes widen when they saw a huge bird with a five-foot wingspan fly directly over their heads, a bird straight out of a horror movie. But they walked on, oblivious.

The great horned owl roosted in the North Woods for three more days. Then it showed up in the Ramble again, hanging out near the Azalea Pond for two additional days. Then poof! It vanished as mysteriously as it had appeared. People searched for it in the North Woods, the Ramble, and even the Hallett Nature Sanctuary near Central Park South. The bird had been with us for forty days—thirty-eight or -nine days longer than any previous great horned owl had stayed in Central Park. Now it was apparently gone for good.

After the news was posted on various Central Park websites, John Blakeman, now a regular reader of all of them, sent a valedictory note:

> From the beginning, I've been impressed with the Fifth Avenue hawks' tolerance of so many humans so close to their daily hunting and perching activities in the park. The hawks have simply accommodated their behaviors to those of humans, recognizing that

those hundreds of two-legged primates down there just don't matter much.

But all winter I've been surprised that the owl hasn't previously taken its leave. I think most great horneds would have exited Central Park after about the second evening of residence. This owl's tolerance of people coming right up underneath its day perches is quite astonishing and, I believe, uncharacteristic. Great horned owls just don't like people (or any other animal) around either their perches or their nests.

Therefore the owl may have finally given up and left, the plethora of easy-to-kill rats notwithstanding. It may have been a young adult, now flitting about from woodlot to woodlot somewhere in New Jersey or up the Hudson.

Of course, the owl may be seen again in Central Park in just a day or so, and it might take up residence, permanently accommodating itself to humans. But if not, owl-watchers have had a wonderfully lengthy encounter with this unique species. Out here in the rural wild, we never, ever get to discover or observe the day-roosting spots of owls or the night roosts of red-tails. You people—in the heart of one of the world's greatest cities—have been able to see things we can't see out in more typical raptor habitat.

We spent the last days of January wandering about the park in search of the great horned owl's chunky silhouette—a short, overweight, double-capped witch in a tree. At the end of the month we gave up. Little Red was back in her black locust pad, but her Riviera lover was as gone as the great horned owl and probably *in* the great horned owl.

Shortly after the owl's final departure, I was waiting in the lobby of Avery Fisher Hall for a concert to begin when I ran into David Monk, a Central Park friend. A good birder, a tree expert, and a self-taught Russian scholar, David had come early too. It didn't take long for our conversation to turn to Central Park and owls. "You know that great horned owl?" he began. "Well, I think it was an escaped captive."

I was amazed. "What makes you think so?"

"Great horneds rarely stay in the park for that long," he said, echoing Blakeman's sentiment. "They show up for a day or two at most and sometimes just for an hour. No, this sounds different. Somebody probably found a nestling that fell out of a tree and took it home as a pet. And then it got to be too hard to take care of it." David spoke with authority. Besides years of owl-watching in Central Park, he had spent much time observing owls and talking to their caretakers at zoos and rehabilitation centers.

I played devil's advocate. "But, David," I argued, "why shouldn't it just be a wild owl that came to Central Park and found a good food supply? Wouldn't that explain why it stayed so long?"

"Two things make me think it was an escaped bird," he answered. "One, a wild owl would never tolerate people getting so close. And two, that owl flew very awkwardly, the way I imagine a bird without much experience of freedom would fly."

"I noticed his ungainly flight," I said. "But I thought maybe all great horned owls fly that way."

"No," David answered. "Their flight is smooth and fast, as fast as red-tailed hawks'."

At home after the concert I reread Blakeman's letter, and everything seemed to fall into place. Not a wild bird. An impostor! Somehow, the thought changed the experience for me, diminished it. A few years earlier at the Hawk Bench, a boy of eight or nine had looked through a telescope at Pale Male and asked, in all innocence, "Who owns him?" We were taken aback, and later a bunch of us moralized about contemporary youth: how pitiful it is that today's kids have no contact with nature, how they think everything can be bought.

But the boy had a point. Nowadays almost everything in our lives *does* belong to someone. A popular song of the 1940s once spelled out a different reality: "The best things in life are free," it proclaimed. It went on to enumerate all the natural wonders free for the taking—the moon, the stars, the flowers in spring, the robins that sing, the sunbeams, and love . . . all are free.

The best things in life don't seem as free as they once were. The air is polluted, the rain is acidified, the weather is globally warmed. Exotic invaders are choking out flowers and trees. The robins must survive herbicides poisoning their worms.

Our almost smug satisfaction was surely rooted in Central Park, our wonderful enclave of wilderness in the heart of civilization. But the flowers in spring weren't free here either. Invasives like Japanese knotweed, lesser celandine, and the sycamore maple were serious threats to the park's horticultural diversity—the Conservancy's valiant gardeners were ever struggling to keep them from taking over.

And what about Pale Male—did he belong to someone? "Oh no, no," we assured the boy at the model-boat pond, "he's a wild free bird. Nobody owns him!" But the arrogant dwellers of 927 Fifth Avenue had succeeded in destroying his nest and perhaps his reproductive future. And now, we realized, the great horned owl was probably a former pet.

The screech owls hadn't come into the park on their own either. Though we loved having owls permanently settled there, we couldn't exactly think of them as examples of nature's bounty. Moreover, the park itself had never been a real wilderness. It had started out an artifact, a never-never-land of fake nature planned by two brilliant landscape architects who designed it to approximate the real thing. Yet a century and a half later, it didn't matter how ersatz its origins had been—real wilderness had taken over. Perhaps the same thing would happen in the case of the screech owls.

11

THE RESCUE FANTASY

After the great horned owl vanished, we began hearing rumors of a screech owl living in a London plane tree on the edge of the West Drive, not far from Strawberry Fields. We were skeptical—surely no self-respecting owl would choose to nest right above a busy road! Still, we needed a new owl to follow. At sunset on February 2 we gathered at the rumored tree. We were not very hopeful but the sight of a tear-shaped cavity on the tree's largest limb, about twelve feet from the ground, was encouraging.

Almost as soon as we raised our binoculars to the cavity, whoosh—a little owl came zipping out. If I'd been alone and not with four other witnesses, I wouldn't have believed my eyes. A moment later, even before we'd quite gotten our breath back, another ear-tufted head appeared at the opening, peered out, then quickly popped back in. A pair of owls! That was the beginning of our adventure with the West Drive owls.

Our new owl tree was not at a scenic overlook like Willow Rock or in the poetic meadow where Little Red's black locust stood. Here was Central Park at its busiest, noisiest, most public. But there was a silver lining: a bench in direct view of the owls' cavity. Like the Hawk Bench, the West Drive Owl Bench demonstrated an important feature of any unfolding wildlife narrative: the importance of being seated.

We began to gather there every night, and as we pointed our binoculars and cameras toward the owls, passersby inevitably stopped to see what we were looking at. We always loved to hear people's surprise at the presence of an owl in the middle of New York City. Everyone knew it wasn't just a bird. This was a *magical* bird, straight out of Harry Potter, and we were Keepers of the Owls.

There was a striking sunset on the evening of February 6. Puffy pink clouds floated over wide swaths of fading blue sky, followed by an intense burning-ember glow at the southwestern horizon. The sun went down at 5:20 p.m. At the same time a single dark gray cloud mass on the other side of the park seemed to loom over the Hawk Building—an ominous portent. Would we ever see chicks there again?

We argued about the reason for the odd color disparity between the dark gray and puffy pink clouds. I figured that the pink clouds were lower, thus catching the colors of the setting sun. Later I learned it was just the opposite: the pink cherub clouds were high enough to intercept "unadulterated" sunlight—light, that is, that had not suffered color loss by passing through the dusty, hazy lower atmospheric layer. Clouds in the high cirrus and altocumulus layers are often spectacular shades of scarlet, orange, and red while low clouds such as stratus or stratocumulus are white or gray.

Just as the evening rush hour was filling the West Drive with cars and taxis, a screech owl appeared at the cavity entrance. What could be more incongruous, I thought as I stared at the creature with its huge, unblinking, hypnotic eyes, tufted ears, and weird little scimitar of a beak, a science fiction beast that eats its prey whole and can see in the dark, looking down at an urban landscape of cars, horse-drawn carriages, joggers, bicyclists, pedicabs, and Rollerbladers, to say nothing of an odd collection of figures (with long, black tubular eye-extensions pressed against their faces) gathered at a bench just across the drive from his tree every evening.

For thirty minutes the owl alternated preening with napping. At 5:40 he drew himself up, stretched lazily, and then zoomed off abruptly, as if he'd made up his mind on the spur of the moment. He headed west, toward the little wooded area between the drive and the park boundary wall. We headed in the same direction.

Lee spotted him almost immediately. But quick as she was he'd been quicker: the little hunter was perched on a low bush with a mouse in his talons. In the gloom we could make out the rodent's white feet and dangling tail. But to our surprise the owl did not proceed to devour his prey. Instead, he adroitly transferred the mouse to his beak and flew back to the West Drive roost hole. He paused at the entrance and then disappeared into the recesses. Less than a minute later, he flew out, empty-beaked. We had witnessed a FreshDirect delivery.*

As we headed home in the darkness, exhilarated, an almost full moon seemed to be following us. Was it waxing or waning? someone asked. I remembered a mnemonic device my father had taught me when I was a child—in Latin, as so many of his memory aids seemed to be—for distinguishing a waxing moon from a waning one. As the moon grows in the sky and then shrinks again over the course of a month, he would explain, the curve of its partial body is sometimes on the left, like the curve of the letter C, and sometimes on the right, like the curved part of a D.

"Remember *Luna mendax*—the moon is a liar," my father would say. He'd spell it out: "D, *crescit*, C, *decrescit*." I came to understand that if the moon's curve was like the D of the word *decrescit* ("decreasing" in Latin), then it was increasing. If its

---

*FreshDirect is an online food and grocery delivery service for people in the New York City metropolitan area—owls, too, if they have Internet access.

curve was like the C of *crescit* ("increasing"), then it was decreasing.

The moon's C or D curve is most conspicuous when it's a
mere crescent, but even a small nibble out of one or the other
of the moon's sides signifies the waning or waxing: you just have
to remember which side is which. That night the shining liar was
like a D—it was waxing.

☾

Two days before the great February blizzard I arrived at the
Owl Bench to find the male screech owl missing from
his usual post at the roost hole entrance. Well, it was only 5:15,
a bit early. Only one other owl-watcher was sitting there, a
woman I'd seen at a fly-out once before—Helga, I'll call her. Before I even had a chance to sit down, she announced: "There's
bad news."

She'd been watching the tree a few minutes earlier, she reported briskly, when she saw a squirrel coming out of the owl's
residence. "You know what that means, don't you," she said,
looking at me with raised eyebrows. "Remember what happened
at the Riviera owl nest?" she added, to make sure I understood.

My heart sank. Of course I remembered. When Little Red's
mate disappeared, squirrels had taken over his Riviera roost hole
almost immediately. Tree cavities are in great demand in Central
Park. Squirrels and starlings are ever on the lookout for nest
holes.

"The owls are gone," Helga said in a portentous tone, as if
narrating a war documentary. I felt like weeping. I also felt like
killing her for bearing the bad news so mercilessly. "Look! I
think I see part of the squirrel in the roost hole right now," the
dreadful woman announced with unseemly excitement.

Reluctantly I trained my binoculars on the opening. Indeed,
the top of a gray, furry thing was poking out at the base of the

teardrop cavity. But it made my spirits lift. It's odd how close in color a gray squirrel and a gray screech owl can be; odd too how furlike a bird's feathers can appear. The gray furry creature who now emerged from the cavity was not a squirrel. I glanced at my watch: 5:25. The male owl took up his pre–fly-out position at the cavity entrance and began to preen. I glared at Helga, who wandered off without a word.

The male flew out at 5:50, twenty-four minutes after sunset. By then Lee, Noreen, Donna, and Jean had arrived. Lee and Donna went owl-chasing into the woods. The rest of us stayed at the bench, waiting for the female to fly out or at least poke her head up for a moment or two. When the owl popped out and quickly disappeared again into the cavity, Jean, in her usual laconic way, made a comment that rang a bell with all of us. "She looks like an unmade bed," she said, "like a little pile of laundry."

By now we'd begun to tell the owls apart by subtle differences in appearance, and Jean was right, the female owl looked frowsy with her odd-shaped beak that resembled a little bucktooth. The slightly darker male, on the other hand, was a regular Beau Brummel. Maybe the little pile of laundry had heard Jean's comment and took offense. We waited until our noses froze, but she did not emerge again that evening. I posted the owl report on my website and included Jean's comment about the unmade bed for comic relief, little thinking it would soon lead to a serious dustup with some hotshot birders.

The next day was Tuesday, the day the Bird-feeder Squad gathers at the Evodia Field between Thanksgiving and Easter (more or less). We fill the big plastic jugs with sunflower seeds, load the mesh stockings with the fine black seeds beloved by finches, and stuff the greasy chunks of beef fat—Lee cadges them from a fancy Madison Avenue butcher—into homemade suet cages. The usual gang was already there when I arrived.

I'm always in a cheerful mood at this weekly gathering—the birdwatching community is at its most cohesive during feeder filling. So I was especially taken aback when a birder I admired for both his birding skills and his general friendliness came up to me and said brusquely, "Marie, your names for the West Drive owls are ridiculous."

"What names are you talking about?"

"Spiffy and Unmade Bed," he replied.

Another ace birder added, "If you're going to name the West Drive owls Spiffy and Unmade Bed, I'm taking your website off my Favorites."

"What a terrifying threat," I said in mock horror, and left it at that. Actually I was delighted to hear that even one of the big guns read my website. But when I posted my next owl report, I felt obliged to defend my honor. "Nobody has named those owls anything," I wrote, "and we're not planning to. We were just kidding around. So lighten up, guys."

In fact the owl-watchers *had* started referring to the pair as Spiffy and Unmade. When you get attached to birds, it's hard to keep calling them "the male" and "the female." But after the Evodia Field pother I firmly nipped the naming tendency in the bud.

It began snowing lightly on February 11. The next day the flurry turned into a full-fledged nor'easter, one of our area's most ferocious storms. Accompanied by wind gusts reaching hurricane force, nor'easters are notorious for producing heavy snow and rain, as well as oversize waves that crash onto beaches along the Atlantic coast. This storm dumped 26.9 inches of snow on the streets and rooftops and parks of Manhattan, an all-time record.

There's a lot to worry about when a storm of that magnitude hits a big city. Snow accumulates faster than snowplows can clear it, and then what happens to people with heart attacks or women with babies on the way? Guiltily, I focused my worries on a pair of small owls. Would they survive the nor'easter?

I longed to be at the fly-out on February 12 but was stymied.

I have neither skis nor snowshoes, and I'd left my boots in the downtown office I use for writing. I sent out a plea to the various owl-watchers to keep me informed. Jean Dane, one of the most faithful, sent the first report:

> Not to worry—everybody's fine.
>
> I thought fly-out might be later this evening, because it was lighter, with all the snow. Wrong: he went out at about 5:50, about ten minutes earlier than we've been seeing. He also flew higher than usual and stuck on a high branch. Still up there when we left.
>
> A couple of minutes after he flew out, the female's head appeared in the doorway just for a few seconds, and then she popped right back in. She did that again, every five minutes or so. We thought she might fly, but all she did was peer out to see what was happening.
>
> What was happening was many many people walking on the West Drive, cross-country skiing or dragging kids on sleds right past the owl tree. Lots and lots of very cheerful people. Good snow today, very good snow, excellent snow.

Another bulletin arrived that evening, this one from Barbara Kent, a newly addicted owl-watcher. An attractive, soft-spoken woman in her fifties, Barbara had become a Central Park regular during the Pale Male nest-removal crisis, as had Jean and Bruce Yolton. Terrible as that episode had been, it had given the nature community's entrenched body a transfusion of fresh blood.

> This evening I cross-country-skied out to see our West Drive Screech Owls. I wasn't going to take any chance of missing the fly-out, so actually this time I was the first out there.
>
> We got a good show. I'd estimate that I arrived around 5:30, when "the spiffy male" was already living up to his name in full view, framed by his tear-shaped hole. I'd say he flew out around

5:50, this time surprising us by perching quite high. He was still at this high perch when I had to leave around 6:45 p.m. Several times we saw the "unmade bed" female pop up to fill the plane tree hole, but she never flew out while we were there.

The next report was sent in by Amy Campbell, a visitor from Maine and a welcome addition to our little band that week.

I saw the fly-out last night! The owl flew from the hole about 5:45 or a few minutes later and, according to regular watchers, flew onto a much higher perch where he remained, feathers all fluffed out, for the half hour we watched. Meanwhile the other bird made periodic appearances at the entrance.

Though the others seemed to call her Unmade Bed, I'd prefer to think of her differently. She was more like Juliet coming to the balcony than the housewife taking time out from chores to look out the window and see who's walking by.°

A few days later I received the last blizzard report, but it was not about owls. It was about the Plaza grackles, and it came from Veronica Goodrich, the Bergdorf personal shopper:

You will be interested to know that your grackles did not return to their perch at the Plaza for three days during the snowstorm. I was worried my total entertainment was over for the season, but on the fourth day they came screaming back in greater numbers!! Quite impressive.

All the owl reporters had noted the screech owls' high perches during the snowstorm. On one memorable occasion Lee and Noreen saw a screech owl beyond the park limits, out in the city proper. The bird had been perched on a brownstone ledge on 75th Street, a few houses west of the park, and was gaz-

---

°I haven't edited Barbara's or Amy's letter, though the references to Spiffy and Unmade may provoke the scorn of the anti-naming hotshots.

ing at a curbside garbage can—a rodent magnet. On the night of the big storm, with small prey animals taking shelter underground, the owls may have chosen the higher perches to look for garbage-can rodents on the city side of the park wall. Or perhaps higher branches are thinner, less likely to be thick with snow.

The following night the male owl flew out at 5:40. He made his first landing on a low branch quite near us. We were about to follow him into the woods when the female appeared at the hole's entrance—yes, Juliet-like. She retreated into the cavity again as she usually did. Then the surprise: she popped up again and zipped out of the hole, heading directly west.

We found her easily. She was perched on a high branch about halfway between the West Drive and the wall. She sat there for a minute and then presto change-o, two owls on the branch instead of one. It was the first time we'd seen the male and the female together. They sat there companionably for quite a few minutes. Then they were gone, not to be seen again that evening.

Were there eggs in the nest? This was a subject of constant discussion. There must be, we thought. But why had she left the eggs that night? According to a species account, "Males feed females during the incubation period of 26–30 days. Females stay in the nest cavity all day but leave briefly at dusk and at dawn." That would explain it. But she'd have to be quick, for it doesn't take long for eggs to cool fatally in midwinter. We'd find out what was going on eventually. For the time being we'd have to stay in the dark.

Mitchell Nussbaum, an amateur astronomer, came for a post-blizzard fly-out. It was a perfect night for stargazing—the air was exceptionally sharp and clear, the snow glittered, and the stars and planets looked bright as country stars.

We pestered Mitch with questions: *What's this one? What's that one?* and the young man patiently identified them. The brightest star we'd been seeing all evening low in the east was

Sirius the Dog Star, he said. (Sirius is the bane of crossword puzzlers. When the clue is "dog star" and there are six spaces, the solver writes in . . . Lassie.) We all recognized Mars without help—we'd been watching its progress for months. But now Mitch pointed out Saturn shining brightly and steadily in the east—we'd had no idea.

The next star was not a star but a space satellite. It was gliding past Betelgeuse, at the upper-left-hand corner of Orion. Pronounced *beetle-juice*, it is one of the two brightest stars in the sky, said Mitch. Antares, in Scorpius, is the other. For the benefit of us nomenophiles,* Mitch had all the names at the ready, including the name of the satellite and the two stars it passed between. The stars were Castor and Pollux in Gemini, the Twins, and the satellite was Lacrosse-III, launched in 1989 and now flying at an altitude of four hundred miles. Though the Internet site Mitch had consulted said it would appear at 6:37, the bright, steadily moving speck of light didn't heave into view until 6:39. We wondered about the delay. Light pollution, Mitch explained, and perhaps some atmospheric drag. Atmospheric drag! The term delighted us. We didn't know what it meant, but we didn't encourage him to explain. A moody dance? An airy cross-dressing disguise? On a note of high silliness we did a little cha-cha-cha and headed for home.

In *The Psychopathology of Everyday Life* Freud describes a not-uncommon delusion that has come to be called the rescue fantasy. In his example a man fantasizes about saving "a great personage" from certain death, whereupon the rescued one presses the rescuer's hand and says, "You are my savior. I owe my life to you. What can I do for you?"

On a bitterly cold February day the great personage did not shake the hand of his fearless rescuer and say, "I owe my life

---

*There *should* be a word for people who love names, even if there isn't one yet.

to you" as, indeed, he did. Instead, he looked Lee Stinchcomb fiercely in the eye and said clearly—though nonverbally—*If you come one inch closer, I'll bite your nose off.*

This was not a fantasy. Lying in the middle of the West Drive was something that resembled a little pile of feathers. It was the male screech owl, alive and glowering.

Collision with cars is a major source of mortality for all owls that live in the vicinity of roads and highways. But screech owls are by far the prime victims of car collisions. Here's why: Most birds leave a stationary perch in a straightforward way, heading directly for their destination at a fair height. Screech owls drop straight down as they exit, leveling off two or three feet from ground level. Then they continue to their destination low off the ground.

That makes good sense in the woods, where flying low is the best way to search for small rodents. Evolution to screech owl: *Get down as low as you can as quickly as possible.* For millions of years screech owls have been obeying that command. But this peculiar flight pattern makes no sense if the owls' roost tree is at the edge of a busy car road that they must cross to reach their hunting grounds.

That was the situation of the West Drive owls. Every evening they left their roost to hunt in the little wooded area behind the Owl Bench. But to get there they had to cross a perilous car drive. Plummeting straight down from their high roost hole, they'd cross the road at a height of two or three feet above the ground. Unfortunately, their flight did not exceed a car's height. It wasn't a question of *whether* a collision between car and owl would occur. It was a matter of *when.*

The West Drive, a one-way road going south, loops around to the east near Central Park South, then joins up with its north-bound, east-side counterpart to make a complete circuit around the park. Both drives are heavily used, especially by taxis trying to avoid traffic on busy city avenues. Since owl fly-outs are asso-

ciated with sunset and a specific level of light, everything was
fine in the summer—rush hour was over by sunset. Consequently traffic on the drive was light when the owls made their
exit. But for most of the winter months owl fly-out time fell right
in the middle of the heaviest traffic period.

In Central Park the traffic signals at various intersections and
pedestrian crossings on the drives are coordinated so that cars
moving at the legal speed (35 miles per hour) never have to stop
at a light. Most drivers in the park understand the pacing. That's
why you'll find cars making their way down the drive in little
herds, proceeding at the optimal speed from one end of the park
to the other without having to step on their brakes.

From our usual viewing spot we could see a considerable distance up the road, almost as far as 79th Street, where the drive
curves out of sight. As fly-out time approached, we kept our eye
on that distant curve, waiting for the herd of cars and taxis to
materialize. If fly-out was imminent, as the cars headed our way
we'd freeze and issue warnings to the owl under our breath: *No,
no, don't go now. Wait there just a few seconds.* If the owl was
still there after the herd departed, we'd heave a sigh of relief and
send another urgent message to the owl: *Now! Go now!* Irra-
tionally we felt that if we wished hard enough, we could save the
owls. It was the ESP version of a rescue fantasy.

Was there something we could do to help the owls avoid
crashing into cars? We could see two ways to proceed: either
slow down the cars, or impel the owls to fly higher when they
crossed the road. In pursuit of the first, we considered standing
upstream with signs saying SLOW DOWN—OWLS AHEAD. But
would New York drivers pay any attention to a ragtag group of
people with patently absurd signs? Might they not even speed
up just to get away from us?

Altering owl behavior seemed the easier alternative. For
many days we positioned ourselves at precisely that place across
from the roost tree where the owls usually entered the woods at

fly-out time. As an owl was about to take off, we'd raise our arms stiffly over our heads as high as we could—we were trees! We hoped the owls would fly a few feet higher in order to clear our hands. But our strategy didn't work. It simply made the birds cross the drive a little to our right. They avoided us without changing their flight altitude. We abandoned these efforts after a few weeks. But the rescue fantasy lingered.

It was freezing on February 24—only the hard-core owl-watchers showed up that night: Lee, Noreen, Jean, Donna, Bruce, Gabriel (the raccoon feeder), and I. Seeing Bruce with his camera aimed at the roost hole, several passersby stopped to see what we were looking at but none of them stayed for the fly-out. How could they fail to be excited about owls flying off into the dark? we couldn't help wondering.

At 5:40, one minute before sunset, the male popped up at the nest entrance. He looked sleepy, eyes blinking, ear tufts down, the way you might look if you'd just awakened from a twelve-hour nap, if your eyes were the size of grapefruits and you happened to have little feathers where your ears ought to be. He began to preen. At 5:50 he drew himself up at the entrance of the hole, alert, his chest fluffed out a bit, eyes wide open, ear tufts erect—a beautiful thing.

At 5:55 as he was standing there ready to go, we saw the pack of cars approaching the 79th Street traffic signal. We willed the light to turn red before the cars got there. *Turn red.* But of course it didn't. One second later the owl took off.

Slow down, cars! Speed up, owl! But our ESP power failed us that night. A car passed the tree at the exact instant the owl began crossing. We heard the terrible thud of impact.

When disaster strikes, some bury their head in the sand while others rush into the fray. I'd always hoped my instincts would be heroic. But in the absence of sand I simply collapsed on the side of the road and covered my head with my arms for almost a full minute.

Lee followed a different inner imperative. Without a moment's hesitation she rushed into the road. Brakes squealed. By some miracle the cars chose not to run over an apparent lunatic who was imperiously commanding them to stop.

The first car kept going, its driver probably unaware that he'd struck a little owl. The next car would have gone right over the stricken bird if an elegant woman hadn't by now been kneeling in the middle of the road. The car—I seem to remember it was a black sedan—came to a standstill inches from Lee. After pausing a few moments—*What's going on here?*—the car's driver made a quick decision. He turned the wheels to the left, drove around the woman in the road, and continued his journey. The rest of the car pack followed suit. Jean the violist had the sense to walk to the traffic light at 77th Street. There she signaled the next group of cars to proceed with caution—woman and owl on road up ahead.

Lee inched her way toward the little mass of feathers, not knowing whether the owl was alive or dead. Either way she was planning to scoop it up and then get off the road as quickly as possible. As if mesmerized, the rest of us watched Lee creeping closer and closer to the owl. She seemed cucumber cool. At that moment a scene Lee had once described to me flashed into my mind: Lee, aged six or seven, holding a pearl-handled pistol, shooting real bullets at a target her grandfather had placed in a tree at his Long Island summer home. A tough little cookie.

Lee was almost within reach of the owl when the little raptor revealed that he was very much alive. He swiveled his head, fastening his huge eyes on his would-be rescuer. The owl, she could see, was showing no gratitude. He looked furious. Indeed, his look and posture, and especially the clacking of his bill, were clearly menacing. Another tough little cookie. Lee paused, and at that moment the owl took off.

I was crying. Bruce shouted, "He's flying! He's all right!" And when I opened my eyes, the heap of feathers on the road was gone.

Back on my feet, I saw that Bruce was focusing his camera on a low branch just a few feet away. There sat the owl, staring directly ahead, with no visible injury. "He *must* be all right. He was flying perfectly well," said Bruce, taking picture after picture, *click, click, click.* No flash, of course. He always used a very long exposure to avoid damaging his subject's retina. Five minutes later—it was just about 6:00—the female owl flew out of the cavity as if nothing had happened. In fact, she probably had no idea that anything *had* happened. She headed northwest. But uncharacteristically the male did not fly to join her.

The little male continued to sit on the same branch. As the minutes went by, ten or twenty minutes, we grew alarmed. He had never stayed at his first landing spot for more than a minute or two. Now a half hour had passed, and he hadn't moved. Something was wrong. Should we call a local wildlife-rescuer? I even thought of calling Len Soucy in Millington, New Jersey, though he was a two-hour drive away.

But why call a rehabilitator if the owl could fly? Surely that was a sign that everything was okay? Besides, how could we possibly catch him?

It was completely dark at 6:45 when the owl finally flew off. He took the usual downward trajectory but after the dive we couldn't see where he went. Perhaps he'd fallen to the ground. We searched with flashlights. We walked back and forth, looking for the little owl on the ground. Was not finding him good news?

All through the night I replayed the accident: owl taking off, owl diving, owl beginning his low traverse, cars approaching, owl in road, Lee stopping traffic, owl eyes glowering, owl flying to branch, watchers waiting, waiting, owl taking off into the night.

The next morning I arrived at the Owl Bench an hour before sunrise. At first with a flashlight and then by the light of a new day, I searched the woods where we'd last seen the little male, looking for a body we might have missed the night before. To my relief, I didn't find one. But I did find something.

Under the tree where the bird had perched, I discovered a large splotch of fresh owl whitewash, and one small pellet. A pellet? It didn't figure. He hadn't cast a pellet before he took off into the darkness the night before—I was sure of that—we hadn't taken our eyes off him for a second. Could he have returned to the same perch later on?

I placed the pellet in a black film canister and headed for home. It wasn't even eight in the morning, not too late to go back to bed for another hour or two. But sleep didn't come. In my mind I kept hearing a relentless inner dialogue between two familiar selves, one of them doom prognosticating, the other foolishly denying.

DOOM: He's dead.

DENIAL: Stop worrying! He's fine. Didn't he pick himself up and fly perfectly well to the branch?

DOOM: Then why did he sit there for an hour? He always starts hunting five minutes after fly-out. He was hurt.

DENIAL: Well, of course. He'd gotten a bit banged up. He'll be a little sore for a few days, but he'll be fine.

DOOM: Obviously he has internal injuries from the collision. He'll just get worse and worse.

DENIAL: He'll be at fly-out tonight. You'll see.

The day seemed interminable—would fly-out time never come? I whiled away some of it dissecting the little pellet. After I dropped it in a cup of warm water the fur came off almost immediately. I used tweezers to remove two tiny fragments from the cup: a matched set of upper and lower mandibles. There were a few other miniature bones, none recognizable. I'd never seen bones so small. The biting surfaces of the tiny teeth had no discernible pattern. Unidentified rodent. I'll take the bones to the museum for identification, I thought, but I never did.

I left for the fly-out with a grinding feeling in the pit of my stomach. It was only 4:30, much too early to stand and wait at the owl tree on a freezing winter day. As I rounded the curve from West 72nd Street onto the drive, I kept thinking about those tiny mandibles. Was that minuscule creature our little owl's final meal? I wondered. Hardly a feast.

I dawdled, not really wanting to know the bad news. Then I saw a familiar shape in front of the owl tree, a man wearing a brown leather bombardier jacket I knew well. Bruce! His tripod was set up, the camera pointing up to the owl's nest. He waved from a distance—he must have recognized me by my shape and winter jacket too. I looked with binoculars to get a forecast of his expression and saw that he was not only waving but giving a thumbs-up signal. I broke into a run. And there he was, the handsome screech Beau Brummel, peering out of the tear-shaped cavity as if nothing had happened.

I've had anxious times in my life—who hasn't? A scary medical report, a kid unaccountably late from school—*kidnapped?* I can tell you that worrying about an injured owl is up there with the worst. And when owl anxiety ends, the relief is equally powerful. Biophilia must be the simple explanation: life is life.

The joy was short-lived. Though the male was back in his usual place at the cavity entrance, the fly-out routine was different. Before he finally took off a few minutes before six, the female kept popping up in his place at the nest entrance, as if jockeying for position. That was something new . . . and ominous somehow.

On the next night, a Sunday, the temperature had dropped to 25 degrees and a penetrating wind made it feel like zero. If there were eggs in the nest, this was not a night to expose them for long. Nevertheless the female was the first to appear at the tear-shaped nest entrance and the first to fly out. We were dumbfounded—she had never preceded the male. The male followed a few minutes later. He didn't look injured, but once more the change in routine made us more than uneasy.

The photo Bruce took that evening documents the last time we ever saw the male West Drive screech owl, our handsome, dapper, spiffy little guy. From that day on there was only one owl at the fly-out. For the next six days, with diminishing hopes, we watched the female fly out alone.

On March 4 at about 6:00, as we watched the female preening at the cavity entrance in preparation for takeoff, somebody said, "Hey, what was that?" Everybody stopped chatting and started really looking. A mysterious, grayish-white shape had appeared to the left of the preening owl. The female immediately popped back down into the hole. The thing remained briefly at the entrance. Then it too dropped out of sight.

"It looked like a head!" someone said.

The female popped up again, filled the entrance, stretched, and flew out—the fastest fly-out ever. None of us followed her into the woods—we kept our eyes glued to the roost hole, Bruce aiming his camera at the cavity and clicking away.

A minute later we saw it again, a ghostly head at the lower part of the entrance. The head moved up and peered out, huge-eyed. Was it the missing male?

Jean said, "Marie, look! That's *not* the *male*!"

No, it wasn't. It had neither his tawny-yellowish color nor his handsome physique. But what in the world was it? We were slow on the uptake.

As we gaped, we saw another head poke up. Now there were two spooky creatures peering out into the world. Slowly the truth sank in. Owl babies! Without the characteristic screech-owl ear tufts, they looked like spectral shmoos. Examining his photos later that night, Bruce did a double take: one photo revealed *three* distinct shmoo shapes.

The next day was Sunday, and a big crowd gathered to view the West Drive fly-out. Only a few knew about the babies—most of the viewers were tourists attracted by the cameras and scopes. Several luminaries happened by that night: Betsy Barlow Rogers, founder and first president of the Central Park Conservancy, and Wendy Paulson with her husband, Hank, whose new appointment as secretary of the treasury had recently been announced by the President.

At 6:00, the two baby owls appeared at the cavity entrance, crowding their mother and each other. Then they popped down again. The female took off five minutes later, and a few regular owl-watchers stayed on in hopes of another baby sighting—Bruce, Lee, Noreen, Jean, Martha, Gabriel, and the blackbird chronicler, Bob. We waited and waited until it was too dark to see. Then Jean said her usual parting words, "Safe home," and we went our various ways. We never saw the owl babies again, though the female owl continued to fly out with perfect regularity night after night.

For two weeks we waited at the nest after fly-out, hoping for another spectral sighting. Had the baby owls been figments of our collective imagination? No, we had photographs to prove they were real. We began coming up with other theories to explain what had happened to them.

By far the most popular theory concluded that the babies had already fledged. They must have been on the verge of leaving the day we first saw them. But there was a hitch to that one: newly fledged owlets, like newly fledged red-tailed hawks, require a lot of parental care during their first weeks out of the nest. Mom was still spending her days sleeping in the West Drive hole—we saw her fly out every evening. Who then was taking care of the youngsters, feeding and educating them?

I had an answer: It had to be Dad. Unlikely as it seemed, maybe Dad wasn't dead after all. After the accident he'd moved to another cavity to convalesce, and now, completely recovered, he had taken over child care in another part of the forest. My theory was a masterpiece of double denial: the babies were fine, and Dad, poor Dad, was fine too.

Jean had a certain way of raising her eyebrows whenever I voiced the Dad-is-minding-the-store hypothesis. If the rest of her face had vanished, you would still read total disbelief in those eyebrows. Nevertheless, during daylight hours we kept searching for the babies in all the places where we'd ever found owls: the Upper Lobe, Bank Rock Bridge, Hernshead. We prowled around the little glades and copses directly to the north or south of the nest hole. Nothing. Of course, this didn't eliminate the possibility that the baby owlets were alive somewhere. The park is big. But it made my scenario unlikely. I didn't really believe the Dad-as-babysitter yarn, but during our time of uncertainty I repeated it to keep our spirits up.

Bruce was wedded to an even more outlandish narrative. He proposed that the kids were still down there in the hole. Here's how he elaborated it: Dad's accident had made the female preternaturally cautious; after the babies' first appearance on March 4, Mom scolded the children and said, "No, no, kids, it's a jungle out there. You stay down here until you're ready to go out into the dangerous world."

Nestling owls have to be fed, but as we waited at the cavity every night, we never saw food being delivered. Well, maybe deliveries were made after we left. Maybe these owls liked to hunt in the small hours of the night. Maybe, maybe.

Back and forth we went from one theory to another as we waited for the little female to fly out into the night and then as we waited for the babies to appear again.

Spring was on the way. The days were getting longer, fly-out was getting later and later. Finally one day we failed to have our what's-with-the-nestlings discussion. Two weeks later we stopped waiting at the nest and began following the female into the woods after fly-out. Maybe she'd give us a clue. We did get a clue, though it broke our hearts.

There in the quiet woodlands we heard what we couldn't have heard from the noisy West Drive: the little female singing her one-tone trill song, *Hu-hu-hu-hu-hu*. She sang it again and again and again. Had she been singing it night after night all those days we hadn't followed her? Probably. Was she calling her babies? Was she singing for her lost mate? Or looking for a new one? We didn't know. We followed her from tree to tree and heard her song from each one. A year earlier Cathy, a woman in a wheelchair who loved to watch the North Woods owl family fly out of the pine tree above the Ravine, had given me a poem by Ted Kooser, the poet laureate of the United States from 2004 to 2006.

> *All night each reedy whinny*
> *from a bird no bigger than a heart*
> *flies out of a tall black pine*
> *and, in a breath, is taken away*
> *by the stars. Yet, with small hope*
> *from the center of darkness*
> *it calls out again and again*

Our uncertainty ended on April 11. The Tuesday Bird-feeder Squad had gathered for its last meeting until fall—Central Park's birds are on their own once the trees are full of seeds and fruit. Someone there told me that he'd seen a strange feathery thing hanging out of the West Drive cavity a few hours earlier. "Better check it out," he said.

Lee and I finished our assigned duties—she was the suet lady, while I was part of the sunflower seed bucket brigade—but instead of going to the Boathouse for our usual bowl of soup, we headed for the West Drive London plane. Our anxiety level was high—we both knew something terrible had happened.

Just as we feared, the feathery thing was a dead baby owl. A squirrel or a starling must have been trying to prepare the cavity for its own use and dragged out the pathetic little body. I called Regina, the Woodlands Manager, on her emergency cell phone, and she arrived with a bucket truck a few minutes later. First she removed the owlet hanging at the nest entrance. Then she reached deep into the cavity and drew out two more little bodies. Three baby owls—they must have starved to death.

Regina laid the little corpses out on the ground, our three fuzzy white owlets now looking dirty gray and bedraggled. She photographed them and packed them up to send to the wildlife pathologist. We all stood and watched her put the bodies in a box. We might have stayed a bit longer and sent the babies off with a little poem or prayer, but the smell was too terrible.

That evening we met at the Owl Bench as usual. We needed to talk, to relieve our odd feeling of guilt. Could we have helped somehow? Brought mice or mealworms or done *something* weeks earlier to keep the babies alive? Such thoughts tormented us, rescue fantasies of one kind or another, even though we knew that humans shouldn't interfere in the lives of animals in the wild. Hadn't it been human interference—the car—that killed our spiffy male?

As we sat there for the last time, we finally did some math. The period between hatching and fledging for screech owls is about thirty days. The three ghostly babies we saw at the nest entrance on March 4 must have been at least two days old— newly hatched owls are barely feathered and their eyes are closed. So hatch day had been no later than March 1, and the babies should have been ready to fly by April 1.

The truth stared us in the face: the West Drive female had shared the nest with her dead babies for almost two weeks. And we had watched her fly out every night during that time! We tried to put the unbearable thought out of our minds. Yet the image of a grieving owl Niobe living in a small cavity with three lifeless children haunted me for weeks afterward.

The female didn't fly out that night. Her family drama had come to an end—the cavity belonged to a squirrel or starling now. That evening when we finally said our goodbyes at the Owl Bench, we knew that our singular community had come to an end too. We'd been gathering there night after night for more than two months, drawn together by the magic of owls, of night, of nature unfolding. Now our reason for being together had ended. I don't know about the others, but I've felt a hole in my life for some time, as if a friend had died.

But the West Drive female had not disappeared from our lives forever. Before long we found ourselves entangled in another owl mystery, a murder mystery this time, and the owl we'd once called Unmade Bed showed up as a prime suspect.

☾

Remember Little Red, the rust-colored screech owl who lived up the hill from the Boathouse? Back in January, when her gray Riviera boyfriend disappeared, the red-phased owl continued to live in her old black locust pad, but not for long. After a few weeks she became harder to find. Had she moved to a different roost? Most of the owl-watchers were haunting the West Drive nest, and we rarely ran into Little Red.

Other birdwatchers were more ecumenical in their owl-worship. Though Bob Levy often joined us at the Owl Bench during the next three months, he continued to wander through the woodlands at night, where he enjoyed a few more sightings of the red owl. Mainly he reported "soundings." He heard her singing the monotonic trill song many nights that winter: on January 12, for instance, he noted nine repetitions of the tremolo trill song; on January 20 she was singing at the entrance to her old black locust cavity—Bob counted six trills in total before she flew out. One night in late February, not long after the West Drive male disappeared, Bob documented forty-four consecutive trills.

Jack Meyer, a popular walk leader then—he retired the next year—was the first to hear the bad news: a dead owl had been found near the boat rental stand at the Loeb Boathouse. A park worker took the body to the rangers at the Castle, who identified it as a screech owl. What was the dead bird's color? We hoped against hope the answer wasn't red.

But it was. Yvonne McDermott, the chief ranger at the time, sent the body to Ward Stone, the wildlife pathologist at the New York State Department of Environmental Conservation in Albany.

Ward Stone! All things converge. I knew him from the hawk-watching years. The bodies of two ill-fated Pale Male mates and two redtail nestlings that had sickened and died had ended up in his lab. The females had eaten poisoned pigeons and the babies had died of trichomoniasis, a protozoan disease carried by pigeons. Now Ward held the key to what had killed Little Red. Had it been disease, or poison, or, as I expected, internal injuries from a collision with a car?

I hadn't talked to Ward Stone for years. Would his phone number be the same? Would his assistant still be Rose, the woman who had always put me through to the boss after a pleasant little chat? As I dialed the old number, I could almost hear the gloating little electronic voice saying, *The number you have dialed is not a working number*.

But nothing had changed, neither the number nor Rose. The great pathologist's voice was unchanged, too, and his fervor remained strong for protecting wildlife from man-made chemicals that assail them on all sides—pesticides, herbicides, rodenticides. He was equally devoted to protecting mankind from dangers that birds and mammals might carry, rabies and West Nile virus and bird flu, for example.

When I asked him about the red-phase screech owl he'd recently been sent from Central Park, he quickly found the file. The final report had not come in yet—toxicology tests always take a long time—but I was too curious to wait a month or two. "Can you give me a hint of what killed the owl?" I asked. For some reason he didn't want to tell me on the phone. "You'll be surprised," he said, and promised to fax me the preliminary report, or necropsy, as soon as he could.

The fax arrived within an hour, and I can hardly describe my astonishment when I read it. It was the last thing I would have imagined. But it left no doubt about what caused the little owl's death.

Marie:

This is a summary of what I have: the Eastern Screech Owl (WPU case 061108).

The red phase screech owl was found dead on the west side of Central Park (around 73rd Street) on March 26th of this year. Yvonne McDermott of the Urban Park Rangers (NYC) submitted the bird to the Wildlife Pathology Unit and it arrived three days later. The owl was an adult female with a gross weight of 192 grams. She was in good flesh and had visible subcutaneous and coelomic cavity fat supplies. She had a brood patch and developed ova, and probably was nesting.

She had two punctures in the skin of her head. One in the skin of the left dorsal skull that measured 2.2mm. The other a thin gouge through the skull. The gouge that went through the bone was 17.7mm long and the trauma extended into the brain parenchyma. Another hole in the skin over the right ventrocaudal skull (at the base of the "ear") measures 4.6mm in diameter with the skull punctured. A puncture was also observed on the right side and the ribs 4 and 5 were fractured.

The stomach contents were small mammal hair and insect fragments. The owl was negative for West Nile Virus and High Path Avian Influenza.

Diagnosis: Traumatic injuries most likely inflicted by *another screech owl* [italics mine].

Ward B. Stone
Wildlife Pathologist

Another screech owl? As far as we knew, there was only one other screech owl left in the Ramble—the West Drive female, widow and bereaved mother of three dead chicks. We began to call her the Little Murderess.

After Regina removed the three baby owl corpses on April 11, the West Drive cavity was quickly taken over by starlings. We saw them flying in and out, grateful to Regina, no doubt, for putting their spanking-new nest cavity into ship-shape order. Of course this meant that the little female would not be returning to the nest. And we knew that without a fly-out location to point us in the right direction, we had only the slimmest chance of finding her, day or night. Where would we start? She could be anywhere. To find her now we'd have to depend on a screaming bird mob or the report of a lucky birdwatcher.

Sixteen days after the West Drive female abandoned her closely watched nest, Anne Shanahan located her snoozing in the afternoon sunlight on an old dead tree at the Point. A phone and e-mail alert went out to the Owl Bench regulars, and that very evening we enjoyed a reunion at the little promontory up the hill from the Boathouse. By then we had already received Ward Stone's necropsy report about Little Red, which is why Jean Dane gave the owl a quick glance and said: "Yup, it's her, the Little Murderess."

The significance of the owl's new location was not lost on us. It was nowhere near her old West Drive territory. The Point was right smack in the heart of Little Red's territory. If we'd had any doubts before about who had done in the red owl, they vanished now. As we watched her prepare for fly-out that night we all agreed on her identity; though most screech owls are hard to tell apart, this one had a special look. We tried hard not to call her by the new name, but Little Murderess stuck.

At the beginning of June, Bob Levy, the young chronicler of red-winged blackbirds who was now intensively studying Central Park's cardinals, found our owl again. She was high in an oak at the Upper Lobe. More than a month later, on July 26, Bob heard a screech owl trilling near Balcony Bridge. On August 4 the noted photographer Cal Vornberger chanced on a screech owl at the Point. We studied the photo he posted on his website, and that clinched it—it was the Little Murderess beyond doubt. A year earlier he had included a photo of the West Drive female peeking out of her old tear-shaped cavity in his book *The Birds of Central Park*. But now that nest was abandoned and we didn't know where to look. Nobody found her again that summer.

Little Red was past history. We hadn't seen the Little Murderess for ages—maybe she was dead too. Was anyone left? Eight years after the stormy meeting at which we'd aired our doubts about Project X, we began a quest to find out if *any* of the twenty-eight owls were still around. Our original forebodings about the screech owl reintroduction now seemed justified. The rangers had just dropped the project, abandoning the birds to their dismal fates. In fairness, they had never intended to monitor the owls for more than a couple of years. But that seemed short-sighted. They had launched the project with so much fanfare. Didn't they want to know how it all turned out?

Then I remembered Chris Nagy, who had been one of the Project X owl monitors during the second phase. For several years after the birds had sloughed off their transmitters, Chris had continued to monitor them by broadcasting taped screech owl trills and whinnies from his boom box recorder. We'd been critical of the playback method back in the early days; it seemed haphazard. Well, we'd been critical of pretty much everything at the beginning. But now it seemed our only chance to get the scoop on the Central Park screech owls.

I'd always wanted to meet Chris Nagy and talk to him about his Project X experiences, but somehow an opportunity never came up. Now when I called him to see if he'd be willing to undertake an organized playback survey of the park, he agreed without hesitation. Then he paused and asked an odd question: "Are you the nightgown lady?" For a moment I didn't know what he was talking about. And then it came to me in a flash. "Oh my God! That was *you* in Riverside Park?" I asked. "Yes," he answered. "I thought I recognized your voice." It turned out that I *had* met Chris Nagy, after all, on two decidedly odd occasions.

When the second odd occasion occurred I was at the Moth Tree with Nick. It was a hot August evening, too hot for most of the other (nonmaternal) mothers and maybe even too hot for moths—hardly any had shown up. At about 11:00 Nick and I decided to call it quits. As I was gathering up my gear in the darkness, I heard an unexpected sound. I must be imagining it, I thought, but Nick stopped what he was doing and listened too. It was the unmistakable whinny of a screech owl!

We grabbed our stuff and headed down the hill toward the model-boat pond—that's where the sound was coming from. We knew we were going in the right direction because the owl song kept getting louder and louder. Something jogged my memory, and I began telling Nick about the *first* odd occasion. One night a few years earlier, I'd heard a loud screech owl call coming from Riverside Park, a strip of green directly across the street from my house. Though it was late and I'd already gone to bed, I threw a shawl over my nightgown and dashed into the park. All the while the screech owl call kept getting louder and louder, just as it was now. That time, it was coming from the bottom of the 91st Street hill. When I got there I was bewildered—the owl seemed to be right on top of me. Then I saw the car parked on the sidewalk with a big boom box on its roof. It was playing a tape of a screech owl call, repeating the owl's distinctive whinnies over and over again, with a long pause after each repetition.

A young man was standing in front of the car. I stared at him. "What in the world are you doing?" I finally asked.

He stared back at me as if I were an apparition—I must have looked a sight. Then he explained that he was trying to locate some of the missing Project X screech owls.

I finished my story as Nick and I were approaching a little outcrop just north of the model-boat pond. There we saw a young man and woman sitting on the rocks, partly obscured by low shrubbery. They seemed to be listening to the same screech owl we were. We peered into a nearby tree with our binoculars, trying to find the owl. The young man looked at us for a moment and said quietly, "It's a recording."

It took a minute for this to sink in. Finally I figured out that there *was* no owl up there.

"Why in the world are you playing a screech owl recording?" I asked them a bit belligerently.

"We work for the park, and we're trying to locate any screech owls that might be here."

I looked at the young man again. He looked familiar. And then it came to me. "Are you the guy from Riverside Park?"

He looked at me with dawning recognition. "Are you the lady in the nightgown?"

We both began to laugh

"I was just telling that story to Kerry," he said.

"I was just telling that story to Nick," I said.

Our screech owl survey was a model of simplicity: Chris would bring in his boom box and the playback tapes he'd used when monitoring owls with E.J. He'd broadcast the calls in every possible place where screech owls might be residing throughout the park, while four or five of us owl-watchers would help him listen for responses. The young graduate student was confident that the tapes would bring out any screech owls still living in Central Park. Though we'd been skeptical about playback surveys in the past, we were desperately trying to believe in them now.

We began our systematic search in mid-November. Beginning in the North Woods we encouraged Chris to spend extra time playing tapes at the Pool, because that's where owl babies had been discovered two years earlier. He did. He also played tapes at the Loch, the Harlem Meer, the Wildflower Meadow, the Great Hill, the Conservatory Garden, and the North Meadow. In each place we'd place the box on the ground, hold up the special speaker, and turn on the tapes. Out came real screech owl music recorded by the Cornell Lab of Ornithology. Each song was followed by a moment of silence to give any nearby owl a chance to respond. But no owl responded in the North Woods.

We tromped up and down the Ramble, stopping to play tapes at Willow Rock, the Azalea Pond, Little Red's black locust, and the Riviera London plane. We broadcast screech owl trills and whinnies at the Evodia Field, Turtle Pond, and the Great Lawn, at the old West Drive cavity and at the Upper Lobe, where years and years ago we'd watched a screech owl family practicing togetherness. In each familiar place we strained our ears during the silent intervals, hoping to hear a far-off owl calling back. But no owl responded in the Ramble either.

After our fourth session we decided to call it quits. The owls were gone. It wasn't an open-and-shut case, to be sure. Two of the four days we'd searched had been windy, which would limit the distance the recorded songs could travel. And maybe the local owls just weren't feeling communicative on the days we tried to serenade them. Certainly we hadn't covered every inch of the park, though we tried to include every location screech owls had been known to roost or nest in the past. But we'd done our best and found nothing. Not an owl anywhere.

So much for Project X, we thought self-righteously, for hadn't we opposed it from the start? Who can resist saying *I told you so?* Unfortunately, there was no one to say it to. Project X no longer existed. A new commissioner was running the show by then, and reintroducing species was not one of his pet projects. No one had been monitoring the Central Park screech owls for years—no one, that is, except us.

Chris Nagy, now our only connection with the original project, was not so dismissive. "Any small population can easily be wiped out by one bad year, which seems to be the case last winter," he said. A "city-core" park like ours, he said, cut off from the adjacent countryside from which new owls could emigrate, might need occasional replenishment. "You might want to throw in a few more owls every ten years or so, just to get new genes in there," he suggested. Undoubtedly many owls are available for throwing in: rehabilitators like Len Soucy always have orphaned owls to spare.

In all our discussions with Chris, the original question came up again and again, the one that had made us hold back approval of the owl program in the early days: If screech owls had once thrived in Central Park, why had they all died out by 1950? This time I had a theory I wanted to try out on Chris, and he didn't reject it out of hand.

My theory began to percolate on the day the West Drive male crashed into a car. I had a sudden insight into what was behind the extirpation enigma: the answer must be cars! Cars were the culprit, cars and other motor vehicles, in conjunction with the peculiar screech owl flight pattern. I began to study mortality statistics for eastern screech owls and then I looked into the history of car traffic in Central Park. When I put the two together, it clicked into place.

A striking account of the effect cars have on overall screech-owl mortality appears in a 1927 issue of *The Auk*, the scientific journal of the American Ornithologists' Union. There, the ornithologist and bird artist George Miksch Sutton noted that of the 113 requests for permits to retain specimens of screech owls presented to him as game commissioner of Pennsylvania, 82 individuals had been killed by flying into automobiles. "These birds were found on or near roads, and broken bones, battered plumage, internal hemorrhage or blood-shot eyes indicated that death had been caused by a terrific blow." Sutton wrote with a degree of surprise that would vanish after cars became widespread and roadkill so ordinary that no one paid any attention to it. "During the past three years, the writer has personally observed along the roads the remains of sixteen additional Screech Owls thus killed, and has once witnessed the death of an individual which flew into the windshield."

In recent years state and federal surveys have often pointed to motor vehicles as major causes of screech owl mortality, and the websites of numerous rehabilitation centers provide example after example of screech owls injured during car collisions.

The timing of screech owl extirpation in Central Park around 1950 coincides neatly with the history of car traffic there. Screech owls were common nesters in Central Park when it first opened its doors to the public in 1859, long before the automobile era. The park drives were used only for horse and carriage traffic, which posed little threat to the small owls.

As I read about the horses and carriages once popular on the park drives, I remembered something E. J. McAdams once told me when he was in charge of the Project X owls. Later he wrote up his observation in *Topic* magazine:

One night we watched an owl perch on the outer edge of a great oak surveying the field for rodents. When an ambulance came blazing around the bend, sirens blaring, the owl did not turn from its work. A couple of minutes later a carriage horse neighed. Reeling around, the owl zeroed in on that intruder, sussed him out, and again turned its attention to the rustling in the bushes. The owl's

total dismissal of machines is as impressive as it is threatening; cars
are still the biggest killers of screech owls.

In 1899 the Automobile Club of America challenged the ban
on cars in Central Park, and a judge ruled that cars were indeed
"pleasure vehicles" that could not be banned from the drives. To
be sure, the speed limit was 8 miles per hour then, not very
threatening to wildlife. In 1913 the dirt-surfaced drives were finally asphalted, and the speed limit was raised to 15 miles per
hour. By the mid-1920s even as cars were becoming increasingly
common, the speed limit went up to 20 miles per hour. In 1932
traffic lights were installed—at last it was clear that car traffic required some kind of control. But the speed limit continued to
rise—it is 30 miles per hour today.

The greatest change occurred after World War II, under the
aegis of Parks Commissioner Robert Moses. That was the beginning of a car-friendly era. The park drives were straightened for
drivers' convenience, the Marble Arch at the south end of the
mall was removed to allow cars to drive through more easily, and
traffic-light patterns were altered to allow drivers to maintain
the higher speed. These radical changes coincided with the gra-
dual decrease in number and finally the extirpation of the park's
screech owl population.

Central Park's abundance of woodlands and water makes it a
haven for many kinds of wildlife. But this one element of its
landscape—the car drive that loops around it—conflicts with the
needs of the screech owl, which might otherwise thrive there.
Because of its unusual flight pattern, the screech is particularly
vulnerable to encounters with automobiles. Unless cars are permanently banned from Central Park's drives, these lovely little
owls will always be endangered there.

12

UNHAPPY AND
HAPPY ENDINGS

Something was wrong with the Moth Tree—by mid-July we were sure of it. We'd been waiting and waiting for the moth-alluring sap to start oozing. Now we were well into moth season and the tree's rough, flaking bark was still dry. Here and there we could see a small, dark spot of the sticky stuff, one at the base of the tree and another at about the eye level of Aidan Smith, our youngest mother (*author*)—he would turn eight in a few months. But that was it.

Every night after sunset we gathered at the Moth Tree to wait for the mysterious Catocalas to arrive, or any moth at all, for that matter. But they stayed away in droves, as MGM's Sam Goldwyn once said about audiences of bad movies. Toward the end of July a few ilia underwings in all their bright glory did show up to sip at the wet spots. But not one of our favorites came by, the ones assigned romantic names by lonely lepidopterists of the past: not a sweetheart, or a girlfriend, or a darling, or a bride, not even a tedious old oldwife, a pathetic widow, or a sinister Delilah.

Jimmy came up with an odd idea: maybe something was *right*, not wrong, with the English oak. If the oozing sap was a sign of disease, perhaps the absence of it meant good health returning. You might think that a group of nature lovers who vigorously defended every Central Park tree slated for removal would rejoice at the idea of a sick tree's recovery, but that was not our reaction. No, we didn't want the tree to get well. We wanted it to keep attracting rare and beautiful moths. We had always assumed the tree was doomed, but we hoped it would take a nice long time to die. If, in fact, it was actually getting better, we were the doomed ones, doomed to spend our summers without a Moth Tree.

Once again I wrote to Hugh McGuinness, the Long Island moth expert. I had told him about the Moth Tree in the course of the clouded underwing correspondence. Now I asked him if he had any information about trees such as ours. What causes the sap to ooze? What actually is the strong-smelling stuff? Is it a sign that the tree is diseased, and if so, what disease? If he didn't know, I ended, would he steer us to a tree expert who might have the answers?

His response came a few days later: "If it is fermented, then you are getting fluid from the phloem, which is filled with sugar and that is what is fermenting. As to whether this means the tree is diseased, I don't know. You could try my friend Brian Kane, who is a certified arborist and an assistant professor at the University of Massachusetts."

I wrote Brian Kane the same day, invoking Hugh McGuinness, and received a quick response. I knew at once that I'd hit the jackpot. The man was a treasure trove of arboristic knowledge:

> In general, trees oozing sap have a condition known as bacterial wetwood (aka slime flux). It's a bacterial infection, although I think the causal organism(s) are not fully known. Previously, one could commonly find it on American elms, but since there are few elms around, the disease is not seen as often. The slime is rather pungent, mostly because the infection takes place under anaerobic conditions. Hydraulic pressure in the vascular system of the tree pushes slime out of wounds like old pruning cuts or cracks in the bark. To the best of my knowledge, the infection is not fatal, al-

though it may be a secondary pathogen. Once the slime is pushed out, saprophytic fungi begin to colonize it, which perhaps contributes to the staining and aroma. The infection usually does not structurally undermine the tree.

Slime flux! A quick Internet search confirmed the diagnosis. Many websites included photos of diseased trees that looked just like the Moth Tree. Many sites mentioned a symptom that left us no doubt that Kane had nailed it: "Various types of insects are attracted to the slime flux," wrote the authors of "Ornamental Disease Note No. 8" from the North Carolina State University Plant Pathology Extension. "Insects feed on the slime," observed a tree expert at Colorado State University. Walter Reeves, a gardening commentator on Georgia Public Radio, wrote that "the ooze is usually surrounded by insects," adding a bit censoriously, "some of whom seem inebriated!"

Reeves noted that there are two types of slime flux: alcoholic and acidic, with the acidic smelling like vinegar. The Moth Tree was afflicted with the alcoholic type—the area around it smelled like a brewery, or used to in the good old days. I thought back to the occasions we'd found a moth so absorbed in its feeding that it wouldn't budge, even when we poked apart its forewings with a leaf petiole or a thin twig. Now it made sense: the moth had been drunk as a skunk.

When I sent Brian Kane several digital images of the Moth Tree—thank heavens for little point-and-shoot cameras—he answered with more certainty than before:

It looks like bacterial wetwood to me . . . One can clearly see the typical orange-y ooze of bacterial wetwood. I suspect that because of the anaerobic nature of the infection there are fermentation products in the ooze, which make it more palatable to insects. I bet if you looked into it further, you could determine its chemical composition.

What was the prognosis for the Moth Tree? The answer depended on whether you were looking at it from the tree's point of view or ours. As Jimmy had guessed, the outlook was promising for the tree. Kane had already noted that the infection didn't structurally undermine it. The North Carolina State University Plant Pathology Extension wrote that the disease was self-limiting: "Sap may continue to ooze for several weeks or months, but usually it stops after some time, with no treatment and no apparent damage to the tree."

From the viewpoint of the mothers (*authors*), the news was dismal. Unless we found another victim of wetwood or slime flux in Central Park, our Catocala run was over. To be sure, it didn't mean the end of moth-watching—we still had the black light and battery pack, the sheet with the paint stain, and the wheelie for transporting it all from Lee's closet to the park and back again. But most Catocalas are attracted to bait, not light. And even if we created a superpotent moth-bait mixture and smeared the disgusting stuff over a broad swath of Central Park, we knew we'd never get the underwing riches that nature's own bacterially powered moth bait provided.

Though we didn't realize it at the time, it wasn't only underwing moths we were losing, but one of our most important nocturnal narratives as well. Without the Moth Tree we'd have one less reason to venture into Central Park after sunset. Night was our cloak, our surround, but it couldn't be our purpose. We'd always need the powerful impetus of a good story, if only to override the ancient mammalian instinct of dark avoidance. The moth story, the owl story, the star guys' celestial happenings, the Robin Boys' Dormitory epic—all these drew us into the darkness.

Of course we'd always have our daytime dramas. That year red-tailed hawks provided an incredible show. Eleven active hawk nests had been discovered in unlikely urban locations, the most spectacular of them atop the Unisphere (just above Indonesia) at the former World's Fair grounds in Flushing Meadows, Queens. Another redtail pair had built their aerie on a structural support of the Triborough Bridge. There were three nestlings again at the Cathedral of St. John the Divine, three nestlings at the Rose Hill campus of Fordham University, and nests in Prospect Park, Inwood Park, and Green-Wood Cemetery. To think that *Buteo jamaicensis* had long been considered a shy woodland hawk!

Bruce Yolton commuted among the eleven nests, taking baby-hawk pictures at ten of them and posting them on his website. Only one nest failed. Alas, it was the one closest to our hearts—Pale Male and Lola's twelfth-floor stick palace on Fifth Avenue and 74th Street. Bruce's images of the twenty-three new red-tailed hawk chicks growing up in other parts of the city helped many Pale Male and Lola fans get over the disappointment of the pair's third failure in a row.

☾

It was winter now, owl season, but there were no owls in Central Park. We'd broadcast the screech owl's eerie songs from the North Woods to Central Park South, throughout woodlands and lawns, meadows and glens, lakes and streams. And no bird sang back. It would be our first winter without owls in a decade and our third winter without Charles.

It would also be our first winter without Lee. Back in August, while Lee was fishing, kayaking, painting, and sketching at her weekend hideaway on Long Island, she ran into Sonny Staniford, an old family friend. The handsome widower courted her with flowers and billets-doux, and when Lee began showing up at the Moth Tree looking radiant we knew it wasn't from the heat and humidity. Now she and Sonny were planning to spend a chunk of the winter in Florida, and we would have to carry on without her.

In early December I sent the disappointing results of our

boom box survey to various owl-watchers I'd met along the way: Marianne Girards, a shy, diminutive birder who had become one of the most faithful owlers of us all; Donna Browne and Bill Stifel, intrepid owl trackers; Bob Levy, the blackbird chronicler; Anne Shanahan, the sharpest hawk and owl spotter in the park; Mitch Nussbaum, the space satellite maven; Barbara Kent; Martha Marshall. I sent the report to everyone I could think of. Almost as an afterthought, I also sent the report to Chris Karatnytsky, the effervescent owner of the best-behaved dog in the world—I hadn't seen the two of them for more than a year. She had once written me for advice about binoculars and so her name was in my e-mail address book.

Chris Karatnytsky's reply on December 19 knocked my socks off:

> I read your note saying that there are no more Eastern Screech owls in Central Park. Never fear, though I don't know where they live I have seen one or two screech owls hunting in the familiar areas near the Pool on more than one occasion when I'm walking Fig after dark. The most recent sighting was last week when a screech owl did a flyby as I watched a raccoon shamble down from a tree for her evening dumpster foraging. So they're still around, probably enjoying the peace and quiet that comes when one's avian celebrity has waned a bit.

We were skeptical. With so many birdwatchers patrolling the park, surely one of them would have come across owls if any were there. As for Chris Karatnytsky: she certainly sounded convincing. But she was a new birder, and though we admired her enthusiasm, we weren't sure how accurate her observations were. Could she have mistaken bats for owls, for instance? Not hard to do in failing light. There had been a few unseasonably warm days that December, and bats do come out when the cold lets up.

Two days later, at 4:30 p.m., a sextet of owlers—Noreen, Jimmy, Bruce, Jean, Marianne, and I—gathered at the park entrance on Central Park West and 100th Street to check out Chris K.'s owls. It was the shortest day of the year and the sun was already setting. They say that light deprivation can cause a form of depression called seasonal affective disorder—SAD is its appropriate acronym—but we were all unreasonably happy as we entered the park. Jimmy put it into words: "It's so great to be owling again."

As we entered the park everyone else seemed to be leaving. We were bucking the tide. At the Pool, we stopped at the rustic footbridge that crosses a stream west of Glen Span Arch* to plan our evening's itinerary. We'd start at the Pool and the woody strip surrounding it—we were already there. After that we'd descend to the Ravine beyond. Then the Loch and the Wildflower Meadow to its east, known owl haunts of the past. Dusk was falling as we stood there reminiscing about the time we'd seen three young raccoons catching crayfish in that very stream. Then the moment came that we all recognized. All color had faded— everything was gray. Owl time. We fell silent and began our search.

We circled the Pool, from 100th Street to 103rd Street, looking for owlish shapes in trees and listening for trills or whinnies. The streetlamps were on, casting a considerable glow; we didn't need our flashlights. Along the way we carefully searched the area near the Dumpster at the Pool's south side and found Chris's raccoon—he had brought two friends that evening—but nary an owl to be seen. On the north side of the little pond we passed the sweetgum tree where two years earlier we'd first seen three owlets sitting on a branch. What had happened to those owl kids?

*Twenty-one of Central Park's historic spans are Arches built in stone and brick (no two alike); the remaining nine are equally diverse Bridges made of either cast iron or wood.

We crossed the West Drive around 103rd Street and made our way down the steep hillside of the Ravine, flashlights on. We didn't have Fig as our guard dog this time, but we didn't need her: the place had become familiar. This was exactly where the parent screech owls had barked a pussycat warning to their four fledglings two years earlier. And when the great horned owl had moved to the North Woods the year after that, we'd learned a few more of the twists and turns of that less familiar part of the park.

Nevertheless, we were cautious as we made our way along the Loch and tramped through the remains of tall grasses and weeds in the Wildflower Meadow. We stayed close to one another the way ducklings do when they huddle together as they swim across a lake or pond: a snapping turtle might perceive the mass of delicious little morsels as one big unpalatable creature.

We scoured the woods for more than an hour, confident that if owls were to be found, we'd find them. Weren't we owl seekers? Hadn't we been finding owls in Central Park for years and years? And one of us especially, Noreen, a world-class owl-finder, could surely out-Hiawatha Hiawatha himself if given a chance. But neither Noreen nor any of the rest of us found an owl that evening.

"Well, it's been fun anyhow," someone said as we left the park together. But we were just putting a good face on it. We were bummed. The screech owls were gone, another story ended, another gap to fill. Looking for a new story would have to wait, however. Chanukah and Christmas were upon us and we each had our various holiday activities on our minds. That's the only excuse I can think of for having abandoned the search after only one try.

☽

Fast-forward two months. It is February 26, and one of those odd, class-conscious New York love stories is about to begin. In this one, members of the mammalian class are in love with a bunch of owls. Unfortunately, as in so many love stories, the love is one-sided; the owls don't seem to know the humans exist. But it doesn't matter much. Love is love.

SCENE I

At the Pool in Central Park's North Woods. A mob of a half dozen blue jays are screaming at something in an oak tree. Suddenly two fuzzy gray shapes come tumbling to the ground.

PASSERBY: My God, they're baby owls!

He stares at the fluffy, wide-eyed creatures sitting on the grass near the path. They stare at him. They seem unable to fly. The jays continue to scream. The man waves his arms and the blue jays fly away. With one eye on the owls, the man calls over a uniformed park worker, who rings up the Urban Park Rangers on his walkie-talkie. Two rangers arrive with a cardboard carton and take the little birds away. Later, we learn, a Parks Department van transports them to the home of a licensed wildlife rehabilitator in Yonkers, JOANNE DREEBEN, *where they join (in a separate enclosure, of course) two squirrels, a wood thrush, a rabbit, and some pigeons.*

SCENE II

The next afternoon. Two neighborhood ladies, CAROLYN KAY *and* BARBARA ZUCKER, *are strolling along the path that circles the Pool. They hear blue jays screaming, stop, look up, and see a little owl standing precariously on an exposed branch directly above them. It is across the path from yesterday's tree. The blue jays are making feints at it, actually hitting it as they do.*

CAROLYN: What *is* that strange bird?

BARBARA: My God! It's a baby owl!

*The jays are fiercely mobbing the little owl. The raptor is cower-
ing, teetering on the branch. A minute later it loses its footing
and falls into Barbara's outstretched arms. She's a birdwatcher,
by remarkable coincidence.*

BARBARA *(looking at the baby owl indecisively)*: We're sup-
posed to leave birds that fall out of the nest right where they are.
The parents usually come to the rescue and continue to feed
them until they're ready to fly.

*Barbara and Carolyn try putting the little owl on a nearby fence.
It just sits there. The women walk away to see what the bird will
do, and the blue jays resume their attack. The petrified owlet
falls to the ground. Several dogs are seen romping in the vicinity.*

CAROLYN: I don't think we should leave it here. Too many kids
and dogs.

BARBARA: You're right. *(She looks at the little owl longingly.)*
What a beautiful bird. I wish I could keep it. But I think I know
just the place to take it.

*She carefully wraps it in her large black cashmere shawl. Cradling it
like a baby, she walks a few blocks to Animal General, an Upper West
Side veterinary hospital on Columbus Avenue. She enters a waiting
room full of people, some with dogs on leashes, some with cats in car-
riers or birds in cages. She hands the bundled-up owl to KAREN
HEIDGERD, the owner and manager of the hospital. Heidgerd
opens the shawl and everybody in the room crowds around, oohing
and aahing at the little owl. There are exclamations of "An owl in
Central Park!" and "Amazing!" and "Is it real?" and so on.*

KAREN HEIDGERD *(examining the owl, who is hissing and
clicking its bill)*: Looks healthy, just a little scared. A juvenile,

about four weeks old. It's in the process of fledging, but can't fly yet, not for another week or two. Wow, it's awfully early for an owl baby! *(to Barbara)* We really can't handle raptors here, don't have the space or equipment. We'll call a car service and deliver it to Len Soucy at the Raptor Trust. We send a lot of birds there. It's a great place.

BARBARA: I've heard a lot about it. But isn't it far from here, somewhere in southern New Jersey? That'll cost a pretty penny.

HEIDGERD: About $150, but we're glad to pay it. *(She hands back the black cashmere shawl to Barbara.)*

BARBARA *(proudly holding up the shawl and pointing to a large white stain)*: Owl poop!

HEIDGERD *(thoughtfully)*: I wonder where the parents are.

INTERLUDE

At the Pool, same night, about 8:30 p.m. A waxing gibbous moon, three days from full, is shining directly overhead. A pretty, dark-haired woman, CHRIS KARATNYTSKY, *is seen walking around the Pool with her dog, Fig. It's cold; the woman's breath is visible in little puffs of smoke. She stops walking, stands for a minute as if listening. Fig seems to be listening too. Then the distinctive trill of a screech owl is heard, once, twice, three times. Chris smiles. She does a creditable imitation screech call back.*

SCENE III
The next day, in Maine.

NARRATOR: Coincidences are best avoided in fiction. But amazing ones happen all the time in real life. Amy Campbell, the

same lady who found her way to a Central Park owl fly-out during a big blizzard, sends an e-mail to a writer in New York City.

AMY CAMPBELL *(at her computer, writing)*: Just heard about
a four-week-old screech owl chick rescued from mobbing blue
jays in Central Park. I think it was found today, and was taken to
Len Soucy at the Raptor Trust. Do you know anything about
this, Marie? If not, try calling Soucy.

SCENE IV

The Raptor Trust—a week later. LEN SOUCY, *a handsome man
in his mid-seventies, bearded, sturdy, vigorous, is standing in
front of a huge flight cage filled with branches for birds to perch
on. Within are four or five adult screech owls. One by one the
camera picks out three fluffy gray immature birds, each on a different perch.*

SOUCY: Now I've got all three of the Central Park owls here.
Last week Karen Heidgerd sent over the one found in the park
on Monday. But the other two had gone to Joanne Dreeben, a
rehabilitator in Yonkers. When she heard I had a third owl she
called me and said she didn't have the facilities to raise screech
owls. So I told her, "Bring the two over here. I'll raise the three
of them." She drove them down today.

Well, Dreeben and I agree it would be a big mistake to take
them back to Central Park now. Nobody knows where the nest
tree is, or whether the parents are still around, or anything about
the food supply.

I know the Central Park birdwatchers are looking for the
nest. One of them keeps calling, asking how the birds are doing
and begging me to return them to the park. She's worrying about
the parents—thinks they're like human parents whose kids have
been kidnapped. *(makes a familiar shrugging and palms-up ges-*

ture of helplessness) I hope she and her friends will understand when I tell them that owls are not people, and that it's better to wait until spring to bring them back to the park.

INTERLUDE

The Pool, about 2:00 p.m. the same day. Six bundled-up owlers are looking up and down trunks of bare, wintry trees, searching for cavities that might house a screech owl family: Bruce, lugging heavy photographic equipment; Jean, a viola case strapped over her shoulder; Lee, in town from Tampa for a week; Jimmy, holding up a cell phone in front of every tree being scrutinized. His phone's ring tone is a real screech owl trill—God knows how he managed that—and he hopes it will get an answer. Noreen, the only one without binoculars, is walking a little apart, gazing at various trees in the dreamy way that often precedes a discovery. It's freezing cold.

Near the Grotto, a picturesque deployment of rocks and cascading water that feeds both the Pool and the Loch, they inspect a promising red maple that has a cavity of just the right size. Jimmy plays his ring tone, and something moves at the entrance to the hole. They freeze—not from the cold. Then a squirrel pokes its head out. A starling flies into another perfect, oval-shaped cavity in an adjacent tulip tree.

Noreen's voodoo isn't working, nor is the owlers' diligent scanning. As they face failure in their quest to find the nest tree, they're filled with anthropomorphic pity. Poor parent owls, to have three beautiful children suddenly disappear off the face of the earth.

JEAN: I couldn't sleep last night. If only we could *tell* the parent owls that the kids are all right.

SCENE IV *(continued)*

SOUCY: But even if the birdwatchers find the parent owls and locate the actual nest, it's way too early to put those young owls back
in the park. It's still winter! No leaves on the trees, no cover. That's
why screech owls usually fledge in May or June, not February. The
jays will keep attacking and the nestlings will keep falling to the
ground. No, we'll hack them here, teach them all the things they
need to know to survive in the wild. We get other owls to teach
them how to fly and hunt for themselves. And mainly we keep
them away from people so they don't get imprinted. They have to
hate people—people and their cars are dangerous for owls. Then
we can release them into the wild again and they'll have a chance.

Here's how we do it: We put them in a big flight cage with
adult screech owls—ones we can't release because they've been
injured but who can still take fledglings under their wing. *(He
laughs heartily at his joke.)* We keep them for this purpose, to be
surrogate parents for fallen nestlings. The young owls learn imi-
tatively. They watch the adults do it. I buy crickets, mealworms,
anything that moves. Screech owl young are mostly bug eaters in
the wild too. Then I graduate them to larger prey.

I'll return them to the park in May, when the trees are in leaf
and the kids have some protection from the pesky blue jays. I
have a long connection with Central Park, you know.

Telephone rings. SOUCY *answers.*

SOUCY: Hello? *(aside)* It's one of the Central Park birdwatchers. *(into phone)* Yes, I've got all three of them now. *(pause)* Yes,
I know you're looking for the nest. *(pause)* No, don't worry about
the parents, they'll be fine. But here's what I want to tell you:
Even if you find the nest, the kids will be better off at the Raptor Trust until April or May. It's too cold out there. No leaves on
the trees, no cover for the young ones. Probably not enough

food. *(longer pause)* Good, I'm glad you agree. I'll let you know when it's time to release them. And no press conference with Isabella Rossellini this time. *(He laughs. Hangs up.)* I think they understand. My God, owl babies in February! It's another crazy Central Park story, like the one with the Fifth Avenue hawks. But if screech owls are still breeding in the park ten years after the experiment began, this one looks like a success story.

It's 7:00 p.m. on March 27 and still daytime when the usual band of owlers gathers at the entrance to the Pool—daylight saving time has started, so everything seems to happen an hour later. The moon is visible high in the sky, a children's moon, Jean calls it. If it's visible in the day, children can see it before their bedtime, she explains. (The term must have been coined in the days when children still went to bed early.) In Central Park the trees are not in leaf yet. On the grassy slope west of the Pool, masses of daffodils and narcissi are blooming.

Fifteen minutes later the sun is setting. Chris and Fig are walking briskly along the south side of the Pool, the owlers following close behind. We're wearing fewer layers today; everyone looks five pounds lighter. Our mood is lighter too: anticipation has replaced anxiety, for Chris has discovered secrets that have eluded us and tonight she is taking us to see what she has found.

We pass the Grotto, where the red maple we'd inspected for owl cavities a few weeks ago is now in full flower. The rich red of maple blossoms is the surest sign of early spring in Central Park; it's the first tree to flower if you don't count witch hazel and Cornelian cherry. Chris and Fig walk about thirty feet past the Grotto, and both stop in front of a large London plane. "Please sit down," Chris says to Fig in a quiet, conversational tone, the way you might say, "Please try this piece of cake"—she never commands. The dog immediately sits. We look at the tree. What, *that* tree, right out in the open? we ask, chagrined. "Yes, look up the trunk a little bit past the place where it begins to branch out."

And there it is, a beautiful tear-shaped cavity, perfectly visible. How did we miss it? Easily—the cavity blends in with the irregular scaly spots that characterize the bark of *Platanus acerifolia*. Then Noreen exclaims, "Look, there's an owl in the entrance!" And when each of us has finally located that hiding-in-plain-sight cavity, we all see that indeed a screech owl is sitting in the entrance.

We can also see that Chris is bursting with excitement, and we think it's simply because she discovered the nest and is eager to show us the parent owls. We don't know that she has made another discovery, the most thrilling of all, and saved it as a surprise for us.

It is 7:20 when we first see the nest with the owl in the entrance. Seven minutes later the owl flies to an oak just across the path leading to the North Meadow and perches on a low branch. "Keep your eye on the nest," Chris says urgently when we turn our attention to the flying owl. We look back at the cavity and see that a second owl is now peering out of the entrance. Mom and Dad are together! Less than a minute later, that one also flies to the oak and perches beside the first. Owls at last! Owls to follow! We watch them intently to see which way they'll go.

"No, keep watching the nest!" says Chris eagerly. "Don't look away." We don't understand at first. What is there to look for? We'll lose sight of the two owls in the oak. "No, no," Chris insists, "the parents are staying there. Don't worry. Keep watching."

We gasp when we see another owl fly out of the cavity. A third owl! But it's flying strangely, not like the previous two. It is flapping its wings heavily, too much flapping. What's wrong with this one? It seems to be aiming for the oak where the first two owls are waiting, but it overshoots. Then it makes a little circle, tries again, and settles in awkwardly on the branch. There it begins to bob its head in a weird way that we recognize immediately. It is a baby!

That was Chris's glorious secret. The owl parents hadn't become empty nesters when the three owlets dropped out of the sky and were sent away to their foster homes. There had been four nestlings to begin with, and one of them—the cautious one? the clever one?—was still living at home.

For almost two months thereafter, while three erstwhile members of the family were being educated at Len Soucy's academy in Millington, New Jersey, we watched the nightly fly-outs of parents and remaining child from their London plane. Thanks to Bruce's steady stream of photographs, we learned to tell the male from the female by the different markings on their chests. We watched the juvenile's plumage change day by day from fuzzy fluffy gray to the mottled brown barrings and spottings of an adult owl.

And we acquired another skill. We learned to recognize the moment of imminent fly-out by a conspicuous change in the local soundscape. The instant an owl makes its appearance, the neighborhood robins abandon their steady chorus of gentle night-night chips and begin blasting out loud, louder, loudest alarm chips. Chip! Chip! Chip! Somehow we'd never noticed the chip change. Once we became sensitized to it, however, we never had to worry about missing the fly-out moment. The robins never failed to alert us.

As the weeks went by we watched the fourth fledgling, once an awkward bumbler, turn into a swift aerial navigator and a cool hunter. Mainly, alas, he captured moths, large moths. We were happy our little owl was becoming independent but sorry to see beautiful moths disappearing down a raptor's gullet before we had a chance to identify them.

I wasn't there on March 30 when an event occurred that held the greatest promise for the future of screech owls in Central Park. Fortunately, Bruce took a series of once-in-a-lifetime photographs that night. He posted them on his website for the world

to see, along with a description that still chokes me up when I
read it:

> As it got dark, the female adult, followed by the fledgling, appeared
> on a tree east of the Grotto. While there, the female adult sang one
> soft song. It was the trill song, the one we used to hear the West
> Drive screech female singing after her mate disappeared.
>
> The female and fledgling headed west along the edge of the
> Pool and then flew across the water, landing in a tree at the east
> end of the Pool. Then the female alone flew into a bare tree just to
> the north.
>
> Suddenly the male appeared right above the female. And
> there, silhouetted by the almost-full moon, we saw an amazing
> sight—owl sex.

☾

Just after sunset on May 21, a day when Central Park is at the
height of tender greenness, in an unidentified woodland in
the park's north quarter, a man and a woman come into view,
both wearing Smoky the Bear uniforms. They are walking
slowly, carefully carrying a bulky object—the cardboard cat carrier Len Soucy uses for owl transporting. The ingenious rehabilitator has modified it for avian comfort, carpeting its floor so
small birds won't slip around. Stopping at the edge of a small
meadow, the rangers gently put the box on the ground. In it are
three wide-awake screech owls. The woman stoops down and
opens a hinged flap door Soucy has cut in the carrier's side. The
birds hesitate—they don't seem in a hurry to leave. The other
ranger gives them a little nudge with a gloved hand, and reluctantly, one by one the owls step out. A long moment passes. Could
they possibly know they are coming home? All at once, *whoosh*,
the three young owls fly off into the night.

AFTER
THE ENDING

And they lived happily ever after in a park blessed with owls.

No. Too many puzzles needed solving. It was time to seek out Chris Nagy again. We had questions that had accumulated over the years and I sent him a note with a few of them. A week went by without an answer. Well, maybe he was working overtime on his dissertation. Or maybe he'd had enough of our endless applications for help. But biologists, it turns out, are people with broad interests. Chris's rock band Pale Horse (A Near Deaf Experience) had been touring that week. His answers, when they came, were illuminating:

First question: Why do Central Park's screech owls consistently lay eggs two months earlier than do owls anywhere else in the country? "It's a real mystery," Chris answered, "but here are three possible explanations."

1. The photoperiod: Screech owls may be physiologically cued to breed by changes in the relative duration of day and night. That is, they begin breeding behaviors when they do—at the beginning of spring, generally—because of the increasing amount of daylight. The artificial lighting in the park, together

with increased illumination from the surrounding city, may cause the owls to experience "artificial daylight." Therefore, they might begin to nest earlier. But the photoperiod can't be the whole explanation. If owls have inadequate food to support egg production in frigid temperatures, for example, they are unlikely to try to breed, no matter what the photoperiod is.

·2. The temperature: Scientists often consider temperature a crucial factor in determining egg-laying dates—the higher the temperature, the earlier the laying date. But in Central Park, egg-laying dates are much earlier than in places with considerably higher temperatures, in warmer parts of Texas, for instance. So even though the temperature in Central Park *is* a bit warmer than in surrounding parts of the city, that doesn't seem to be the answer.

3. Available prey: This is the one that makes sense to me. Lower temperatures generally bring down the numbers of available prey species. So birds would want to wait until there's enough food for the young, which usually happens when the temperatures go up. Maybe because of the great numbers of people who visit Central Park year-round (and the food remnants they leave behind), there are abundant rodents in the park at all times of year. It may turn out that nesting dates are determined not by light or temperature but primarily by food supply. That would be my hunch.

Our next question was specifically about our most recent owl experience at the Pool: Why so many owl foundlings this year? You hear of one bird falling out of a nest, and maybe, by chance, another one might tumble out. But *three*?

That sort of thing happens everywhere, not just in Central Park. Owls fall out of the nest all the time, just at the age they start learning how to fly. They go out on a branch, they try to fly, then they fall to the ground. Out in the wild it's not a problem because there's no one around to bother them. The parents have to keep an eye on them for a couple of days, that's all. And even though the young owls aren't ready to fly, they can climb very well. They'll scramble up a tree trunk and perch on a limb and the parents will keep feeding them until they fledge.

These owls might have been okay if the nest hadn't been in Central Park. When the nestlings were found, the parents were probably right nearby somewhere, watching them. Normally the best thing to do would be to leave them there. But you couldn't just leave them there in Central Park. Dogs come running up or a person could grab them in the normal scheme of things. That's why three of them were found. It happens.

About the boom box survey—it turned out that there *were* more owls in the park. Why had Chris failed to find them? Nagy was not defensive:

No survey method is 100 percent accurate, especially since animals move around. So you have to repeat the surveys a few times in a reasonably short period of time to get an accurate picture. We did go out four times, but we covered large parts of the park. We were only up in the Pool area one evening.

There's another thing. When I started with one particular recording it worked okay at first, but I noticed that after a while it stopped working. So I made a new one, the one I have now, and that worked really well for quite a while. But it could be that since I played it in Central Park so many times over the years, all the owls had gotten habituated to that CD. It happens.

Our final question was about the West Drive female, the one we had dubbed the Little Murderess. We wanted to know more about its history. Bruce had a few photographs of her that clearly showed the band on her foot—you could even make out some numerals. I attached a couple of these as JPEG files.

Chris knew the owl at once by the style of the band: it had a different crimp from any of the thirty-two Phase 2 owls. Our West Drive female turned out to be one of the six original Len Soucy owls, a female. The sole survivor of the first lot, she was not part of the scientific study Chris was involved in. But over the years the young man often ran into her in the course of his monitoring job. We were amazed to hear her history.

Shortly after the Phase 2 owls began to settle into Central Park, our little female hooked up with one of them, number 18 on Chris's chart. The pair nested near the Upper Lobe—they must have been the very ones we watched there so many evenings during our early owling days. But the male disappeared at a crucial stage of the breeding cycle. Though around that time we'd heard of two dead fledglings found in the park, we never made any connection between those dead babies and our closely watched female. Now we knew her tragic past.

How did Chris know the details of this failed nesting attempt, while we avid owlers were left in the dark? The owls were still being monitored by radio transmitter in those days and the rangers quickly noted the male's absence. But we were not part of the Project X network then. After all, we had vehemently opposed the whole plan at a Woodlands Advisory Board meeting. Looking back, I can understand why such an unhappy owl story would not be widely publicized.

When her first love disappeared it didn't take the owl femme fatale long to snag a new mate—number 25 in the official survey. And who was number 25? None other than our spiffy Beau Brummel owl, the ill-fated male that collided with a car on February 24.

While making his rounds one day, Chris captured the little Soucy owl in a bal-chatri trap, thinking she was one of his official birds. But before releasing her he took down her band number.

It was 70527460. Sounds familiar? Yes, she was the owl Isabella Rossellini sent off into the darkness on that long-ago August evening as flashbulbs popped and people marveled.

Where is she now? Well, maybe the West Drive female is still in Central Park. Maybe her sad story will still have a happy ending. But the odds are against it. She'd be ten years old this year, an advanced age for an eastern screech owl. "The oldest screech owl in the wild is way under ten years old," Len Soucy observed when I told him that his Central Park owl was still alive.

As I write these last words at the last possible moment before my book goes to press, the owl scene is hopping in Central Park. Three pairs of screech owls are nesting in various parts of the park—owl etiquette prevents me from telling you the exact location, I'm sorry to say, but someone will show you the way. Wear binoculars—that's the key. And beware—owl-watching is addictive. It's also enchanting. Good night. Safe home.

Selected Bibliography

BIRDS: FIELD GUIDES AND GENERAL INFORMATION
Ehrlich, Paul, David S. Dobkin, and Darryl Wheye. *The Birder's Handbook.* New York: Fireside, 1988.
Leahy, Christopher W. *The Birdwatcher's Companion.* Princeton, N.J.: Princeton University Press, 2004.
Sibley, David Allen. *The Sibley Guide to Birds.* New York: Knopf, 2000.
Terres, John K. *The Audubon Society Encyclopedia of North American Birds.* New York: Knopf, 1987.

OWLS AND OTHER NOCTURNAL BIRDS
de la Torre, Julio, and Art Wolfe. *Owls: Their Life and Behavior.* New York: Crown, 1990.
Johnsgard, Paul. *North American Owls.* Washington, D.C.: Smithsonian, 1997.
Martin, Graham. *Birds by Night.* London: T. & A. D. Poyser, 1990.
Maslow, Jonathan Evan. *The Owl Papers.* New York: Vintage, 1988.
Skutch, Alexander. *Birds Asleep.* Austin: University of Texas Press, 1989.
Soucy, Len. *New Jersey's Owls.* Millington, N.J.: The Raptor Trust, 2002.

MOTHS AND CATERPILLARS
Covell, Charles V., Jr. *A Field Guide to Moths of the Eastern United States, 2nd Edition.* Martinsville: Virginia Museum of Natural History, 2005.
Himmelman, John. *Discovering Moths.* Camden, Me.: Down East Books, 2002.
Sargent, Theodore D. *Legion of Night: The Underwing Moths.* Amherst: University of Massachussetts Press, 1976.
Wagner, David L. *Caterpillars of Eastern North America.* Princeton, N.J.: Princeton University Press, 2005.

OTHER INSECTS

Capinera, John L., Ralph D. Scott, and Thomas J. Walker. *Field Guide to Grasshoppers, Katydids and Crickets of the United States.* Ithaca, N.Y.: Cornell University Press, 2004.

Eisner, Thomas. *For Love of Insects.* Cambridge, Mass.: Harvard University Press, 2003.

Marshall, Stephen A. *Insects: Their Natural History and Diversity.* Buffalo, N.Y.: Firefly Books, 2006.

MAMMALS

Griffin, Donald R. *Echoes of Bats and Men.* New York: Doubleday Anchor, 1959.

———. *Listening in the Dark.* New Haven, Conn.: Yale University Press, 1958.

Nowak, Ronald M. *Walker's Mammals of the World (Sixth Edition).* Baltimore, Md.: The Johns Hopkins University Press, 1999.

SLUGS

Runham, N. W., and P. J. Hunter. *Terrestrial Slugs.* London: Hutchinson University Library, 1970.

Western Society of Malacologists. *Field Guide to the Slug.* Seattle: Sasquatch Books, 2002.

TREES

Barnard, Edward Sibley. *New York City Trees.* New York: Columbia University Press, 2002.

CENTRAL PARK

Burton, Dennis. *Nature Walks of Central Park.* New York: Henry Holt, 1997.

Knowler, Donald. *The Falconer of Central Park.* New York: Bantam Books, 1986.

Miller, Sara Cedar. *Central Park, An American Masterpiece.* New York: Harry N. Abrams, 2003.

Rosenzweig, Roy, and Elizabeth Blackmar. *The Park and the People: A History of Central Park.* Ithaca, N.Y.: Cornell University Press, 1992.

MISCELLANEOUS

Darwin, Charles. *The Descent of Man* (Book IX). New York: Penguin Classics, 2004.

Gallagher, Tim. *Parts Unknown: A Naturalist's Journey in Search of Birds and Wild Places.* Guilford, Conn.: Lyons Press, 2001.

Heinrich, Bernd. *Winter World.* New York: HarperCollins, 2004.

Lévi-Strauss, Claude. *Myth and Meaning: Cracking the Code of Culture.* London: Routledge Classics, 2004.

Quinn, Stephen Christopher. *Windows on Nature: The Great Habitat Dioramas of the American Museum of Natural History.* New York: Harry N. Abrams, 2006.

Squire, Larry, and Eric Kandel. *Memory: From Mind to Molecules.* New York: Henry Holt, 2003.

Thoreau, Henry David. *The Journal of Henry David Thoreau.* Salt Lake City: Peregrine Smith Books, 1984.

The Holy Bible (King James Version)

Websites

Central Park Nature News And Photography
PaleMale.com
Palemaleirregulars.blogspot.com
urbanhawks.blogs.com
www.calvorn.com
www.lloydspitalnikphotos.com
www.mariewinn.com

Moths
mothphotographersgroup.msstate.edu. (Includes more than seven thousand photos of living moth species.)
www.hmana.org/mulberry. (NYC Butterfly Club site, includes links to B Moth sites.)
www.silkmoths.bizland.com/catocala.html. (John Oehlke's website.)
www.texasento.net/witchna.htm#Aug. (The Black Witch website.)

Birds
birdsbybent.com/contents.htm. (The online version of Arthur Cleveland Bent's *Life Histories of North American Birds.*)
bna.birds.cornell.edu/bna. (The online version of *The Birds of North America.*)
elibrary.unm.edu/sora. (Searchable Ornithological Research Archive.)

Stars (including sites of Central Park's amateur astronomers)
aa.usno.navy.mil/data/docs/RS_OneDay.php
novahunter.blogspot.com/index.html
topofthelawn.blogspot.com
www.skyandtelescope.com/resources/darksky/3304011.html. The Bortle Scale.
www.space.com. (Widely read astronomy website.)

NYC Organizations
www.nycaudubon.org
www.centralparknyc.com.org (Central Park Conservancy's website.)
www.linnaeanewyork.org

Articles Cited

Brewster, William. "Summer Robin Roosts." *The Auk*, 7:360–63. (Cited by Arthur Cleveland Bent in *Life Histories of North American Birds*.)

Carleton, G. C. "Supplement to the Birds of Central Park." *Proceedings of the Linnaean Society* (update for 1974).

Conant, Helen S. "A Ramble in Central Park." *Harper's New Monthly Magazine*, vol. LIX, no. 135, 1878.

Grant Watson, E. L., "Unknown Eros." Reprinted in *Nature Writing*, edited by Robert Finch and John Elder, New York: Norton, 2002.

Hedenström, A., L. C. Johansson, M. Wolf, R. von Busse, Y. Winter, and G. R. Spedding. "Bat Flight Generates Complex Aerodynamic Tracks." *Science* 316: 894–97.

Humphries, S., R.H.C. Bonser, M. P. Witton, and D. M. Martill. "Did Pterosaurs Feed by Skimming?" *PLoS Biology*, vol. 5, no. 8, e204.

Kelber, A., A. Balkenius, and E. J. Warrant. "Scotopic Colour Vision in Nocturnal Hawkmoths." *Nature* 419: 922–25.

MacDougall-Shackleton, S. A., D. F. Sherry, A. P. Clark, R. Pinkus, and A. M. Hernandez. "Photoperiodic Regulation of Food Storing and Hippocampus Volume in Black-Capped Chickadees." *Animal Behaviour* 65(4): 805–12.

McAdams, E. J. "Wilderness on 68th Street: Why We Need Owls in Central Park." *Topic*, Issue 3, Winter 2003.

Pyle, Robert Michael. "Carnal Knowledge." *Orion Afield*, Winter 2000–01.

Rattenborg, Niels C., and Ruth M. Benca. "Migratory Sleeplessness in the White-Crowned Sparrow (*Zonotrichia leucophrys gambelii*)." *PLoS Biology*, vol. 2, no. 7, e212.

Rydell, J., N. Skals, A. Surlykke, and M. Svensson. "Hearing and Bat Defence in Geometrid Winter Moths." *Proceedings of the Royal Society B: Biological Sciences* 264(1378): 83–88.

Torrey, Bradford. "Robin Roosts." *Atlantic Monthly*, October 1890.

Woodruff, L. B., and A. G. Paine. "Birds of Central Park." *Forest and Stream* 26(1886): 286–87.

Acknowledgments

This book is dedicated to four people and an ever-present spirit who shared most of my nighttime adventures in Central Park: Lee Stinchcomb, Noreen O'Rourke, Jimmy Lewis, Nick Wagerik, and the late Charles Kennedy. Their curiosity, passion, and perseverance will always inspire me. I want to single out a few other members of the park's nature community, notably: Regina Alvarez, Donna Browne, Ben Cacace, Tom Clabough, Marianne Girards, Veronica Goodrich, Chris Karatnytsky, Bob Levy, Naomi Machado, Jack Meyer, Charlie Ridgway, Lloyd Spitalnik, and especially Bruce Yolton. Thanks to all. I couldn't have done it without you.

Rebekah Creshkoff and Jean Dane are two Central Park Regulars to whom I owe a special debt. Besides being vital parts of the story, each took time off from owling, birding, mothing—and sleeping—to scrutinize the manuscript as a whole. It's a better book because of their corrections and suggestions. Others who read parts of the book and made important editing suggestions are Nick Wagerik; Brad Klein and Danielle Gustafson; Julia and Davie Rolnick; Tom Clabough; Charlie Ridgway; and Peter Tagatac. Needless to say, any mistakes you'll find here are fully my fault, not theirs, as I added a lot of material after they sent back their pages. (I'd still be adding stuff if it weren't, finally, too late.)

Chris Nagy and E. J. McAdams helped me figure out the screech owl mystery. I'm thankful to them and to many other Central Park friends who helped in innumerable ways: Carol Abrahams, Karen Asakawa, Chanda Bennett, Ardith Bondi, Mike Bonifanti, Samantha Browne-Walters, Shale Brownstein, Dennis Burton, Neil Calvanese, Annabella Cannarella, Norma Collin, Sylvia Cohen, Marianne Cramer, Jim Demes, Alice Deutsch, Sarah Elliott, Joe and Mary Fiore, Tom Fiore, Tare Gantt, Dick Gershon, Kelley Harrison, John Holland, Lincoln Karim, Barbara Kent, Ed Lam, Harry Maas, Martha Marshall, Charles Matson, Gabriel Molnar, David Monk, Malcolm Morris, Mitchell Nussbaum, James O'Brien, Wendy Paulson, Irene Payne, Dorothy Poole, Betsy Barlow Rogers, Kellye Rosenheim, Starr Saphir, Anne Shanahan; Aidan, James, David, and Paula Smith; Cal Snyder, David Speiser, Brian St. Clair; Bill Stifel, John Suggs, Eleanor Tauber, Cal Vornberger, Irene Warshauer, Chris Wood, and Elliott Zichlinsky. We're all tremendously grateful to Karen Heidgerd, Carolyn Kay, Barbara Zucker, Joanne Dreeben, the Urban Park Rangers, and—of course— Len Soucy, for saving the owl babies of Chapter 12.

You might call Len, John Blakeman, and Ward Stone honorary members of the Central Park nature community. Each played a major role in the real-life dramas you'll find here, and they also answered my endless questions over the years. Steve Quinn, an eminence in the Department of Exhibitions at the American Museum of Natural History as well as author of an invaluable book about the museum's wildlife dioramas, helped in more ways than he knows. Seeing the dioramas through Quinn's eyes, and especially the depictions of sunrise and sunset in the displays' masterful background paintings, led me to a startling conclusion: the light and color at both times of day are identical! Also thanks to Hugh McGuinness and Brian Kane for a cyberspace correspondence about moths and the Moth Tree. Hope to meet you in real life one of these days.

Among the experts I must thank for their generous time: Carl Herzog of the New York State DEC; David Wagner, author of the great caterpillar field guide; and Jay Holmes of the American Museum of Natural History's education department.

One important person on my thank-you list is connected to Central Park primarily by marriage: Allan Miller, filmmaker, palindromist, and husband extraordinaire, whose enthusiasm, encouragement, and help at every stage of this book transformed the task into a true collaboration. Six other Millers helped behind the scenes: my sons, Mike and Steve, and my grandkids, Izzy, Abby, Eli, and Clara. Huge thanks to my daughters-in-law, Sarah Paul and Jennifer Durand, and as ever to my sister, Janet.

I owe thanks to Elisabeth Sifton, my distinguished editor at Farrar, Straus and Giroux, for her splendid editorial suggestions and for her friendship and trust. At FSG, thanks are also due to Charles Battle for many kindnesses; to Wah-Ming Chang for endless patience and endurance; to Matt Kaye, Jonathan Lippincott, and Sarita Varma; and to Audrey Jobson, a cheerful presence at the reception desk.

At Picador, I'm grateful to another fine editor, Sam Douglas, and to Lisa Mondello in the publicity department.

To Lee Stinchcomb, huge thanks for the drawings on the chapter pages, and for the incredible Clouded Underwing pin you made for me. To my brilliant niece Anne Malcolm, who created the dark and wonderful map on pages viii and ix, auntly gratitude and love.

Finally, a grateful bow to the American composer Charles Ives (1874–1954) for the title of this book.

INDEX

"Passim" indicates an entry that occurs frequently throughout the text. The entry's first mention is included here, for identification, as are occasional highlights.